THE LIFE DIAMOND

Your mini map to life

Copyright ©2007 by Louise Storey

All rights reserved. No part of this publication may be reproduced or transmitted in any form, or by any means – electronic, mechanical, photocopy, recording or otherwise – without prior written permission of the copyright owner or publisher, except as provided by international copyright law. For further information please contact:

Louise Storey
Email: info@numbersalive.com.au
             lifedmnd@numbersalive.com.au
Web Site: www.numbersalive.com.au
Mail: Numbers Alive, P.O. Box 584, Mount Martha, Victoria, Australia, 3944

Library of Congress Cataloging-in-publication data

    Storey, Louise
    The Life Diamond: your mini map to life

       ISBN 9780980392906 (pbk.).

       1. Numerology. 2. Tarot. I. Title.

       133.335

Designed and produced by Allan Cornwell
Text set in Times New Roman PS MT

Disclaimer

No responsibility for loss or harm occasioned to any person or entity acting on any of the material in this publication can be accepted by the author/composer or publisher. The subject matter is for the information of readers only. Any extreme practices resulting from any of the information contained herein are absolutely negated.

Illustrations from the Rider-Waite Tarot Deck® reproduced by permission of U.S. Games Systems Inc., CT 06902 USA. Copyright © 1971 by U.S. Games Systems, Inc. Further reproduction prohibited. The Rider-Waite Tarot Deck is a registered trademark of U.S. Games Systems, Inc.

THE LIFE DIAMOND
Your mini map to life

LIFE PATHS AND SOUL DIRECTIONS
How to figure them out

L. STOREY

Published by
Storey Publishing

DEDICATION

This book is lovingly dedicated to my son, Tim,
who provided the inspiration needed
to tackle such an awesome task.

ACKNOWLEDGEMENTS

Grateful thanks go to Cynthia, Julie and "Reg" who openly shared
their life events in full awareness that they were being
guiding stars to others.

Special thanks to Donna, Betty and Alan, Pam and Ruth
who were all "angels in disguise", appearing just at the right moment
to offer their highly valued support.

Lazarus – so special – thank you.

Ellen Green. My goodness; such generosity and support – thank you.

Allan Cornwell for his major role in helping make something majickal manifest.

CONTENTS

PREFACE		10
INTRODUCTION – the Advent of Esoteric Numerology		12
✧ From the Past to the Present		12
✧ Evolution of New Theories, Methods and Terminology		12
✧ Traditional Numerology+Number-Pairing+Magickal Symbols=Esoteric Numerology		13
✧ Major Differences Between Systems		14
✧ How to Use This Book		15
✧ What You Will Learn from This Book		15
✧ A Brief Overview of What This Book Covers		16
✧ To Sum Up		17
✧ Handy Tips		17
CHAPTER 1: FROM PINNACLES AND CHALLENGES TO LIFE DIAMOND		19
✧ New Terminology		20
✧ From Broad Generalities to Specifics		21
✧ "An "Accidental" Breakthrough		22
✧ New Discoveries Lead to New Hypotheses		22
✧ A Test Case: BILL CLINTON		23
CHAPTER 2: YOUR LIFE DIAMOND AS YOUR MINI TREE OF LIFE		27
✧ Introducing An Esoteric Perspective		28
✧ Proposed LG and LC Interpretive Guidelines		30
• Your Life Goals Reveal This Life's Budding Potential		30
• Your Life Challenges Reveal Your Past Lives' Legacy		31
✧ An Esoteric Depiction of a Life Diamond (LD)		32
✧ Achieving the STAR of DAVID		33
✧ The HEART Number of the LD		33
CHAPTER 3: PYTHAGORAS' GENIUS		35
✧ Esoteric Symbols Showing the Emergence of the LD		38
• The VERTICAL CROSS		39
• The DIAGONAL CROSS		39
• The PENTAGRAM		40
• The STAR of DAVID		41
• The WHEEL of LIFE		41

CHAPTER 4: A LD's MAGICKAL FACETS — 43
- ◇ Establishing Associations Between Magickal Symbols — 44
- ◇ Identifying the Magickal Facets of a LD — 45
- ◇ A LD's Basic Components — 46
- ◇ A LD's Magickal Symbols — 46
  - The PENTAGRAM or HEART NUMBER — 46
  - The LD's BASELINE — 47
  - The INNER SQUARE — 47
  - The STAR of DAVID — 48
  - The GRAIL — 51
  - The COSMIC DIAMOND — 51
  - The WHEEL of LIFE and its CONSTELLATIONS — 52
  - The LD's RULER CONSTELLATIONS — 52

CHAPTER 5: CALCULATING SDLDs AND THEIR CYCLES — 55
- ◇ How to Calculate a SDLD and its Age and Calendar Cycles — 56
  - Step 1: How to Calculate a SDLD from a Birthdate — 57
  - Step 2: How to Calculate LGs — 57
  - Step 3: How to Calculate LCs — 57
  - Step 4: How to Calculate Age Cycles for Life — 58
  - Step 5: How to Calculate Age Cycles by Calendar Years — 60
  - Step 6: Extending LG/C Age Cycles *BEYOND* the 4th LG/C Cycle — 61
- ◇ Table for Extending Age Cycles *Beyond* the 4th Life Cycle — 61
- ◇ The Three Major Life Cycles — 61
- ◇ Overlooked Numbers — 62
- ◇ Handy Tips — 63
- ◇ Example WORKSHEET — 64
- ◇ Life Diamond WORKSHEET — 65
- ◇ A Handy CHECKLIST of Notable LD Features — 66

CHAPTER 6: NUMBER-PAIRING TECHNIQUES — 67
- ◇ Introducing Number-Pairing as a Numerological Technique — 68
- ◇ CASE STUDY: JULIE — 70
- ◇ How to Apply Number-Pairing Rules to a LD — 71
- ◇ Step 1: Number-Pairing within the First Cycle — 72
- ◇ Step 2: Number-Pairing within the Second Cycle — 74
- ◇ Step 3: Number-Pairing within the Third Cycle — 75
- ◇ Step 4: Number-Pairing within the Fourth Cycle (The COSMIC DIAMOND) — 76
- ◇ Step 5: Pairing the Two Top and Bottom LGs and LCs — 77
- ◇ Step 6: Pairing the Two Vertical Core Numbers — 78

- ✧ Step 7: The INNER SQUARE — 79
- ✧ Step 8 The STAR of DAVID — 80
- ✧ Step 9: The WHEEL of LIFE'S NUMBER LINE RULERS — 82
- ✧ A Handy CHECKLIST of Notable LD Features — 83

CHAPTER 7: INTERPRETATION GUIDELINES — 85

- ✧ How to Decode a LG/C Cycle — 87
  - Life Cycle For Analysis — 87
  - Single Digits — 87
  - Paired Compound Numbers — 87
  - Corresponding Tarot keys — 88
  - Ruling Numbers of a Life Cycle — 88
  - Hidden Numbers — 88
  - Magickal Facets — 89
  - Final Analysis — 89
- ✧ Interpretation Beginnings — 89
  - General Impressions — 89
  - Homing in on Major Themes — 90
  - Julie's Inner Square — 91
  - Julie's Star of David — 92
  - Julie's Cosmic Diamond — 93
  - Julie's Wheel of Life — 93
  - Julie's Current Life Cycle — 94
  - Prevailing Indications — 94
- ✧ Handy Tips — 95

CHAPTER 8: LIFE DIAMOND EXTENSIONS — 97

- ✧ Introducing Life Goal Rulers (LGRs), Life Challenge Rulers(LCRs) and Life Diamond Rulers (LDRs) — 98
- ✧ How to Calculate the LGRs, LCRs and LDRs — 99
- ✧ CASE STUDY: JULIE — 99
- ✧ CASE STUDY: BILL CLINTON — 102
  - Interpreting Bill's LGRs — 103
  - Interpreting Bill's LCRs — 104
  - Interpreting Bill's LDRs — 104
- ✧ Handy Tips — 105
- ✧ CASE STUDIES: NICOLE KIDMAN and WALLIS SIMPSON — 105
- ✧ CASE STUDY: The 14th DALAI LAMA — 107
- ✧ CASE STUDY: GANDHI — 109

CHAPTER 9: THE WHOLE NUMBER LIFE DIAMOND (WNLD) — 113
- ✧ Introducing the WHOLE NUMBER LD – Using Your *TRUE* Numbers in a LD — 114
- ✧ How to Calculate WNLDs — 117
- ✧ CASE STUDY: BILL GATES — 118
  1. Bill's SDLD — 119
  2. Number-Pairing Bill's SDs — 120
  3. Bill's WNLD — 121
     a) How to Calculate Whole Number LCs (WNLCs) — 122
     b) How to Calculate Whole Number LGs (WNLGs) — 124
     c) How to Calculate Whole Number LPNs (WNLPNs) — 127
     d) How to Calculate Whole Number LGRs, LCRs and LDRs — 128
- ✧ Number-Pairing Large, Whole Number LGRs and LDRs — 128
- ✧ CASE STUDY: HUGH HEFNER — 130
- ✧ CASE STUDY: OPRAH WINFREY — 133
- ✧ CASE STUDY: St JOAN of ARC — 136
- ✧ Handy Tips — 143

CHAPTER 10: WHEN ZERO CHALLENGES "DISAPPEAR"! — 145
- ✧ Zero Challenges *Replaced* — 146
- ✧ Examples: Sir EDMUND HILLARY and ALBERT EINSTEIN — 147
- ✧ Handy Tips — 147
- ✧ CASE STUDY: CYNTHIA — 148
  - Do Challenges represent Past Life Works and Karma? — 148
  - Esoteric WNLC10 — 149
  - Esoteric WNLC18 — 150
  - How WNLC10 and WNLG66 Work in Unison — 150
  - How One Cycle Carries Over Into the Next — 152
  - Outcomes — 152
- ✧ CASE STUDY: REG — 153
  - From Four Zeros to Four Numbers — 154
  - When *True* Challenges Indicate Present Life Trends — 154
- ✧ CASE STUDY: AMELIA EARHART — 155
  - Numbers That Signify a Potential Tragedy. — 155
  - How Do You Ascertain the *Time* for a Tragic Event? — 156
  - Putting the Pieces of the Puzzle Together — 157

CHAPTER 11: HOW TO CALCULATE AN INTERIM LD — 159
- ✧ How to Calculate Three Types of *Interim* LDs — 160
  - Example 1: Daniel Radcliffe (HARRY POTTER) — 161
  - Example 2: Emma Watson (HERMIONE GRANGER) — 162

✧ CASE STUDY: MOZART	163
• Example 3: BILL GATES	167
• Example 4: ANNIE BESANT	168
• Example 5: "50 CENT"	169

CHAPTER 12: THERE *IS* LIFE BEYOND THE FOURTH LIFE CYCLE! — 171
- ✧ The Fourth Life Cycle and Beyond – A Second Chance at Life! — 172
  - • What Reactivated 9-year Cycles Involve — 173
- ✧ CASE STUDY: REG — 174
- ✧ CASE STUDY: LOUISE — 176
- ✧ CASE STUDY: BILL CLINTON — 178
- ✧ CASE STUDY: ALAN BOND — 180

CHAPTER 13: THE NATURE OF NUMBERS AND TAROT KEYS — 183
- ✧ Ways That Numbers and Tarot Keys are Influenced — 184
- ✧ The Nature of Numbers and Tarot Keys — 185
- ✧ The Role of Tarot — 186
- ✧ Single Digits have a Compound Number Reversal — 187
- ✧ The Roles of the Ten and its Unit Digit within Compound Numbers — 187
- ✧ Tens Numbers — 188
- ✧ Master Numbers — 189
- ✧ Where to Lay Emphasis – the Authentic or the Reversed Number? — 189
- ✧ Numbers and Tarot Keys as Individual Operators — 190
- ✧ Opposite Depictions in some Tarot Key Pairs — 190
- ✧ Number, Tarot Key or Tarot Suit Intensification — 191
- ✧ Finally — 191

PREAMBLE TO APPENDIX 1 — 194
- ✧ How Numbers from 0 to 99 are Set Out in Appendix 1 — 194

APPENDIX 1: NUMBERS 0 to 99 AND THEIR MEANINGS — 195

APPENDIX 2: 0 to 78 NUMBERS APPENDED TO THEIR TAROT KEYS — 232
- ✧ The Major Arcana — 232
- ✧ The Minor Arcana — 235
- ✧ The Suit of Wands — 236
- ✧ The Suit of Cups — 237
- ✧ The Suit of Swords — 238
- ✧ The Suit of Pentacles or Coins — 239
- ✧ TABLE: Easy Referral to 78 Tarot Keys NUMBERED in SUITS — 240

APPENDIX 3: DELINEATIONS FOR THE 78 TAROT KEYS — 242

RECOMMENDED RESOURCE LIST — 262

PREFACE

As seems to be so typical for many on the Path, a health crisis in 1982 precipitated my sudden, unexpected interests in theosophy, astrology, numerology and Tarot. I am self-taught in these areas. Although astrology was my first love, my interest in numerology and the Tarot grew over the years. While teaching numerology in the late 1980s, I happened to find one of its forgotten branches. Immediately sensing that it was profound, and that it contained in it everything that one would ever wish to know about their life, I could not stifle a compelling urge to decipher it and uncover its many secrets. What I had stumbled across was Pythagoras' ultimate arrangement of letters and numbers, based upon the magical Qabalistic code called the "ABRACADABRA". I have renamed it the "Numeroscope". The Numeroscope represents one's entire lifetime from birth until death in more detail than the Pinnacles and Challenges do.

Several new numerological discoveries emerged from learning how to decode the Numeroscope. It was instrumental in revising and opening up other fields of numerology such as Pythagoras' *Pinnacles and Challenges* – the subject of this book. The Pinnacles and Challenges have enjoyed a total overhaul due to these new discoveries. Prior to developing a pioneering approach to them, I simply had no interest in this branch of numerology due to its very restricted applications. However, innovative ideas and methods penetrated their exoteric guise to reveal an astonishing amount of information regarding spiritual and everyday prospects. As a consequence, my attitude towards them completely reversed. They captured my attention until, over a period of many years, I had completely transformed this branch of numerology into a highly sophisticated, self-help tool. As a result, their transformation brought about their renewal and, consequently, a new title.

The *Life Diamond* is the new title given to this ancient branch of numerology. Its meagre array of numbers represents a map to life that addresses an *overview of a lifetime*. For centuries, this tiny map ingeniously masked guidelines to individual destinies in meticulous detail. Mystic, highly personalised information was secreted in its numbers all along but out-of-date thinking and methods failed to penetrate their enigmatic veneer that had all the while hidden their esoteric content.

Many years were spent unravelling the Life Diamond's secrets. Hunch after hunch led to uncovering hidden geometric symbols woven into its framework. All along I suspected that Pythagoras, who invented this branch of numerology, had secretly created it out of mystic, geometric symbols. For years I wondered if they had been intentionally put there by him but needed proof to verify this notion. It took until this book was almost finished before the proof finally came via a very special friend who brought a book on occult philosophy to show me.

Quite unexpectedly, while my friend was flicking through the book's 900 plus pages to find the illustrations she wished me to see, a tiny diagram flashed by which I immediately recognised as being very similar to the one I had used to portray the "Wheel of Life" diagram in Chapter 3. Seeing it, I knew that I had found the final piece to the puzzle. It left no doubt in my mind that Pythagoras had indeed created the Pinnacles and Challenges upon geometrical symbology which was steeped in deep, occult principles.

The Life Diamond - Your Mini Map to Life, is the first in a series of four books. It is anticipated that each book will be appearing in the following order: Book 1: *The Life Diamond - Your Mini Map to Life;* Book 2: *The Yearly Diamond - Your Destiny in Action* and Book 3: *More Magickal Diamonds.* (This book addresses other exciting areas of numerology). Finally, Book 4: *The Birth of the Numeroscope – The Abracadabra Decoded,* the last book in the series, is actually responsible for bringing the other three into being!

The four books are first and foremost about *you.* They are dedicated to exposing the Divine Intent secretly encoded in birthdates and names. Therefore, *self-disclosure and self-direction that lead to self-empowerment* are their primary focus. Their new methods help you to get to know who you are, what your birth potential is and how to capitalise on its indications. They are written with the aim in mind that from what you uncover about yourself, you will achieve a fuller, richer understanding of your innate capabilities, when you apply their enlightening methods to your numbers. The principle behind this is to learn how to activate and live to the fullest, the promise that they contain.

It is my hope that what is presented in this and my other books will be used as a springboard to reawaken the esoteric counterpart of this ancient, occult science.

In Light and Love,
Louise

INTRODUCTION
THE ADVENT OF ESOTERIC NUMEROLOGY

FROM THE PAST TO THE PRESENT

Importantly, this book introduces a new system of numerology that radically modifies and extends the Pinnacles and Challenges. It requires serious study as it is by no means superficial in approach. Everything being introduced is brand new in an effort to meet the changing requirements of this most auspicious time – a time that is not only ushering in a new millennium but also a new age. It is my opinion that numerology has failed to keep pace with these changes – changes that accompany each transition from one period to the next – changes that shatter crystallised forms while ushering in new ones that are continually evolving and seeking expression through each new cycle and phase in time. As a result of this failing to move with the times, out of date numerology practices have ceased to serve our needs as traditional numerology has, in many respects, ceased to grow and evolve in-keeping with changing times.

The Pinnacles and Challenges fall into the above category. They have enjoyed a major place in the field of numerology for aeons but have failed to keep abreast with the processes of change. In fact, they have fallen so far behind that they no longer appropriately or adequately address past, present and future trends. They are seriously in need of updating if they are to suitably reflect today's acceleration in consciousness and the endless possibilities that are now available and achievable.

However, it needs to be remembered that the Pinnacles and Challenges were originally devised to cater to ancient, not modern times. Hence, their old parameters being severely restrictive and generalised could only ever produce superficial generalities and deal with the mundane; *but,* all the while, their esoteric counterpart was waiting to be uncovered! Their true significance and meaning has remained untapped due to a fixated concentration on outmoded methods. This fixation has hindered our ability to recognise the fact that they represent both spiritual and everyday aspects of the self in one.

EVOLUTION OF NEW THEORIES, METHODS AND TERMINOLOGY

Transitional periods, such as the one that we are experiencing now, serve as gateways to eternal growth. At every moment, the present is changing and determining the future. Every moment of every day is a gateway in time, birthing new beginnings and new possibilities. Therefore adjustment, modification and adaptation are necessary companions in order to keep abreast of these changes. So are re-evaluation, reform and revision. New forms, new concepts and technology are birthed as natural by-products of the forces of change. Creation of new language is another, in order to explain and describe whatever is emerging or being modified. Auxiliary means such as these present and describe ways that ensure progress.

Awareness of an inability to keep abreast of changing times made it plain that this branch of numerology was long due for an overhaul. To achieve this end, it was necessary to develop new theories methods and terminology in order to revive it and bring about its restoration. Their express purpose is designed to raise this branch of numerology from obscurity into the light of present times while at the same time keeping its time-honoured integrity in tact. What this means is to anticipate that numerology procedures and terms, used in this text, have been modified in some instances while totally replaced in others to accommodate each new concept and method being introduced. This follows the inevitability of the pattern of cyclic change and its need for consequential back-up systems, to assist with ushering in that which can progressively develop new understandings, ways and forms.

A major pioneering technique that was particularly instrumental in facilitating the Pinnacles and Challenges' transformation, resulted from applying number-pairing techniques to their single digits in order to create compound numbers from them (Chapter 6). It powerfully impacted on the Pinnacles and Challenges by opening up their restricted number-range from being confined to single digits only, to being able to work with all numbers from 0 – 99 and beyond. The fusion of Tarot to this greatly extended number-range caused a further monumental change. Their synthesis transformed the Pinnacles and Challenges to grow from something stereotypical into something quite remarkable.

As a consequence, the Pinnacles and Challenges' interpretive capacity is greatly increased. This is chiefly due to their now vastly increased number-range and the availability of the Tarot's time-honoured interpretations. Its abundant reservoirs of "ready-made" interpretations provide an enormous amount of highly dependable and relevant data that can be appended to their projections. This increases the accuracy, detail and amount of information that can be derived from their numbers. Hence, their innate potential can now be tapped and exploited to the fullest. Access to extremely *personalised* qualities, that highlight each individual's undeniable uniqueness and inestimable range of possibilities is the happy result.

TRADITIONAL NUMEROLOGY + NUMBER-PAIRING + TAROT + MAGICKAL SYMBOLS = ESOTERIC NUMEROLOGY

Years of exploration and experimentation have generated the multifaceted, mystical approach to numerology shown in the "equation" above. It includes the merging of occult philosophies, geometric symbolism, numerology, Tarot and a little borrowing from the Qabalistic Tree of Life and Theosophy. *They spawned the advent of an esoteric numerology; one that synthesises seemingly disparate occult sciences to more appropriately address our multi-dimensional natures and infinite possibilities.* This composite approach is better able to appropriately address what transpires in our lives and our worlds today.

Merging doctrines and dramatically increasing the number-range has erased generalisation and speculation, as specific details and unerring accuracy take their place. You only have to compare the existing, limited number range from 0 to 9 along with a few master numbers, to one that now embraces all numbers from 0 to 99, and beyond, to realise what a tremendous benefit this will prove to be to those seeking help with finding their true Path in life.

Breaking through old barriers meant that *whole numbers* could also be utilised thereby introducing yet another, new approach as well as extending this branch of numerology further. Instead of reducing whole numbers as they are found in the birthdate to their root digits, they are retained and analysed to uncover their unique contribution to life directions thus enriching findings further. This approach is introduced in Chapter 9.

Another aspect of this branch of numerology needed modifying to bring it in line with modern times. It was the very important issue of longevity. The Pinnacles and Challenges' age cycles traditionally culminate when the fourth life cycle is reached. This is totally unrealistic as it fails to address that people born into modern times enjoy much longer life spans than those of Pythagoras' time. Consequently, a new system for extending life beyond this cycle is proposed in Chapter 12.

MAJOR DIFFERENCES BETWEEN SYSTEMS

The following table shows the salient differences occurring between the Pinnacles and Challenges and the modifications made to them to develop the Life Diamond system.

TRADITIONAL APPROACH (PINNACLES & CHALLENGES)	NEW APPROACH (LIFE DIAMOND)
Based on REDUCTION methods	Based on NON-REDUCTION methods
Therefore, CONTRIVED numbers used	Therefore, AUTHENTIC numbers used
RESTRICTED number range	UNRESTRICTED number range
Therefore, GENERALISED	Therefore, SPECIFIC
Therefore, NON-PERSONAL	Therefore, PERSONALISED
Therefore, ACCURACY DUBIOUS	Therefore, ACCURACY ASSURED
An ISOLATED SYSTEM	Incorporates MULTI - SYSTEMS
Therefore, RIGID	Therefore, FLEXIBLE
Produces one LIFE PATH No. only	Produces a LIFE PATH No. *FAMILY*
None	Introduces NEW TERMS and EXTENSIONS: Life Goal Rulers; Life Challenge Rulers and Life Diamond Rulers and Constellations
Life Cycles CEASE ROTATION once fourth cycle is reached	Life Cycles ROTATE OVER AGAIN after nine years spent at fourth life cycle
EXOTERIC	ESOTERIC
None	Utilises HIDDEN MAGICKAL SYMBOLS
PERSONALITY/MATERIAL based	SOUL/SPIRITUAL based

By following and mastering the instructions outlined in each chapter, the dedicated student, teacher and counsellor are led to uncover many layers of hidden truths about themselves and others that they could not otherwise have imagined that their Life Diamond's numbers could ever contain. This is because outmoded methods fail to produce definitive, detailed information that contains spiritual as well as everyday (mundane) indications that are specifically unique to each and every individual. Herein lays the exceptional difference between traditional and esoteric methods.

Just your birthdate is required for this work. It is difficult to conceive that only a birthdate's numbers were needed by Pythagoras to create a tiny array of numbers which are capable of producing such amazingly accurate Spirit, Soul and Personality directions for an entire lifetime. This unassuming configuration conceals, in unimagined detail that belies its size, copious amounts of personalised guidelines that are totally unique to you and your world. But, do not be fooled by its modest appearance, as it veils the profundity of what is hidden behind its enigmatic façade.

HOW TO USE THIS BOOK

Primarily, this is an advanced discourse on numerology and Tarot. It is expected that you, the reader, possess a good working knowledge of both sciences. However, those who do not have an advanced knowledge of both sciences will be able to follow the in-depth instructions given for each step along the way. Hence, the text is essentially along the lines of a **"How To" or "D.I.Y."** workbook.

Each new concept and technique is introduced alongside self-instructive and easy to comprehend text. Many detailed diagrams and numerous case studies exemplify teaching points. Each chapter builds on the one before, exposing more and more advanced techniques and interpretive guidelines. In this way, greater depth and meaning is methodically explored with new ideas receiving systematic reinforcement and consolidation throughout. To make the most of what this book offers, endeavour to master each step by allowing sufficient time for practice, research and reflection before moving on to the next.

WHAT YOU WILL LEARN FROM THIS BOOK

The following points list the most basic things that you will learn.
- A new system of numerology
- How to use your numbers as tools; your personal guides and signposts, to uncover your hidden birth potential
- How to time life events
- How to recognise the individual nature of your life cycles and their prospects
- Automatic use of number-pairing techniques
- How to work with large numbers whether paired or whole
- Automatic Tarot Key/number combinations

- How to cultivate a multifaceted approach to numerology
- How to accurately forecast present and future trends
- How to use this knowledge to successfully manage and plan your life
- How to access Past Life brought over gifts and debits (Karma)
- How to live your life by the Life Diamond – perceiving it as your personal Wayshower
- How to successfully live your Dharma

A BRIEF OVERVIEW OF WHAT THIS BOOK COVERS

Perhaps a brief outline of the main points and methods used to extract the wealth of information to be found in each Life Diamond (abbreviated to LD) will help to prepare you for the practical work ahead. The points given below give you an idea of what to anticipate.

1. A first requirement is to keep an open mind when exploring the new esoteric theories and propositions being presented, most of which modify traditional, numerological procedures. The Preface, Introduction and Chapters 1 through 4 introduce the esoteric foundations upon which this new system of numerology is based.
2. Basic instructions for calculating age cycles are to be found in Chapter 5. **Worksheets** and a **Handy Checklist** are provided at the end of this chapter.
3. The new concept of applying number-pairing techniques to the Life Goals (LGs) and Life Challenges' (LCs) root digits is introduced in Chapter 6. Appending the Tarot to these numbers is gradually introduced at this stage.
4. Chapter 7 introduces basic interpretation guidelines followed by chapter 8's introduction of Life Goal Rulers (LGRs), Life Challenge Rulers (LCRs) and Life Diamond Rulers (LDRs), classified as the LD's **CONSTELLATIONS**.
5. Whole Number LDs are introduced in Chapter 9 and 10 and interim LDs are introduced in Chapter 11 as further extensions to the basic LD. In all, you will be learning how to calculate and delineate three basic types of LDs. By now, the Tarot is a familiar part of the work.
6. Extending the LD's age cycles to eternity! This is introduced in Chapter 12 where a new numerological concept is revealed that explains the continuation of life cycles beyond the fourth life cycle. *Rounds* **of life cycles** are its new numerological feature.
7. The "Nature of Numbers" appears in Chapter 13. It provides many tips on how to work with numbers and Tarot Keys before accessing the interpretation guidelines in the three appendixes.

8. Working with the ongoing development of a greatly extended number range from 0 to 99, as numbers in their own right when not linked to the Tarot, is a main feature of this work. Their delineations appear in Appendix 1. An explanation of how to follow their interpretation guidelines is contained in the "Preamble to the Appendices".

9. A table that links a number to its Tarot Key and vice versa appears in Appendix 2. Many handy tips are given in this Appendix to help you to quickly memorise the numbers with their Tarot Keys. Automatic recall is essential to this work.

TO SUM UP

As you become skilled at decoding the Life Diamond's map to life and decipher what its numbers esoterically represent, you will learn how to bring to light major spiritual and day-to-day pathways that act as your unique signposts to your life and your world. Layer upon layer, personality traits, gifts, skills and potential, as well as personality blocks, challenges and limitations, can be methodically exposed, as you become more and more adept at using these combined, innovative procedures to reveal your birth possibilities. Apart from disclosing present eventualities and insights into past lives, the past and the future can also be brought to light. The experience and expertise of the interpreter is the only thing that limits the amount of significance and meaning that can be uncovered from Life Diamonds when applying this new system.

 HANDY TIPS

1. You are expected to have additional resource material on numerology and especially, the Tarot. See the *Recommended Resource List* after the Appendices.
2. Have pen and paper at the ready to work along with the instructions.
3. Also, have your Tarot cards at the ready. (My preference is for the time-honoured *Rider-Waite Deck* because I find that its pictorial images depict our everyday circumstances so explicitly, that it makes it easier to interpret both long and short term directions from its Keys' illustrations.)
4. Progress slowly. Master each step before attempting the next.
5. Practise, practise and more practise

FROM PINNACLES and CHALLENGES TO LIFE DIAMOND

Abbreviated Terms used in this Chapter:
- ✧ LD = Life Diamond
- ✧ LG = Life Goal
- ✧ LC = Life Challenge
- ✧ LG/C = A Life Goal, Life Challenge combination

CHAPTER 1
FROM PINNACLES and CHALLENGES TO LIFE DIAMOND

Most importantly, the theme of this work is not only to provide soul-based directions that facilitate the growth of self-awareness and the right determination of spiritual aspirations, but also to modernise and spiritualise the Pinnacles and Challenges without detracting from their original precepts.

In order to achieve this, the Pinnacles and Challenges had to be seen *into* with "new eyes" and worked with in new ways to make possible their transformation. As mentioned in the introduction, the merging of occult philosophies, geometric symbolism, numerology, Tarot and a little borrowing from the Tree of Life and Theosophy were all instrumental in bringing this about. Their contribution has greatly facilitated the emergence of the Life Diamond to take the place of the old Pinnacles and Challenges. All levels of sensory experience, possibilities and potential from spiritual, mental and emotional to the physical can be addressed as it is a much expanded version of them. Best of all, it is now tailored to suit all individual levels of attainment and Life Paths, no matter how diverse.

NEW TERMINOLOGY

Employment of a multifaceted approach meant that new terminology became necessary to describe the emergence of a new approach. An example of this was the need to choose a term that would sum up the Pinnacles and Challenges in their entirety. Accordingly, the title *Life Diamond* (from now on abbreviated to LD) was settled upon.

This title covers more than one observable feature. It serves the dual aim of addressing the obvious that: firstly, it rules for *life*, and secondly, that it has a *diamond shape*. Mental impressions of a diamond-shaped array of numbers are then instantly conveyed to the mind to differentiate the LD from all other numerology branches. However, there was another important reason for selecting this title; the LD, for purposes of numerological discourse, had to be made readily distinguishable from the *Yearly* Diamond, which addresses *yearly* trends.

Further developments meant that it was also found necessary to replace the term "Pinnacle" with "Life Goal" and to add the word "Life" to the word "Challenge". Exchanging and modifying these terms distinguished them from similar goals and challenges that constitute the *Yearly* Diamond (Book 2) – again, for the purposes of numerological discourse.

Another reason for exchanging "Pinnacle" for "Goal" was that "Pinnacle" translates as "height", "peak", "apex", "zenith" and so on, which fails to impart that it is actually referring to "a point or points of *attainment* in life". "Life Goal" on the other hand relays this meaning, giving a clearer message of striving for something in a bid to extend and better oneself. "Life Goal" also serves to modernise the outmoded term "Pinnacle'" The new term is more applicable and readily understood. The term "Life Goal" and its initials "LG" will be used to replace the term "Pinnacle" in the text from here on; similarly, "Life Challenge" will be abbreviated to "LC" from here on.

For you to be able to embrace what has been suggested so far will require an open mind, lateral thinking and a willingness to work with new theories and methods. This will prepare you to be open to the introduction of innovative and creative ways to interpret the LGs and LCs. They expose the LGs and LCs in a new light, making their spiritual intent and content easier to recognise, decipher and understand. Once applied, relatively "insignificant" looking LDs of old, will be found to camouflage one of the most potent and self-directional configurations that numerology has to offer.

FROM BROAD GENERALITIES TO SPECIFICS

The "Divine Marriage" between an extended number-range and the Tarot has dramatically increased the ability to arrive at exclusive directions and extremely accurate forecasts. It provides the main vehicle for moving away from overly generalised interpretations to those that are extremely specific, detailed and personalised. Consequently, the intricacies of human nature can at last be fathomed due to their union.

To cite an example of this, the days of trying to fit persons into a traditionally limiting system of root digits, such as describing a "6 typology" or a "9 typology", are over. There are many types of sixes and nines that stem from their "parent" (whole) numbers. By including whole numbers in the calculations, these new techniques reveal each "true" type of 6 or 9, by being able to distinguish exactly *what kind* of a 6 or a 9 is being represented in each and every case, no matter where they appear in the calculations. That is because these new methods find, uncover and work with "actual" or "true" numbers by not adhering to traditional reduction methods to obtain root digits. As a direct consequence, remarkably authentic data is exposed that relates solely to *individualised* aspirations, character development, life directions and possibilities.

Retaining the parent number (Chapter 9 introduces whole number methods), that spawns its single or root digit, unveils the true nature of what its root digit represents. *You need to know exactly what kind of a 4, 6, 2 or 9 that you are dealing with to generate accurate forecasts*. Essentially, this is the emphasis of this work. It retains the parent numbers or compound numbers derived from number-pairing techniques (Chapter 6) that are creating the root digits. In this way you know precisely what the root digits represent so that through them and what they signify, you can get to know exactly who and what you truly are and what you are capable. You are able to come to these realisations because your numbers and your Tarot Keys will indicate exactly what you have at your disposal in order to achieve what you desire from life.

Before going further, and not wishing to give the wrong impression, you may be thinking that the numbers from 0 to 9 have lost their significance. On the contrary, these numbers must be included in all prognostications and their attributes embodied in all findings. They form the very foundations upon which the science of numerology is built and they are present, whether obvious or hidden, in all that is being presented.

AN "ACCIDENTAL" BREAKTHROUGH

Reference was made in the Preface about how I used the Numeroscope's methods years ago, to decode a LD but the actual incident that instigated the advent of the LD was left untold. It was all due to a young man exhibiting 39's negative behaviours. I felt it just *had* to be somewhere in his numbers because he was graphically exhibiting its negative qualities and characteristics since he was in very serious trouble due to drug and alcohol abuse. The idea dawned to experiment with applying number-pairing techniques to his LD because I had exhausted all other numerology configurations, including the Numeroscope, in my search. (You can see from this progressive search, I did not hold the LGs and LCs in high regard at that time.) Not one but *two* 39s were found in its goal sector! The ramifications of this "accidental breakthrough" became apparent. Upon finding his elusive 39, I had absolutely no idea that it would lead from tentative beginnings to a burgeoning desire to understand as much as I could about LDs; there was no thought of lectures, much less a book at the time. This book is a testimony to the huge ramifications that this discovery had. It was this discovery that literally catapulted a foundering, archaic science into the 21st Century – the discovery that unlocked the LD's long hidden secrets and brought about its revival!

NEW DISCOVERIES LEAD TO NEW HYPOTHESES

After conducting many years of research into LDs, to validate its new methods and terminology, old notions, practices and theories faded as new ones replaced them. Many adjustments in thinking had to be made, as it became increasingly obvious that the LGs and LCs behaved quite differently to traditional practices when these new methods were applied to them. As a result, major inconsistencies surfaced which meant that more appropriate ways of working with LDs were necessary.

Discrepancies like the LGs and LCs were not set in concrete as traditional methods would have us believe were commonplace. Their parameters are actually pliable, not rigid, and, not confined to set time frames. What this meant was, that each of the numbers in the LD has a constant influence, being an integral part of a person's character, regardless of whether its cycle is activated or not. If it is not standing out in the foreground being actively expressed, then it is latently or unconsciously stored in the psyche awaiting activation at any given time! To embrace these contradictions was never considered a possibility under traditional practices. It was never taken into consideration that a number or numbers could operate outside their designated cycles – yet they can, and do!

Another major anomaly was that each LG and LC number can be expressed in a *positive, passive* or a *negative* manner regardless of which position it occupies in the LD. These discoveries also unequivocally broke with tradition. As in the case of the young man above, his 39s were hidden within his LGs. LGs are traditionally viewed as being *positive*. In traditional numerology, it was just not considered that a LG could be anything other than positive and a LC anything other than negative. Yet, he was expressing his negatively! By being so rigid one ignores the fact that each number inherently contains every layer of expression ranging from the highest through to the lowest within its own, unique field of activity. In this case, the LGs were definitely being expressed in self-destructive ways.

This possibility was totally ignored because, up until now, LG/Cs have literally been taken at face value. The LGs were always being written up as being a "bed of roses" and the LCs as a "bed of thorns" – precepts that were never questioned. What my research consistently uncovered was that LGs are quite capable of expressing themselves negatively and LCs, positively – what a paradox! This contradiction became more and more evident as further research continued. Many examples of this "interchange" of basic modes of expression between the LG/Cs are illustrated in each case study. The frequency of these revelations, in itself, makes it conclusive that traditional principles regarding how the LG/Cs operate need fundamental revision and updating.

A TEST CASE: BILL CLINTON (born William Jefferson Blythe)

A very brief cameo of Bill Clinton's LD brilliantly exemplifies the above statements, highlighting the need to transform traditional ways of working with LG/Cs. It graphically demonstrates radical changes appearing in the manner that his LG/Cs were expressed by him. You will be shown how they can be expressed both positively *and* negatively regardless of being a goal or a challenge. For example, the publicity that Bill was receiving about his affair with Monica Lewinski and other related indiscretions, lead to intuiting that his behaviours reflected true, negative 39 traits – he had all of the earmarks of a "39 typology"! So 39 had to be an intrinsic part of his nature, just as it was with the young man. On creating his LD, two prominent 39s (due to number-pairing) emerged in his LGs, *not* LCs.

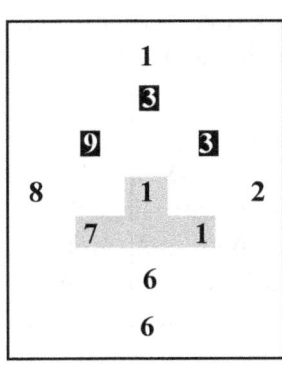

Bill Clinton's birth date is: 19-8-1946 = LPN: 47/11/2

Two, strong 39s appear in Bill's LG's sector. He has expressed them at their highest and lowest levels. 39's *positive* attributes brought forth Bill's talents as orator, statesman, and peacemaker and lover of music. 39's *negative* traits appeared when he used his good looks and charm to beguile his constituents and women. The two 17s in his LC's area fanned Bill's 39s bringing about intensification of expression. Traditionally, *challenge* 17s indicate defamation, scandal, dishonour and lack of support. *Positively*, they stand for fame, respect, admiration and the achievement of one's dearest hopes and wishes – in his case, becoming the President of America!

Bill's LD highlights just how tantalisingly flexible our numbers can be. It serves to demonstrate the need to transform traditional methods and that we need to stretch our thinking about the ways in which numbers can and do operate so that they can more appropriately accommodate our present expansion in consciousness.

For example, the two 39s that are located in the LG's sector of Bill's LD would be traditionally inclined as positive. We know from his gift of oratory (3), humanitarianism (9) and publicised sexual infidelities, deception and disloyalty (39) that he expressed *his* 39 both positively *and* negatively, even though these numbers hold the esteemed position of being in the LG section of his LD! Interchange between positive and negative expression like this kept appearing during research. This repetition not only confirmed a needed break away from traditional thinking but also opened up other thrilling facets of numerology waiting to be uncovered.

Bill's all too brief example also serves to illustrate that our long-standing ideas about *timing* the LG/C cycles need revising and updating. A quick calculation of which of Bill's cycles was active (Chapters 8 and 12), when he was being publicly accused of sexual misconduct, reveals that his 39s would be considered to be inactive using old methods. The fact that he was experiencing the consequences of negative 39 traits, *out of sync with the 9-year LG/C cycles*, clearly demonstrates that the numbers can be activated at any time. Hence the confirmation of the LG/C's flexibility in this way as well! They are not bound to specifically determined time frames, as tradition would have us believe. This becomes obvious when certain traits appear *prior* to the activation of a cycle, or *continue* to be expressed when their traditionally designated time span has expired.

This little cameo about Bill presents just the tip of the iceberg as to what these new procedures are able to bring forth. What I am suggesting from my findings is that we would do well not to set the LD's numbers in concrete. They are much more adaptable, multifaceted and multidimensional than ever previously thought possible. St Joan of Arc, Chapter 9, led an extraordinary short life, one that superbly exemplifies these propositions. It is probably the clearest and most succinct example of just how the numbers in a LD operate in a seemingly "random", yet "controlled", manner.

(For those who are interested, the following "39 type" examples typify, in most cases, rare giftedness coupled with a penchant for self-indulgence, substance abuse, promiscuity and sexual deviance of sorts. These qualities are found in the charts of: Bill Clinton, former US President; Michael Jackson 29-8-1958, incredibly gifted rock idol and alleged paedophile; Michael Hutchence 22-1-1960, popular rock idol with bizarre sexual preferences and drug abuse which lead to death; Dodi Al Fayed 15-4-1955, a dandy and a playboy; John Nash 13-6-1928, mathematics genius with public rumours levelled against his sexual preferences; and Victor Hugo 26-2-1802, great poet, dramatist and novelist whose wife complained of his womanising and insatiable need for sexual gratification with her.)

YOUR LIFE DIAMOND AS YOUR MINI TREE OF LIFE

Abbreviated Terms used in this Chapter:
- ✧ LD = Life Diamond
- ✧ LG = Life Goal
- ✧ LC = Life Challenge
- ✧ LG/C = A Life Goal, Life Challenge combination

CHAPTER 2
YOUR LIFE DIAMOND AS YOUR MINI TREE OF LIFE

INTRODUCING AN ESOTERIC PERSPECTIVE

Previously, I have mentioned that it would help to have a mind that is open and willing to explore new concepts and propositions to accept that this branch of numerology has fallen behind the times. What this chapter presents certainly needs this faculty to be exercised as several new propositions are being proffered for consideration. Whether you share these ideas or not, we do need to view LDs from a different perspective to be able to get them to more appropriately reflect and address our individual Life Paths during this day and age.

One way of doing this is to envisage the LD as a "tree" – a miniature tree that symbolises one's " map to life". To view it from this standpoint, the LGs represent the "budding, blossoming, fruiting part of your tree" – the birth date represents the tree's "trunk", serving as a bridge between old incarnations and new – and the LCs form the "root system" constructed from foundations built upon during past lives. The five-pointed star in the LGs' upward-pointing triangle signifies man, woman, child and their five senses. Through the five senses, on-going experiential, sensory learning is defined by the LD's entire field of numbers.

The following diagram is a graphic attempt at encapsulating the above postulates. It shows what I perceive to be the broad esoteric structure of a LD.

This diagram helps to visualise LGs as depicting that part of life where you meet and embrace new experiences and possibilities that teach you to extend and grow, as you strive to become more during each incarnation. Learning from sensory experience stimulates awareness of innate strengths and weaknesses and the value in learning to adapt to changing circumstances. Learning to move beyond comfort zones opens the way to being able to access increasingly higher "branches of accomplishment". This assures growth, eventual mastery and a sense of personal fulfilment through knowing that you are rising towards unfolding your soul's purpose – your Dharma – by manifesting or living out the "seed" potential in your birthdate.

The work of each new incarnation is ingeniously mapped out in your LGs and LCs. Forming the top sector of the tree, the LGs are like your arms, hands and fingers as they

Chapter 2 – Your Life Diamond as Your Mini Tree of Life

reach out to grasp, take hold of and attract new people, events and circumstances into your life. In this way, they can be seen to facilitate the soul's purpose for this particular incarnation.

Lengthy research consistently revealed that LGs are often expressed *negatively* which went against traditional ways of working with them. This was found to be especially so when new goals were being striven for, new experiences undergone, new things being experimented with or new territory pioneered. It appears that we are at our most vulnerable during periods of transition and self-exploration when we are flexing our spiritual and earthly muscles to extend personal boundaries; new territories and learning which inevitably invite mistakes. These are the reasons why I think negative traits, tendencies and experiences are likely to develop and occur under LGs when they are triggered by the introduction of anything new *or when negative traits are being consciously transformed*. So, prepare to see some "negatives" manifesting under a LG while new things are being explored, developed and mastered.

The LCs represent the roots of your tree. They can be likened to your legs, feet and toes that signify your support structure inherited from the results of past life works – your Karma. Break with tradition and see them as brought over positive *and* negative traits, inclinations and skills. Look to your LCs to uncover what you have that forms this life's foundation. As well as this, recognise that they also represent whatever facilitates or hinders this lifetime *only serving as hindrances until their lessons have been learned and transcended*.

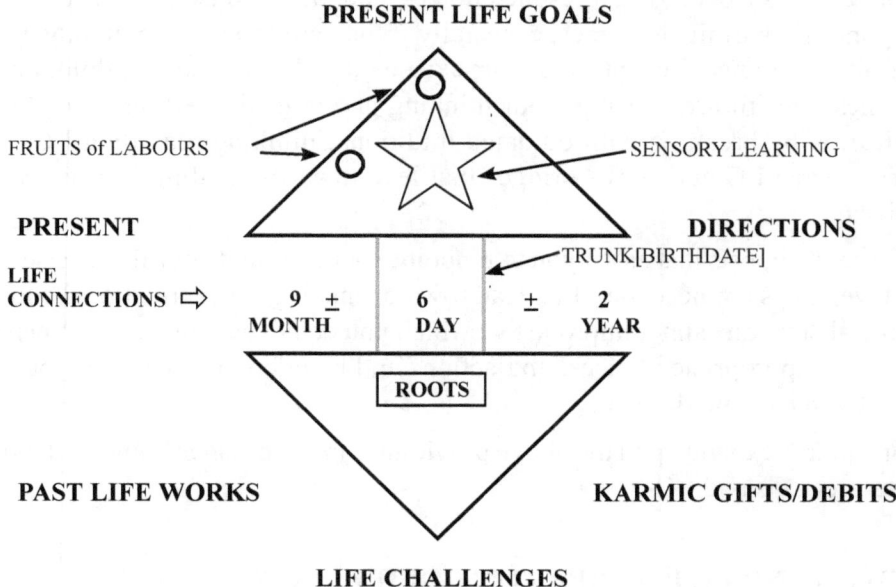

Your LCs contain the antidote to negative effects – all numbers do for that matter. When ready, you will find the right information within both LG/C's to solve your problems and life's mysteries. Perceiving your LCs in this way will supply you with just the right kind of information needed to ascertain what you have at your disposal to improve upon, develop further, consolidate and modify in this life. Bill Clinton's record clearly shows how he used his LC17s both positively *and* negatively, exemplifying the theory that they can be attributed a positive as well as a negative connotation in the challenge sector.

Often, too much emphasis is placed on the bad side of karma at the cost of its good side. Karma is the watershed of good *and* bad work from past and present actions. Because you have also accumulated good work i.e. *good* karma in past lives, it makes sense to think that your challenge numbers can represent *both* good and bad traits if they are a carry-over from past lives. Therefore, your LCs or foundations of your tree can equally represent hard-won esteem, attributes, talents and innate strengths. If this is so, then these would be the special gifts and tools that you have at your disposal to equip you for the life that you have chosen this time around. They may be found in areas of your life where you naturally excel and seem to have a gift for something. They may also explain times when you are highly motivated, feel pressured, or in a crisis and surprise yourself when hidden talents unexpectedly rise to meet the occasion. Bill Clinton's record clearly shows how he used the brought over gifts in his LC17s both positively *and* negatively, exemplifying the theory that they can be given a positive as well as a negative connotation.

It is a fallacy to think that karma cannot be altered. The results of past and present actions cannot be escaped. But, present choices and their consequent actions can significantly modify karmic outcomes, especially if they are founded upon judgements that stem from a deep need to improve your existence. What you know, think and do *now* determines your future. Change your thinking and your life will change. Aim at mitigating Karma by breaking with outdated traditional thinking regarding LCs. Use the positives in each LC number as bridges that lead towards creating Karmic *credits* for future lives.

LGs and LCs are signposts that assist you to pinpoint your gifts and your flaws. Use them to take whatever steps are necessary that lead towards making self-correctional choices. Create a "to-do-list"; you cannot improve that which you do not acknowledge. When you see selfishness, inappropriate choices, and actions and reactions recurring in your life, you know that you have work to do.

The following points expand upon the above providing a much broader framework within which to interpret LGs and LCs.

PROPOSED LG AND LC INTERPRETIVE GUIDELINES
YOUR LIFE GOALS REVEAL THIS LIFE'S BUDDING POTENTIAL:
- ▲ soul influences – assuring continuance of spiritual growth and evolution
- ▲ the facilitation of Destiny (Dharma) – earning credits for future lives

- ▲ new levels of aspiration and inspiration
- ▲ increasing incorporation of higher virtues
- ▲ building on past life accomplishments
- ▲ an inestimable range of new possibilities
- ▲ the new environment, people, paths and directions for this incarnation
- ▲ consistent development of gifts, talents, skills and attributes
- ▲ initiating new ambitions, goals and achievements
- ▲ new tests, trials and triumphs
- ▲ persistence, steadfastness, bravery and strength to overcome negativity and adversity
- ▲ ability to adapt to change often via the pain of adjustment
- ▲ becoming all that you can be

YOUR LIFE CHALLENGES REVEAL YOUR PAST LIVES' LEGACY
- ☐ Personality aspect of the self, "The Shadow"
- ☐ Karmic results of present life works and actions
- ☐ past life gifts, skills and abilities (innate, therefore often taken for granted)
- ☐ brought over traits from past lives that inhibit soul growth
- ☐ positive and negative heredity traits (that which is intrinsic)
- ☐ automatic (unconscious) inclinations, idiosyncrasies and vices
- ☐ inherent weaknesses and predispositions
- ☐ ability to acknowledge, then correct negative thoughts, speech and behaviours
- ☐ opportunities for greater self-awareness through the pain caused from:
    - a) ignorance, fear and guilt
    - b) avoidance behaviours – denial
    - c) failing to adapt or change – remaining "stuck" – inertia
    - d) clinging to that which is comfortable, inappropriate or redundant – inability to "let go"
    - e) not extending oneself
    - f) the pain of adjustment
    - g) making repetitive mistakes and inappropriate choices
    - h) whoever and whatever obstructs and hinders growth
    - i) avarice
    - j) not heeding advice or signs
    - k) not learning from mistakes
    - l) tests, trials and tribulations
- ✡ ability to conquer, transmute, transform and transcend

The Life Diamond

OTHER POINTS TO CONSIDER
- LGs can be likened to the Sun, Mercury, Venus, Mars and Jupiter in nature
- LCs can be likened to the Moon, Chiron, Saturn, Uranus, Neptune and Pluto

The LGs and LCs' true intent and gift to you are for you to learn to unscramble their "Sacred Code", make sense of it, and then *activate* their intrinsic potential and guidelines. Once deciphered, you will know how to define and take conscious, positive steps towards galvanising your Life Purpose, in spiritual and mundane ways. Doing this facilitates your singular quest of uncovering your unique pathways that point the way to becoming.

AN ESOTERIC DEPICTION OF A LIFE DIAMOND

The following diagrams are attempts at encapsulating a symbolic image of the esoteric nature of the ideas presented above. The LCs are represented by a blue, earthward pointing triangle. Imagine it as portraying that part of the Soul that has planted its seed in a fertile domain in which a new life can flourish and prosper.

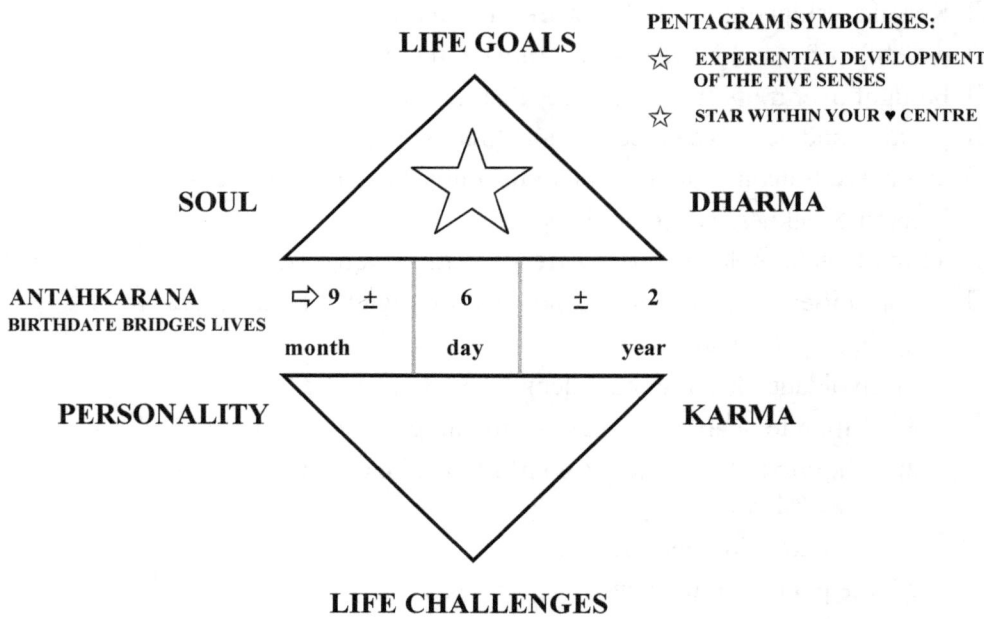

(**NB:** The ANTAHKARANA is the esoteric term used to symbolise the "rainbow bridge" or spiritual line of communication between the Personality (Lower mind) and the Soul (Higher mind). In this instance the birthdate is being substituted for it as an associated idea.)

The LGs are signified by a red, skyward-pointing triangle. Red signifies fiery, male energies and forces – the field of conscious activity. Red also denotes the energy, impetus and drive towards evolution. The LCs' blue, earthward-pointing triangle indicates watery, female energies and forces – the field of subconscious activity; the realm of generation, creation and manifestation. The five-pointed star encompasses the manifestation of one's present qualities, characteristics and capabilities within the LD's dynamic field of activity that all of its numbers represent.

When perceived in this way, these three esoteric symbols portray an incarnation's field of life experience in the microcosm. The LCs represent the past, the LGs the future, and the birth date the present; the bridge between the past and the future.

ACHIEVING THE STAR OF DAVID

The goal of each incarnation is to strive towards integrating and uniting the separated aspects of the self. This is symbolised by merging the red with the blue triangle to create the "Star of David". Perceived in this way, the Star of David becomes your macrocosmic/microcosmic environment with you at its centre, represented by the Pentagram. The Star of David personifies the rotating, spiralling field of activity that caters to all of your spiritual and earthly needs. It represents an extremely high level of human attainment that signifies gaining control over earthly and cosmic forces.

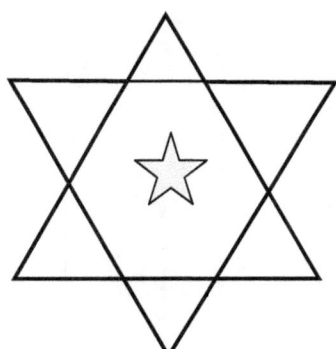

THE HEART NUMBER OF THE LD

When the Star of David and the Pentagram are coalesced, they shed light on a deeper understanding of the significance and meaning that is behind the placement of the birthday number in the middle of the LD's baseline. Being placed thus, situates it not only in the middle of the LD's baseline but also exactly at the centre of the LD itself, as with the Pentagram above! This means that the Pentagram can be considered as the LD's heart. Considering that it is used esoterically to symbolise the Christ centre in everyone's heart, does it not make perfect sense to give the number of the birthday – the most personal number in the birthdate – the day upon which you took your very first life-breath – such a pivotal position in the LD? To emphasise these points helps to appreciate the importance of the birthday's placement within the LD's structure and to name it its "heart number".

To conclude, the broad concepts raised in this chapter set the esoteric background for interpreting a LD. You will come to find it to be one of the easiest and most convenient branches of numerology that we have at our disposal from which to extrapolate a lifetime's projections. By "convenient", it is meant that this tiny, yet profoundly dynamic array of numbers can be singularly used, if pressed for time, to define an outstanding overview of one's life.

NB: Esoteric terms and symbols can be used in general or specific ways to express an association of ideas. In this chapter they have been used in a general sense using associated ideas that draw attention to broad concepts that attempt to describe how a LD operates when viewed in large segments or in its entirety. Chapters 3 and 4, on the other hand, use esoteric symbols to address specific fields of activity within the LD. To avoid confusion when you reach them, they portray the Star of David in a different context than in this chapter. Here, it is being used in its loftiest sense that encompasses the whole of the LD. But from here on, it is used in a much more specific sense to help to isolate and define its occult attributes and the numbers that represent the personality/aspirational field within it i.e. the specific field where soul growth can be initiated, cultivated and nurtured.

PYTHAGORAS' GENIUS

Abbreviated Terms used in this Chapter:
- ✧ LD = Life Diamond
- ✧ LG = Life Goal
- ✧ LC = Life Challenge
- ✧ LG/C = A Life Goal, Life Challenge combination

CHAPTER 3
PYTHAGORAS' GENIUS

Years spent researching LDs gave the sense that they contained much more than their simple numerical appearance conveyed. Little by little, this hunch was proven to be correct. Over the years, different esoteric symbols hidden within the framework of the numbers were uncovered. Each symbol represented an esoteric layer or dimension of the LD. As one layer was examined and understood, another emerged until the realisation occurred that Pythagoras had ingeniously used geometric symbols to create the esoteric nature of the LD then positioned the numbers on them to represent their exoteric nature – not the other way around. Both the symbols and the numbers were masterfully synthesised to create a unified esoteric symbol that was not only couched upon occult philosophies but also embraced macrocosmic/microcosmic principles in perfect harmony. This esoteric template, so ingeniously composed, simulates the field of experience that every individual is allotted for a lifetime. What became obvious was, that this system of symbolic order and relationships, together with its numbers, were intentionally woven together to address most aspects of a human nature and a person's lifetime by describing them in numerological terms.

This was all very exciting but conjecture such as this needs proof! As each symbol revealed itself, the burning question always in my mind was: did Pythagoras *intentionally* create the LD using select occult symbols to meet the singular purpose of providing humanity with keys to their individual destinies? Over time, it became feasible to conclude that Pythagoras had as he was exceptionally well-steeped in occult philosophy, taught that God created the universe by numbers and lived by the code that "God Geometrises".

As mentioned in the Preface, convincing proof came when a very dear friend unwittingly brought a book on occult philosophy to show me. It contained an ancient diagram by Ocellus Lucanus, a Pythagorean philosopher. Written around 150 BC, the diagram, explaining the elements and humours of the time, was tucked away in its 900 plus pages. (See the first diagram below.) This diagram was very similar to the one that I was using to represent the LD's Wheel of Life symbol. Finding this ancient symbol enabled me to put meaning to the diagonal cross; a part of the LD that was an enigma as I was struggling to comprehend its significance in the LD. Not only was light shed upon the significance and meaning of the diagonal cross but more importantly it served to corroborate my feelings that Pythagoras had indeed constructed the LD's numerical arrangement upon a background of deep, occult geometry. Finding that small diagram made everything clear.

When you place both diagrams together, you can see how the LD's Wheel of Life symbol contains the same two crosses as in Ocellus's diagram. See below.

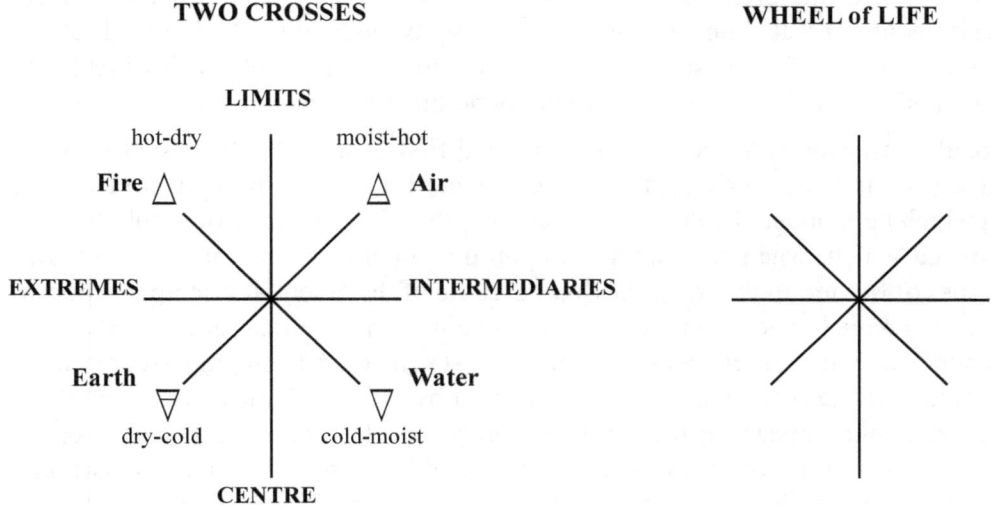

The vertical cross (+) in each represents the cross of matter where spiritual and material experience can be broadened each lifetime. Seeing the four elements placed on the diagonal cross (x) in the ancient diagram explained its relationship to the LD after trying to fathom its purpose for many years. Associations could be drawn from it to acknowledge that its elements symbolised both the composition of and the limits to the macrocosmic/microcosmic field in which we exist. This is beautifully depicted in another way in the Wheel of Fortune Tarot Key. Although the elements are arranged differently on its Key, the basic principle is the same. The fixed signs of the zodiac are allotted to the figures representing each element. Their fixed nature is used explicitly, to symbolise the *limits* of existence that are designated to remain ever the same at the same time allowing sequence and rotation to go on *within* these limits. (Drawing an analogy from this to the physical body, its skin can be seen as the body's limits which supply the framework for its systems and cycles of waking and sleeping and eating, digestion and excretion and of growth and age may be carried on *within* it)

Associations from the two crosses and the Wheel of Fortune Key helped to form the conclusion that Pythagoras had constructed the LD upon occult, geometric philosophies which embraced macrocosmic representations of Deity and the laws of creation. His genius lies in that he then contrived them to represent microcosmic existence. This was

The Life Diamond

achieved mathematically by the adroit use of the birthdate's numbers, plus the element of time, to represent the sequence and rotation of events going on in a human being's lifetime. When placed upon Pythagoras's choice of geometric symbols, the birthdate's numbers represent the microcosmic field of experience to be cultivated and nurtured during each incarnation *within* the cradle of the macrocosm.

Reaching this conclusion has brought about a deep appreciation of the esoteric nature of the LD. It is being aired throughout this and subsequent chapters in an attempt to give credence to the premise that Pythagoras created the LD from different aspects of esoteric geometry that, when synthesised, represents the totality of a human lifetime and the personalised field of sensory experience allotted to it. What follows is a breakdown of Pythagoras' occult philosophy that can be found hidden in each LD's sacred geometry.

Personality aspects within a LD will be treated first. A truly amazing synthesis of four relatively simple geometric symbols reveals what I believe to be Pythagoras's concept upon which he founded the Personality realm of the LD. Four esoteric symbols are being introduced which, when superimposed upon one another, represent the Personality on the Cross of Matter. In this way, they reveal some of the essential principles upon which the LD is created. These simple diagrams begin with a vertical and a diagonal cross accompanied by its four elements to form the first symbol. A Pentagram (representing the Personality) is the second symbol accompanied by its five elements that include spirit. Then a diamond appears in the third diagram which I perceive as being an enclosing square. In this instance, it is used to represent the limits of human existence (the macrocosm). Regarding LDs, I believe this diamond/square is being used by Pythagoras to represent a unified macrocosmic/microcosmic field of existence. (Esoterically, squares can be utilised to symbolise the earth. In this instance I believe Pythagoras has used the diamond-come-square shape of the LD's numbers as a template from which a relationship between it and earthly existence can be established.)

ESOTERIC SYMBOLS SHOWING THE EMERGENCE OF THE LD

TWO CROSSES   +   PENTAGRAM   =   PERSONALITY FIELD IN LIFE DIAMOND

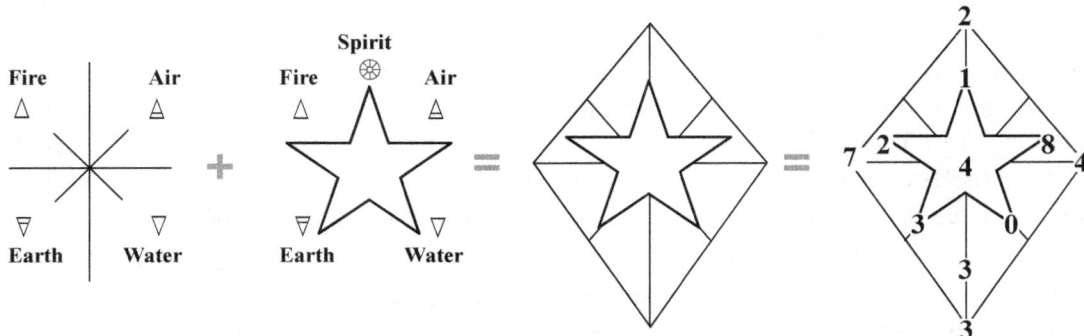

The way in which each of these symbols relates to the LD is profound. Knowledge of what they represent helps to clarify their interconnectedness and associations to the LD's numbers and consequently our lives. The symbols represent most of the inner ordering of the skeletal framework or matrix upon which the LD's numbers are superimposed. Understanding their significance and meaning, their placements and interrelationships and how they can be applied spiritually and mundanely to its numbers, provides a deeper appreciation of the LD's spiritual nature. Then unmistakable links to Deity, creation, generation and formation can be readily comprehended and transposed to a LD's numbers once recognised.

To help with understanding how the symbolic matrix of the LD can be translated into practical terms for use as a divinatory tool, the following briefly addresses each symbol in turn. Some receive a fuller explanation in the next chapter.

THE VERTICAL CROSS (+): The vertical cross is comprised of a vertical arm (active, positive polarity) and a horizontal arm (passive, negative polarity). Spiritual growth is the basic esoteric property attributed to its vertical arm and Personality growth to its horizontal arm. The interconnectedness of the two arms on the vertical cross intimates that vertical and horizontal growth must develop *concurrently* in an aspirant's life; a very important concept to remember.

Numbers appearing on the spiritual arm of the vertical cross provide clues to spiritual aspirations and ways that they may be achieved. Numbers appearing on the horizontal arm of the vertical cross indicate Personality aspirations and materialistic, everyday concerns. Chapter 4 elaborates on the roles of the crosses under the heading of the "Wheel of Life".

THE DIAGONAL CROSS (x): This cross, when placed on the vertical cross, can be seen to have four arms. Each arm represents one of the four elements. The order of the elements on this cross replicates the ancient esoteric assignment of fire, earth, air and water to the Pentagram. When you know how the Pentagram is drawn, you can better understand these correspondences. It is drawn in this way: beginning at the top of the Pentagram, a line is drawn from there to the left-hand, bottom angle representing the descent of spirit into matter to reach its lowest form (earth element – the Bull; fixed sign of Taurus). The next line ascends from this point to the right-hand angle where it represents matter in its highest form i.e. the brain of man (air element – Humanity; fixed sign of Aquarius). From here, a line is drawn across the figure to the left-hand, upper angle that depicts man's developing intellect and progress in material civilisation (fire element – the Lion; fixed sign of Leo). This point also represents the point of danger where man and nations can become corrupted. So, the line from this angle to the right-hand, bottom angle represents man's fall (water element – the Eagle; fixed sign of Scorpio). But, the soul of man having the spark of God within cannot remain at this point. The struggle upward begins from here which is indicated by the closing line ascending to join with the uppermost point of spirit from whence it issued forth at the apex of the Pentagram.

Western Mystery Schools depict the Pentagram's elements in a different arrangement to the above. They follow that of the creatures pictured on the Wheel of Fortune and

The Life Diamond

World Keys: AIR top left; WATER, top right; EARTH, bottom left and FIRE, bottom right. However, I choose to use the version found in the ancient writings of Ocellus Lucanus and Aristotle around 150 B.C. for the LD because it appeared closer to the time of Pythagoras. Their version is being chosen, *in this instance only*, to give credence to the idea that Pythagoras based the LD upon occult principles of Deity, creation, generation and formation.

THE PENTAGRAM: The Pentagram symbolises many things. For the LD's purposes, it can signify: the Christ centre within the heart; the microcosm; the five elements; man/woman's five senses; the Personality and the Quintessential Self.

The Western Mystery Tradition places the four elements in different positions around the Pentagram to Ocellus' ancient diagram. The next diagram uses its placements. In it, you can see how Spirit enters the apex of the Pentagram infusing the four elements (placed on each of the lower points) within it to represent macrocosmic influences. The heart symbol is my addition to the Pentagram. I am using it microcosmically to signify spirit penetrating then radiating out from it to saturate and fill all aspects of the Pentagram like the heart number does in the LD.

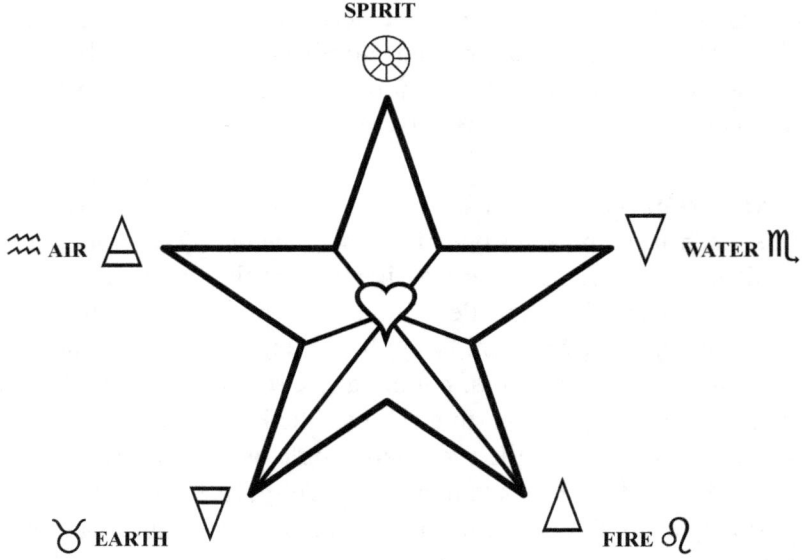

Knowing the Pentagram's esoteric components, you can understand how they translate to your spiritual and physical dimensions. For instance, the apex of the Pentagram represents SPIRIT infusing the FOUR ELEMENTS (the other four points to the star) as it descends deeper and deeper into matter. SPIRIT, at the Pentagram's apex, represents the point of CONSCIOUSNESS (your wisdom aspect) seated in the head. The LIFE FORCE of your SOUL (your love aspect) is situated at the Pentagram's centre (your heart). This aspect of the Pentagram can also be related to your physical heart being the point where your heart is infused with the Life Force of your soul. In this way, Soul essence is then carried by the bloodstream to the cells to permeate every part of your body. These spirit/elemental/physical body associations signify how the Pentagram encapsulates the sum-total of your spiritual and physical being making it, and the heart symbol, correlate to your birthday number which sits at the centre of a LD. Associations drawn between the Pentagram and the heart symbol help to define the importance of the role of the birthday number in it.

Basic aspects of the Personality have been covered by the use of the Pentagram and the crosses. Soul/spiritual aspects can now be addressed by introducing the Star of David.

THE STAR OF DAVID: The Pentagram on the crosses depicts the Personality on the Cross of Matter. When the Star of David is superimposed on the crosses, it represents the Soul on the Cross of Matter. In this way, the Star of David denotes your Soul's field of activity by standing for your subtle counterparts. It epitomises the field in which interactive experiences with the tangible world and that of hidden ethereal worlds can be developed simultaneously. As a consequence, the development of higher principles are stimulated and manifested in everyday life.

You will come to recognise that the position of the Star of David on the crosses provides the link between the playground of the Personality and the transpersonal realms via the cosmic diamond. (Chapters 4 and 6 elaborate on the role of the Star of David in the LD.)

THE WHEEL OF LIFE: If circles are drawn around the cosmic diamond, the Star of David and the inner square (introduced in the next chapter), then a dot put at the centre of the diagram, a Wheel of Life symbol is created. Once created, the element of time and the law of rotation and cyclicity are introduced to the LD. Excellent correspondences can then be made from it to the Wheel of Fortune Key. This Tarot Key specifically represents the law of sequence and cyclicity which governs continuing evolution. I think Pythagoras ingeniously reversed its occult symbology so that the LD could address a *human* lifetime. He modified the LD to represent microsomic life whereas the Wheel of Fortune Key represents macrocosmic life.

Paul Foster Case's book on *"The Tarot"* provides the best description of the Wheel of Fortune. Many associations can be drawn from his descriptions to suit the LD's Wheel of Life. For example, he explains how the 10th Key encompasses ideas of rotation, cyclicity, sequence and such things as fortune, destiny, fate, chance, probability and necessity. All of these concepts can be applied to the LD. He goes on to say that nothing ever really happens by chance; that life is governed by the unalterable law of cause and effect and the sooner this notion is grasped the greater command can be wielded over consequential events. These are facts of life as we know them and can be readily transferred, in a microcosmic sense, to the LD.

In the *microcosmic* Realm of Cosmos diagram below, the large circle which encompasses the LD's Cosmic Diamond symbolises the realm of spirit or the greater Sun. The next inner circle encompasses the Star of David, symbolising the realm of the Soul or the lesser Sun. Then the innermost circle symbolises the realm of the Personality represented by the inner square and finally, the point at its centre symbolises the realm of physical

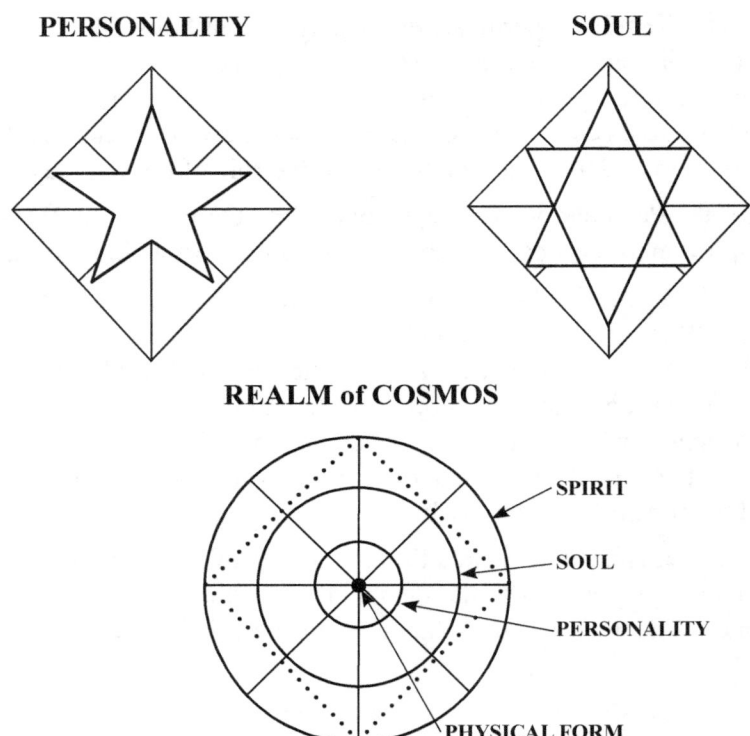

form. The Wheel of Fortune Key does the opposite from its *macrocosmic* representation. Its centre symbolises the archetypal world, the next circle to it, the creative world, the next circle, the formative world and the outer circle the material world. Its eight spokes represent the universal radiant energy that permeates everything which is similar to the way that our life force radiates out from the LD's heart to all parts of the LD.

The Trinity of the Self depicted in the three diagrams above, illustrates the deeper implications that can be drawn from the generational template upon which I believe the LD's numbers to have been intentionally engineered by Pythagoras to create a symbolic representation of a human lifetime.

To support this further, Paul also wrote regarding the Wheel of Fortune: "The affairs of men and those of nations, have a rhythm, a regularity, a steadiness of beat which enables the wise to read the meaning of the present in the history of the past and makes it possible to forecast the events of the future from close examination of present tendencies. The wheel, moreover, is a symbol of progress, advancement, improvement and so represents the march of culture, civilisation and amelioration which in occultism, is called the "Great Work."

Translated to the LD's "Wheel", it can be interpreted microcosmically, to represent the "Lesser Work" i.e. the work of a human lifetime That being so, then it may also be considered that Pythagoras fully intended the LD to be used as a divination tool to enable us to discern the meaning of the present from our past and from that to forecast future possibilities from close examination of our present.

A LD's MAGICKAL FACETS

Abbreviated Terms used in this Chapter:
- ✧ LD = Life Diamond
- ✧ LG = Life Goal
- ✧ LC = Life Challenge
- ✧ LG/C = A Life Goal, Life Challenge combination

CHAPTER 4
A LD's MAGICKAL FACETS

ESTABLISHING ASSOCIATIONS BETWEEN MAGICKAL SYMBOLS

Unlike the broad use of symbols in Chapter 2, this chapter introduces you to magickal symbols that draw your attention to individual facets of a LD, in specific ways, so that the divine intent contained in them and their numbers can be studied in greater detail. The purpose behind this is to learn the significance and meaning of each symbol and its numbers so that willed changes to your life can be initiated with the intent of manifesting desired outcomes that complement your spiritual aspirations. This approach brings an entirely new slant to this branch of numerology where the onus is placed squarely upon you to learn how to interpret, then manipulate your symbols and numbers i.e. to perform magick, by igniting the spiritual intent secreted in them and getting them to work as you would wish them to in your life. Success at this would be to use your numbers in their ultimate sense by liberating and developing their spiritual qualities with the aim of furthering your evolution. However, in order to delineate a LD exoterically, it is not necessary to work with these magickal symbols.

The spelling of the word "magick" is being used here in its esoteric sense. Used in this way, magick portrays an intentional activation of the will with the main objective being to produce desired changes. In this instance, you use magick when you intentionally activate and manipulate the numbers held within each of your LD's magickal facets to cause desired changes to occur that cultivate and nurture sought after spiritual qualities and outcomes that are in line with your spiritual aspirations. To do this successfully, is to be somewhat like "The Magician".

Familiarising yourself with symbols and their basic interrelationships enables you to begin to know and appreciate their essential nature. You will learn to recognise that each symbol, although separate, in some way connects to others within the LD and to the LD as a whole. Their interrelationships trigger ideas of how the energies and forces of each functions: first as a separate entity and then in unison with each other. This fundamental understanding helps you to more easily understand the nature, positions and subsequently the meanings of their numbers as well as serving to substantiate associations and connections between them.

Where applicable, correspondences from the LD's magickal symbols are made to the

Qabalistic Tree of Life to further an understanding of them. (Throughout, the spelling of Qabalah follows that of the Western Mystery Tradition.) The purpose behind making correspondences between the LD's symbols and the Tree of Life helps to provide added weight to their interpretive use when seeking esoteric guidelines. In simple terms, the Tree of Life is a fantastic, symbolic representation that describes the macrocosm and the microcosm in which we live and move and have our being. Having a basic knowledge of the construction and occult philosophy behind the Tree of Life and meanings of the Hebrew letters and the astrological associations from the Tarot Keys to your numbers would be to your advantage when working with these symbols.

IDENTIFYING the MAGICKAL FACETS of a LD

First, construct your SDLD (Chapter 5 provides instructions) and then mentally differentiate between its mundane and magickal facets as listed below. Firmly imprint its different components on your mind. This will enable you to prepare for all interpretation work.

Each LD contains a HEART number or PENTAGRAM, a COSMIC DIAMOND, an INNER SQUARE, a STAR of DAVID and a WHEEL OF LIFE and CONSTELLATIONS. Most require advanced knowledge to be able to decipher their significance and meaning and apply their mystical connotations to mundane life experiences to reflect macrocosmic/microcosmic influences.

A list of the different facets of a LD is outlined below with its magickal facets appearing from numbers 8 through 14. Following them are diagrams of each facet.

Your Mental Image Should Picture:
1. INSIDE the LD are two side-by-side mini-diamonds and two opposing triangles.
2. The TWO MINI-DIAMONDS represent your *first and second* life cycles.
3. The TWO OPPOSING TRIANGLES represent your *third* life cycle.
4. The LARGE OUTER or COSMIC DIAMOND represents your *fourth* life cycle.
5. The birthdate's three major numbers form the LD's BASELINE and produce the LPN.
6. The four numbers above the baseline are the LD's GOALS (LGs).
7. The four numbers below the baseline are the LD's CHALLENGES (LCs).
8. The HEART No. is your *birthday* number.
9. The LD's INNER SQUARE
10. The LD's STAR of DAVID
11. The GRAIL
12. The LD's COSMIC DIAMOND (Large outer diamond)
13. The LD's WHEEL of LIFE (Number-Lines, two crosses and their Rulers)
14. The LD's CONSTELLATIONS (different LD RULERS)

The Life Diamond

A LD's BASIC COMPONENTS

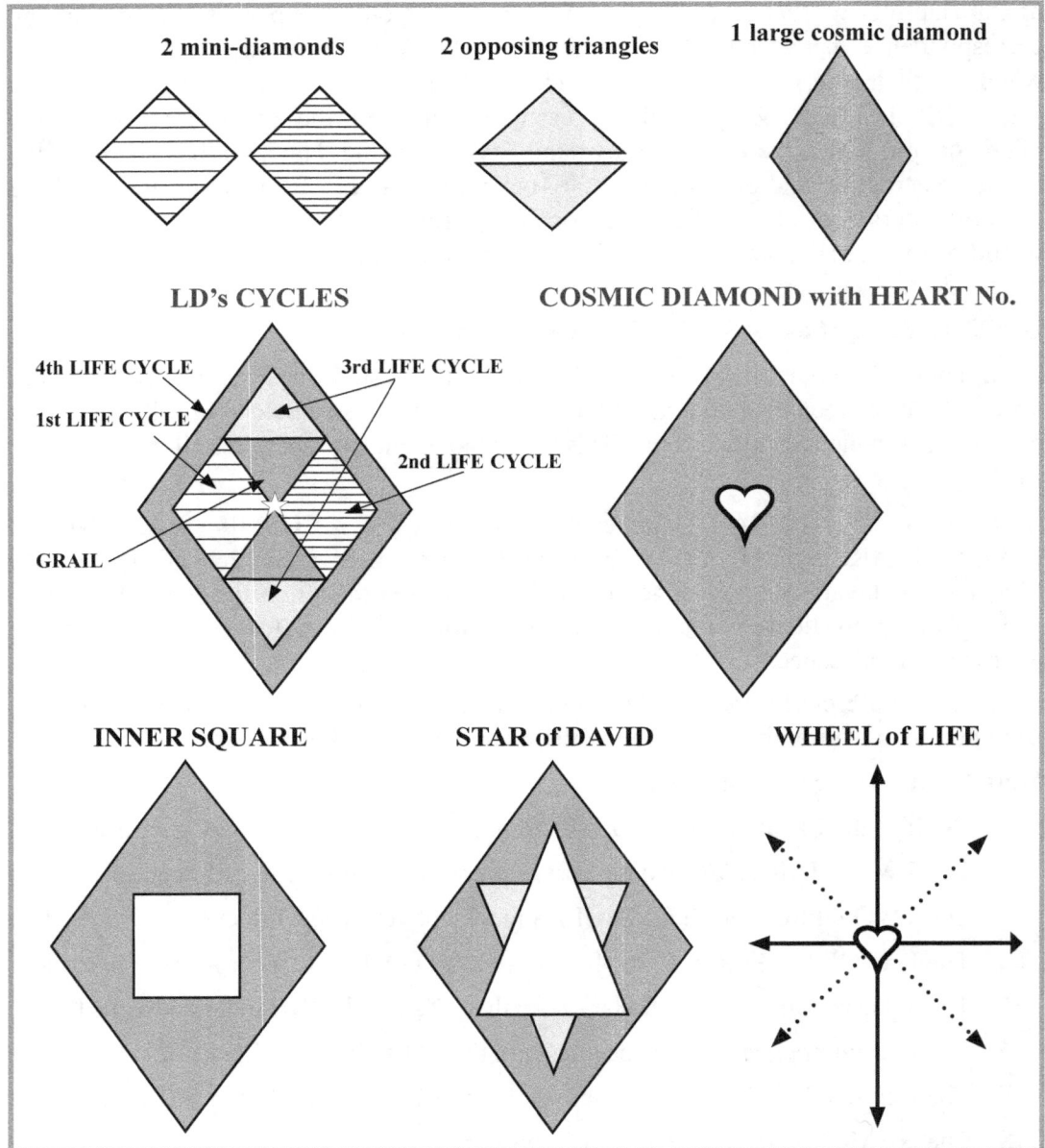

A LD's MAGICKAL SYMBOLS:

The PENTAGRAM or HEART NUMBER can be used to symbolise your birthday number. The Pentagram (Five-Pointed Star) and its esoteric principles were introduced in Chapters 2 and 3.

Knowing what the Pentagram represents and then relating its attributes to your birthday number or heart number, helps you to understand and to appreciate how it is *the* vital point in a LD in that it receives sensory, spiritual and cosmic, soul and earthly impressions which it then radiates and circulates to all parts of your LD somewhat similar to the way in which the spiritual component of the bloodstream does in your body. *From your level of consciousness*, it enables you to translate and transmit combined spiritual and earthly influences into your livingness. Not only that, as a vital part of the bridge between the challenges and the goals, your birthday number also enables you to integrate past, present and future aspects of your life.

Imagine your birthday number as a filter or a funnel through which cosmic energies and forces can be radiated into and through your LD's numbers then percolated into your world. View it as a receiving station, a translation station and a transmitting station. Get to know all that it signifies as best you can and seek out its specific gifts to you as it is pivotal to your means of self expression. Therefore, both its root digit and compound number's meanings (if your birthday number happens to be a compound number) should receive your undivided attention. Make the variety of meanings of your birthday number second nature to you. See how they colour all that you think, say and do and the way that you go about your daily affairs. Also, take out its Tarot Key/s and study them. Doing this will help you to increase self-awareness.

If your birthday number is a compound number, do not forget to use its reverse number and its root number. Those born on the 28th and 29th of the month will use 28/82/10/1 and 29/92/11/2/20 as their numbers. 0 always holds a place before its single digit so those born on the 1st, 5th and 9th, for example will use 1/10, 5/50, and 9/90 for their root numbers.

The LD's BASELINE: In order to gain an understanding of the role of the LD's baseline, similarities can be drawn from it to MALKUTH, the sphere located at the bottom of the Tree of Life; each provide the footing to their structures. Malkuth represents the earth sphere; the realm allocated to the physical body and its sense impressions. It is where our physical consciousness acquires knowledge by penetrating the darkness of ignorance as a direct result of its capacity for translating mental impressions gained from direct sensory experience. From this we can gather that Malkuth symbolises the field where the basis for uncovering the esoteric nature of existence can be initiated. Malkuth's properties that relate to the body and the physical environment can be transferred to the LD's baseline to help you to see it as representing your physical contact with the earth plane. From these associations, the LDs' baseline can be seen as providing the basis from which the actual beginning of progress toward attaining spiritual heights by overcoming inertia is made here, on the physical plane; the field of sensation. Hence, both Malkuth and the LD's baseline represent a fixed field of activity where natural laws and the mechanics of the earth plane can be experienced as a platform from which subtle or inner growth has its initial beginnings.

The INNER SQUARE: Overall, the LD's numbers represent the limits of your total field of activity in this lifetime but the inner square specifically pertains to your everyday field of activity which facilitates the cultivation and manifestation of individuality, sensation and work. It represents your horizontal or personality growth as opposed to your spiritual growth that the numbers on the vertical axis and the Star of David signify. It is a direct result of combining the energies and forces of the LD's earth axis; the horizontal arm of the vertical cross meaning that it serves as a platform from which the senses can be elevated to a higher plane of sensation making it an upward extension of the baseline. This likens it to YESOD which is the next higher sphere on the Tree of Life from Malkuth. Similar to Yesod, the square is intermediate to physicality and soul influences; it partakes of the two encapsulating the Personality aspect of the lower self.

On the Tree of Life, Yesod is called FOUNDATION. This title beautifully links to the grounding, elemental nature of the inner square. Correspondences such as this help you to determine that by position and placement, how both the baseline and the square point to your instinctive, distinctive attributes which are at the root of your personality. Yesod, the second last sphere on the Tree of Life, is also known as the MOON sphere. The Moon represents the Personality in this sphere which equates to the lower self in spiritual terms. Accordingly, to make a cross-link from Yesod as the Personality, to the inner square, helps to cement the concept that the square also represents the Personality. It is from the square that we are able to open up the conscious mind to the subtle, intermediate influences of other realms that Yesod represents. These associations establish a sense of the square's place within the macrocosmic/microcosmic influences represented by these symbols. They help you to fathom your place in the macrocosm and connection to the Divine Plan. Another of Yesod's attributes is to promote your sense of individuality and independence by forcing you to challenge your views so that a secure foundation can be built upon the results of tangible and intangible experiences.

The above notions can be readily applied to the square and to your life. Use "4" keywords and draw associations from DALETH, the fourth Hebrew letter to expand your understanding of what a square can represent. Then you might bring in the astrological sign ARIES (rules the fourth Tarot Key) and planet MARS (rules Aries and The Tower). Further to this: look to The EMPEROR (ruled by Aries) and The TOWER (ruled by Mars) Keys to provide more information. Finally, more insights can be gleaned from CHESED, the fourth sphere on the Tree of Life, ascribed MERCY. Looking for clues from other esoteric sources like this, helps to gain a deeper understanding of what the numbers in the inner square signify. What you take from these correspondences may well be used to bolster interpretive possibilities. (All of the LD's magickal facets may be treated along similar lines.)

Accept that the square's numbers are central to all delineations; especially from a Personality angle due to their fundamental placement and nature. This can be further borne out when you consider that the square is derived from the baseline and that Malkuth rules the realm of appearance and materialisation which would seem to elevate the chances of the square's indications manifesting. Use these suggestions as a basis for interpreting the inner square's numbers and its rulers (Chapter 6, Step 7). They provide palpable clues about your everyday experiences and earthly work. Therefore, extremely reliable indications and guidelines concerning highly probable, major, lifelong Personality traits and tendencies can be accessed.

The STAR of DAVID: The Star of David is being used in this instance to specifically define the six numbers that create it and to establish correlations between it and other symbols in an effort to determine interpretive guidelines. (This is not the same as the way the Star was presented in Chapter 2 where it was broadly used to symbolise the entire LD.)

A good place to begin is with the Star's six points drawing correlations to them. They make strong connections to number six and to other esoteric symbols that share "six" connections. TIPHARETH, centrally placed on the Tree of Life, is one. It is the sixth sphere on the Tree making a "six" connection but it more importantly signifies soul responsiveness being the realm of the soul on the Tree. Sharing similar concepts, the soul aspect of Tiphareth forms a strong link to the Star's realm of soul responsiveness. From these associations, an understanding of how the Star in your LD can represent your "soul infused field of activity" begins to gel. The inner square addresses your everyday world of experiences and now the Star can be seen to address your field of soul impressions that underpin your spiritual aspirations.

The Star is strategically positioned in that it spans the baseline integrating the goal/challenge sectors of the LD. Its numbers are the same as the two, separate mini-triangles of the third life cycle, yet its construction synthesises them. *Integration* is the Star's major keyword. Other major Star keywords are: union, duality and opposites and reconciliation and mediation which beautifully describe how its two triangles (duality) unite across (integrates) the goal and challenge areas (reconciling opposing points) of the LD. Additional keywords to consider are: join, link, connect, unite, blend, combine, harmonise, synchronize, coordinate, mediate and resolve. These keywords provide a basis from which an understanding of how the Star's numbers can be manipulated to facilitate the integration of your soul and personality aspects.

A very powerful interrelationship exists between the Star and the inner square. It is important to acknowledge that they are integral to each other to fully appreciate their separate yet conjoined roles within the LD. This connection becomes obvious when you observe how the base of each of the Star's triangles includes the inner square's top and bottom numbers. This is truly fascinating – the Star is literally emerging from the square promising ascendancy to a higher realm like the phoenix principle! Here we have direct proof that from the desire to aspire, we have within us the art of being able to temper ourselves, our environment and ultimately our consciousness by directing our will-power, imagination and intended purpose to transcend our perceived limitations i.e. our squares, by activating our Stars. As a consequence, the Star is able to integrate the work of the inner square, using it as its foundation (Yesod) upon which to spiritualise daily works (Malkuth). Also note how the Star's upper and lower peaks engage the third goal and the third challenge on the spiritual axis which are the sum-total of the positive and negative aspects of the LD's baseline. This creates a powerful unifying effect between them. Another quite fascinating point to note is that the red triangle's ruler is either the same as the square's ruler or a member of its number family which cements its links to the Star and to Personality ascendance.

The Star, by itself, has its own specific attributes. It contains its own Personality (red, upward-pointing triangle) and Soul (blue, downward-pointing triangle) aspects when you separate it into its red and blue triangles (see Chapter 6, Step 8). As an isolated esoteric symbol, the blue triangle can be perceived as signifying your Soul filtering higher consciousness downwards into and through your Personality. The Star's red triangle can then be perceived as encapsulating your Personality's struggle to embody higher consciousness and sought after virtues as it reaches towards the Soul with the aim of coalescing separated aspects of the self. It symbolises re-emergence from the confining limits of form similar to the occult philosophy behind Tarot Key, 20.

For further interpretation purposes, both the red and blue triangles may be seen to represent what you are having difficulty with acknowledging and overcoming. They depict the constant struggle between the lower and the higher self and with the light and dark forces. They also depict the struggle to achieve inseparable unity of spirit and matter. Both triangles offer the gift of transcending personality flaws and spiritualising daily existence once you have uncovered what their numbers mean for you and consciously work at structuring your life so that their potential can be realised. They may shed light upon inhibiting influences from the past emanating from the square and red triangle (and challenge numbers), reveal inner conflicts between your Personality and Soul and show you where and how you are most likely to limit your evolutionary process. For esoteric interpretations, cultivate your understanding of what the Star's connotations are for you from a spiritual perspective when related to the rest of your LD. Use them as a guide to enable you to pinpoint ways to promote Soul and Personality integration.

Nothing can be attained without effort. If you desire what your Star bestows, become *proactive* about it by viewing it as one of your instruments that can be used to expose your spiritual aspirations. The Star, symbolising a perpetual, rotational field of activity implies continuous movement that can then be translated to suggest the perpetual unfoldment and development of spiritual ambition. This notion of constant activity helps you to understand that the Star won't "work" for you as *you* have to "work" the Star to begin to understand its possibilities and to reap its benefits. There is a secret to achieving this. It is to initiate the Star's Mercurial aspect of discriminative intelligence. The Mercurial aspect of the Star is drawn from making associations to the number six and to the sixth Qabalistic letter Vau (which means to unite or join things) and to the zodiacal signs Gemini and Virgo as well as to the Magician, Lovers and Hermit Keys which are also ruled by Mercury. A study of each of these associations will furnish you with further clues. Simplistically, Mercury symbolises the rational mind, which is the key that leads to attaining the Star's purpose via discrimination. Mercury is assigned to HOD, the third lowest sphere of the Tree of Life; its name is SPLENDOR.

Perhaps the best way to work with the Star is to isolate it from the LD and then isolate its two triangles and rulers keeping uppermost in your mind that you are seeking information that will help you to determine what you need to do to cultivate and nurture Soul growth. To do this, compare the possibilities contained in the various components of the Star and its numbers with your aspirations and the reality of your life circumstances by evaluating how well things are actually manifesting for you along this vein. Be brutally honest with yourself. See all that your Star stands for in the light of your tests, trials and triumphs representing your struggle and desire to grow spiritually. Weigh and consider its positive *and* negative aspects i.e. the positive to access spiritual possibilities and guidelines for initiation of continuous aspiration, growth and elevation of self and the negative to shed light on behavioural attitudes and life choices that have countered Soul growth. *Activate* your Star and any faults and flaws will automatically be taken care of in the process of manifesting higher qualities.

The GRAIL: Merely as a point of interest, when you look at the diagram that represents the LD's cycles, you can make out a Grail enfolding the birthday number. The Grail is an integral part of the inner square and the Star of David demonstrating a consistent Soul/Personality-based interrelationship and interconnectedness between these esoteric symbols and the Pentagram – your heart number. Calculate the Grail's ruling number from those that compose it and decide for yourself whether it is of use or not. It is an intriguing combination of the square and the pentagram.

The COSMIC DIAMOND: The cosmic diamond is the large diamond that, in some ways, sets the limits of the LD. It appears to have a more universal influence representing your "superconscious connections" or your "cosmic-infused field of activity". This is due to its founding numbers being universal in nature. Although this diamond seems detached from all other numbers when you isolate it, it is connected to the heart number at its centre through the month and year numbers when they are paired to it. It also connects to the top and bottom pair of LG/Cs when they are paired to it making a Soul/Spirit connection (see Steps 1, 2 and 5 in Chapter 6). But few could use them at this level so they would be interpreted exoterically for most people. Only when it is isolated as a symbol, can its "cosmic" nature be appreciated because the birthday number, the most personal number in the LD, is not part of its make-up.

An important feature of the cosmic diamond is that it is comprised of the outermost points of the horizontal and spiritual axes, connecting the spiritual with the mundane. From its chronological aspect, it seems to personify the emergence of understanding and wisdom when it is activated in mature years. At its conclusion, the cosmic diamond's cycle culminates into a new beginning when the second round of the "golden years" is begun (Chapter 12).

From an esoteric viewpoint, in order to gain an awareness of the cosmic diamond's role in the scheme of things, it is necessary to consider the interrelationships existing between it, the Star and the square. When you do, you end up with three numerical fields of activity representing three different, spiritual aspects of yourself that can be cultivated and nurtured. To help you to comprehend the way that these fields work together, imagine the square relating to *personality impressions* and YESOD on the Tree of Life, the Star of David and TIPHARETH as your *soul impressions*, and the cosmic diamond and KETHER as your *spiritual impressions*.

I sense that the cosmic diamond's individual impress has more of a spiritual *en*folding/*un*folding component for three reasons. The first is because of its universal make-up. The second is that it appears to have a background influence for life. And the third is that it is not accessed until mature/senior years are reached when its cycle becomes activated.

However, there are exceptions to this notion. Paul Foster Case and Aleister Crowley's cosmic diamonds present us with a contradiction. Their SDLDs are exactly the same even though their birthdates are different. Their cosmic diamond rulers are 10, being the Wheel of Fortune. In this instance, the symbolism of the Tarot Key and its Hebrew letter gave the most illuminating clues. These symbols describe Paul and Aleister's life's magickal work as 10's root 1, being the *Magician* and able to *grasp* (the closed hand of the 11th Hebrew letter; KAPH; allotted to Key 10) the *mechanism* of Universal Laws and learn to control them (The Magician). This follows the Wheel of Fortune's true representation. The point being made is that Aleister and Paul's life's Work began earlier in life, well before the cosmic diamond's cycle was activated. When delineating, their LDs provide an excellent example of how a person's level of evolution can be *the* single, most overriding factor that requires alterations to procedures in order to accommodate them.

The WHEEL of LIFE and its CONSTELLATIONS: The LD's cosmic diamond represents the limits of human existence while the rotation of a lifetime's cycles proceed within its structure. Its vertical (+) and diagonal (x) synthesise to form eight arms which can be likened to an EIGHT-POINTED STAR or to the eight spokes of the WHEEL of LIFE. These symbols help you to understand how the LD is based on the laws of evolution and cycles within cycles.

When you have constructed your LD, draw connecting lines through all of its numbers on the vertical (+) cross then those on the diagonal (x) cross issuing from the heart number. You will find that you have created an eight-pointed star or eight spokes of a wheel with your birthday number at its centre. The macrocosmic meaning of an eight-spoked wheel is that it signifies rotations and cycles – the whirling motion of the Life Force *issuing forth* from its cosmic centre.

Microcosmically, on the other hand, by placing the heart number at the Wheel's nucleus you have the *entry point* of SPIRIT at its hub. Picturing this, you can more easily imagine how the heart number impregnates, then radiates and circulates its influence into and through each of the Wheel's numbers, spokes and cycles, somewhat like the heart circulates the soul force throughout the body's circulatory system. The Wheel signifies the ever-changing cyclic nature of our lives which facilitates, via change, the ultimate goal of attaining higher consciousness.

Add up the four major arms of the LD and you will obtain their number-line rulers (see Step 9, Chapter 6). They can be pictured as CONSTELLATIONS as they fall beyond the periphery of the LD thereby simulating the zodiacal constellations in astrology. See these numbers as transmitting and filtering their unique energies and forces into and through their number-lines and the heart number. Remember that they have a background, life-long influence and can be activated at any time (see Steve Irwin: Chapter 6, Step 9).

The LD's RULER CONSTELLATIONS: In Chapter 8 you are introduced to LD extensions. They are the rulers of different parts of the LD analogous to the number-line rulers in that they also fall beyond the periphery of the LD. To introduce their esoteric symbolism, they can be visualised as constellations, too, because they can also be compared to the zodiacal signs in the way that they transmit their influences into and through the LD just as they do in a horoscope. Like the constellations of the Wheel, they have a lifelong influence and can be activated at any time. They also expand your LD's dimensions thereby putting greater possibilities at your disposal.

When you are working with different facets of your LD, try to inject macrocosmic/microcosmic perceptions into your interpretations. This will help you to get soul-based guidelines and directions.

Perhaps the best way to begin interpreting the LD's magickal symbols is to isolate each from the other and write their numbers on them to reveal their make up so that the spiritual nature and purpose of each can be more readily determined. (Refer to the *worked* worksheet at the end of Chapter 5) Once this is done, the next step is to discern how the symbol chosen for study relates to the other symbols in the LD and to the LD as a whole. The more you try to find significance and meaning from this spiritual network of symbolic ideas and numbers and then manipulate them to improve your life, demonstrates commitment on your part to uncovering your destiny.

NB: Exoteric interpretations do not need to include magickal facets in their delineations. Amazing forecasts can be achieved without them.

CALCULATING SDLDs AND THEIR CYCLES

Abbreviated Terms used in this Chapter:
- ✧ LD = Life Diamond
- ✧ SD = Single Digit
- ✧ SDLD = Single Digit Life Diamond
- ✧ LG = Life Goal
- ✧ LC = Life Challenge
- ✧ LG/C = A Life Goal, Life Challenge combination
- ✧ LPN = Life Path Number

CHAPTER 5

CALCULATING SDLDs AND THEIR CYCLES

This chapter is designed to cater to those who have advanced numerological skills and those who have little or none. Novices will be introduced to the basics along with old and new numerological methods. Those who are advanced in this area will discover new concepts that expand on traditional methods.

As the book progresses from simple to advanced, you will be shown how to construct and interpret three different types of LDs with each one having its own unique features to offer. The first is the *single digit* LD (SDLD), the prototype for all other LDs, given in this chapter. The second is the whole number LD (Chapter 9) and the third is the interim LD (Chapter 11).

Age cycles and calendar year cycles are compulsory to all LDs regardless of their type. Their calculations are necessary to locate current positions within a LD's allotted time spans. Once the current age is determined, the active life cycle can be ascertained and its numbers interpreted. Instructions for calculating them are set out below.

HOW TO CALCULATE A SDLD AND ITS AGE AND CALENDAR CYCLES

This procedure is straightforward requiring simple addition and subtraction methods. The format for the example birthdate below shows how to construct your LD, its LPNs, its life goals and challenges, and finally, its age and calendar year cycles; they can all be calculated in a few minutes.

Steps for Calculating LDs:
1. How to calculate a single digit SDLD and its LPNs from the birthdate.
2. How to calculate its LGs.
3. How to calculate its LCs.
4. How to calculate its AGE cycles.
5. How to calculate its AGE cycles by CALENDAR years.
6. How to extend steps 2 and 3 by calculating their cycles *beyond* the fourth LG/C. This innovative technique will have special appeal for those in their senior years Case studies which explore this new concept can be found in Chapters 10 and 12.

Chapter 5 – Calculating SDLDs And Their Cycles

The birth date's birth *day*, birth *month* and birth *year* numbers are the three major numbers that make up the SDLD's baseline from which the LGs and LCs are created. Once calculated, their precise arrangement defines each sequential, chronological, life cycle within the LD allowing exact age positions within their cycles to be plotted. Pinpointing which cycle is being activated, enables you to isolate the specific field of life experience being currently engaged. Each field of experience, beginning with the first life cycle, demarcates sequential, unfolding stages within a Life Path. Their main purpose is to provide clear signposts during their time spans that lead towards the eventual attainment of a Life Purpose.

STEP 1: HOW TO CALCULATE A SDLD FROM THE BIRTHDATE

To begin, use or make a copy of the blank worksheet at the end of this chapter. Set up the baseline of your SDLD by reducing any compound number within the birthdate to single digits by addition. For example:

Example Birth date: 24-9-1928   24 reduces to **6**   1928 = 20 reduces to **2**
REDUCE ANY COMPOUND NUMBERS: (24 = 2+4 = 6)   (1928 = 1+9+2+8 = 20 =2)

Next, *rearrange* the three single digits of 6, 9 and 2 by putting the birth *month*, 9, in first position on the baseline as shown below. The + and – signs between the reduced numbers on the baseline indicate addition of these numbers to obtain LGs that go *above* the birthdate and subtraction to obtain LCs that go *below* the birthdate. NB: Always include the LPN/s at the end of the LD's baseline as it is one of its extensions – never leave it/them out of your calculations; Chapter 8 explains why.

$$9 \pm 6 \pm 2 = 17/8 \text{ LPN} \quad \text{DHARMA}$$

MONTH   DAY   YEAR

STEP 2: HOW TO CALCULATE LGS
1. To obtain the first LG, add the month and day numbers together and reduce.
2. To obtain the second LG, add the day and year numbers together and reduce.
3. To obtain the third LG, add the first two Life Goals together and reduce.
4. To obtain the fourth LG, add the month and year numbers together and reduce.

STEP 3: HOW TO CALCULATE LCS
1. To calculate the first LC, subtract the month and day from each other.
2. To calculate the second LC, subtract the day and year from each other.
3. To calculate the third LC, subtract the first two Life Challenges from each other.
4. To calculate the fourth LC, subtract the month and year from each other.

NB: Master numbers and tens numbers are not used at this very basic level.

The Life Diamond

WORKED EXAMPLE:

Example Birth date: 24 - 9 -1928   The baseline of the LD = 9 - 6 - 2

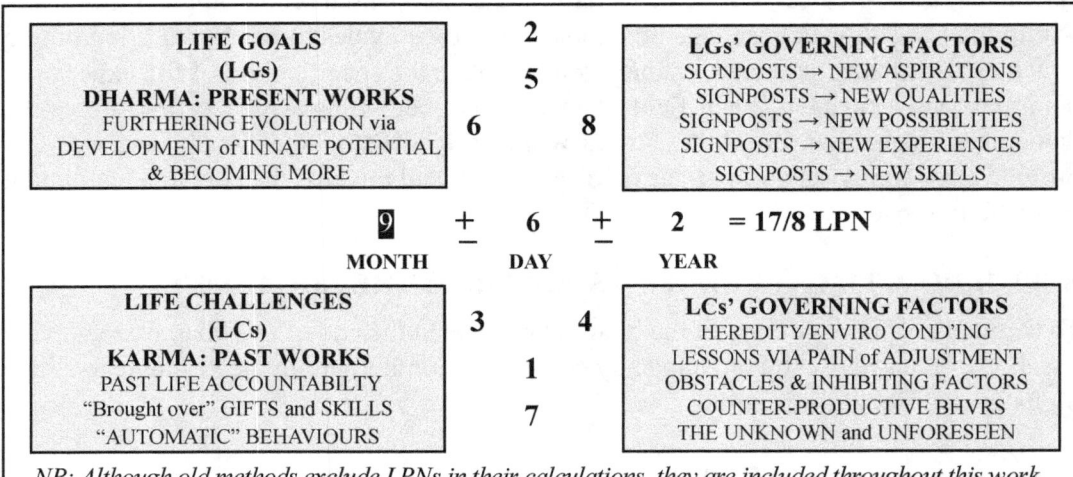

PERSONAL EXERCISE: *Construct your own SDLD.* Once your LGs and LCs are calculated and positioned, you are ready to begin figuring out how they can assist you to know the whats, whens, whys and hows of your life.

STEP 4: HOW TO CALCULATE AGE CYCLES FOR LIFE

Each LG/C pair governs 9-year periods, except for the first pair of LG/Cs. A special formula, provided below, is used to calculate the length of its duration. Pythagoras based this formula upon the "four cycles of man" which he found to have special significance. It simply translates to 4x9=36.

HOW TO CALCULATE THE 1st LG/C's AGE SPAN (using 24-9-1928)

- **STEP 1:** Calculate the **LPN** (2+4+9+1+9+2+8 = **35**) and reduce to a single digit 3+5= **8**.
- **STEP 2:** Subtract the single digit **LPN8** from 36. (36 - 8 = 28)
- **STEP 3:** The result is that the first **LG** and **LC** cycle rules from **0 - 28** years.
- **STEP 4:** Once the age range of the 1st LG/C cycle is calculated, add **9** years to each remaining pair of LG/Cs. This determines the ages for all succeeding **9-year cycles** that follow on from the first, long cycle as shown in the example below.

Chapter 5 – Calculating SDLDs And Their Cycles

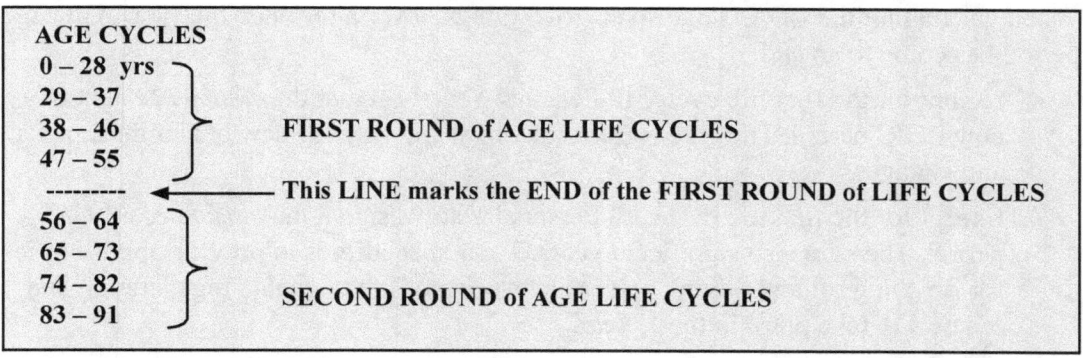

It is my belief that we do not remain "stuck" at the fourth cycle for the rest of our life but *continue reactivating our cycles until we die*. Because of this belief, the age cycles given above extend into a *second round of life cycles*. This new concept is treated fully in Chapter 12.

PERSONAL EXERCISE: *Calculate your personal set of age cycles.* Place your age and calendar cycles close to your LD if not using the format provided in the worksheets. Highlight the current cycle using colours. The LD WORKSHEETS at the end of this chapter show one way of doing this – the example given below presents another. To indicate the end of the <u>first round</u> of age cycles, draw a line under the fourth LG/C cycle to separate it from the second and third rounds (if life continues that far).

The next set of calculations illustrates how to extend the LG/C age cycles beyond the fourth LG/C cycle using a **LPN8**.

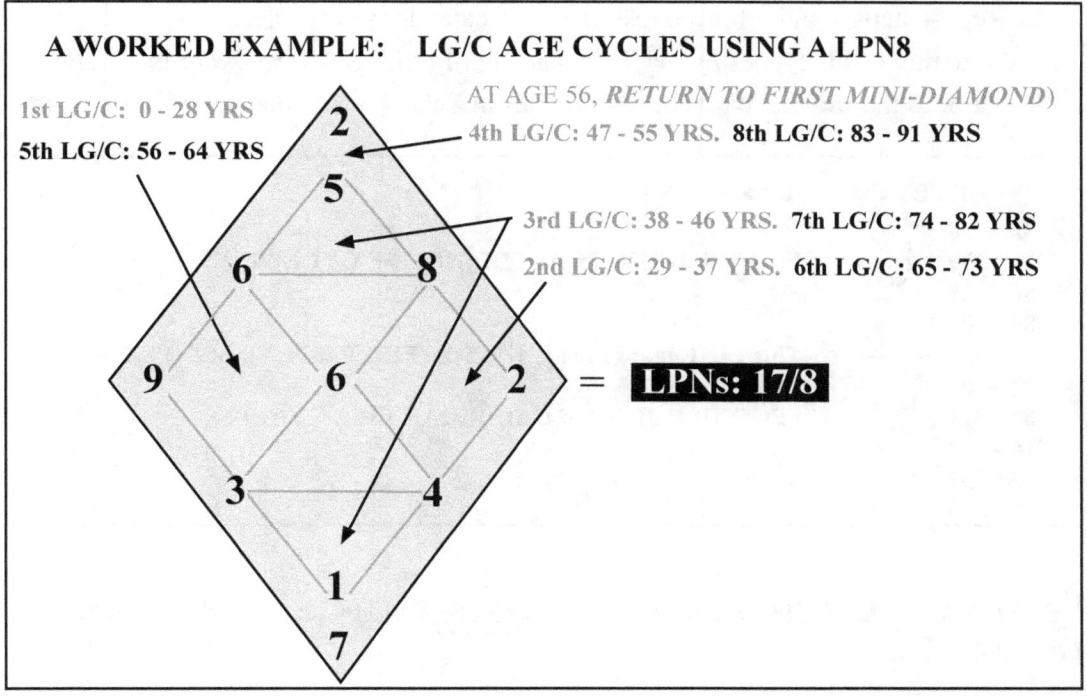

The Life Diamond

When calculating the LG/C's age spans, two things never alter once the first LG/C age period has come to an end:

- ✧ Except for the first life cycle, all Personal Year 1s signal the *commencement* of a new LG/C period. They are significant years; gateways to new beginnings, paths and changes.

- ✧ Except for the first life cycle, all Personal Year 9s signal the *closure* of a LG/C period. They are also significant years. Their speciality is to provide opportunities for finishing off and tidying up certain aspects of life to enable regeneration and renewal to take place in the 1, year.

STEP 5: HOW TO CALCULATE AGE CYCLES BY CALENDAR YEARS

1. Begin with the year of birth. Write it in *abbreviated form* in the "Cycles in Years" box. Eg: Julie's (main case study introduced in Chapter 6) birthyear is 1942 so '42 is written in the first space at the top, left corner of this box.

2. Next, calculate the length of the first cycle. Eg: Julie's LPN = 8. Subtract 8 from 36 to get 28. Julie activated her first cycle for 28 years, so add 28 to 1942 and you get 1970. Shorten 1970 to '70 and place it opposite '42 at the top, right corner of this box. Now you have calculated the calendar years that span Julie's *first* life cycle.

3. For Julie's *second* life cycle, begin by adding *one* year to '70 and writing '71 in the space directly below '42.

4. Add *eight* years to '71 and write '79 opposite it; directly below '70. Now you have calculated Julie's second life cycle that spans *nine* years, inclusively.

5. Repeat steps 4 and 5 for the rest of Julie's calendar year cycles.

6. Note that Cycle 5 goes *below the bar* to signify the *second round of life cycles*.

7. Refer to the *worked* Worksheet's "Cycles in Years" box at the end of this chapter.

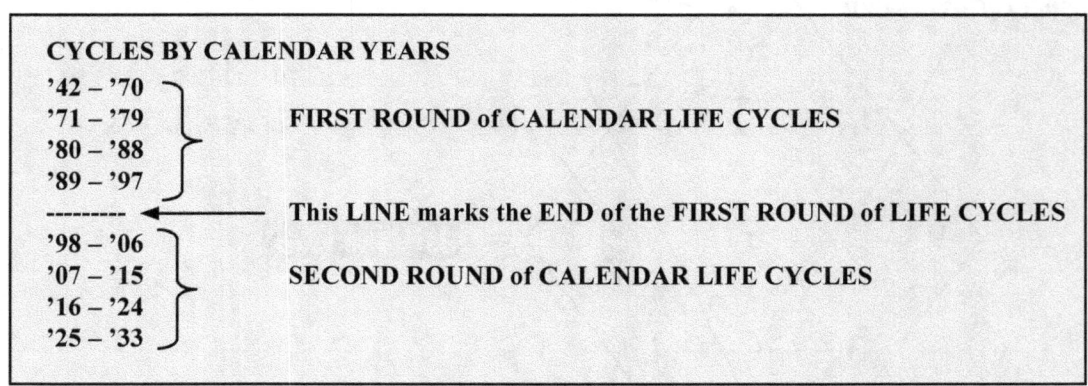

PERSONAL EXERCISE: *Calculate life cycle calendar years* and highlight your present cycle.

Chapter 5 – Calculating SDLDs And Their Cycles

STEP 6: EXTENDING LG/C AGE CYCLES *BEYOND* THE FOURTH LG/C CYCLE

The following table takes the hard work out of calculating future LG/C age cycles. For your convenience, it lays out ages at the commencement and completion of each LG/C cycle in ages for all LPNs from 2 – 22 (in my opinion there is no real LPN1). Going against tradition, this table goes beyond the fourth life cycle to accommodate those who live long lives.

TABLE FOR EXTENDING LD AGE CYCLES *BEYOND* THE 4TH CYCLE

RULING LPNS	AGES FOR 1st LG/C ROUND	AGES FOR 2nd LG/C ROUND	AGES FOR 3rd LG/C ROUND
LPN 2	0-34; 35-43; 44-52; 53-61	62-70; 71-79; 80-88; 89-97	98-106; 107-115; 116-124
LPN 3	0-33; 34-42; 43-51; 52-60	61-69; 70-78; 79-87; 88-96	97-105; 106-114; 115-123
LPN 4	0-32; 33-41; 42-50; 51-59	60-68; 69-77; 78-86; 87-95	96-104; 105-113; 114-122
LPN 5	0-31; 32-40; 41-49; 50-58	59-67; 68-76; 77-85; 86-94	95-103; 104-112; 113-121
LPN 6	0-30; 31-39; 40-48; 49-57	58-66; 67-75; 76-84; 85-93	94-102; 103-111; 112-120
LPN 7	0-29; 30-38; 39-47; 48-56	57-65; 66-74; 75-83; 84-92	93-101; 102-110; 111-119
LPN 8	0-28; 29-37; 38-46; 47-55	56-64; 65-73; 74-82; 83-91	92-100; 101-109; 110-118
LPN 9	0-27; 28-36; 37-45; 46-54	55-63; 64-72; 73-81; 82-90	91-99; 100-108; 109-117
LPN 10	0-26; 27-35; 36-44; 45-53	54-62; 63-71; 72-80; 81-89	90-98; 99-107; 108-116
LPN 11	0-25; 26-34; 35-43; 44-52	53-61; 62-70; 71-79; 80-88	89-97; 98-106; 107-115
LPN 22	AS FOR LPN4		

Chapter 10 and especially Chapter 12 introduce convincing evidence that LG/Cs begin again when the fourth life cycle has ended after a nine-year allotment.

THE THREE MAJOR LIFE CYCLES

Each of the three major life cycles sequentially governs firstly by the birthmonth, then the birthday and finally, by the birthyear. These numbers sustain a background influence on the LD's life cycles during their long periods of reign; hence their importance. Although beyond the scope of this book, a brief explanation follows.

First Major Life Cycle - The Birth Month: The birth month rules this cycle from approximately 0 to 30 years. It holds first place on the baseline because it is considered to be less personalised therefore more general in effect than the birth day number. It is assigned to this position to govern formative years -- a time when others have most control over your life while you learn to develop character, potential, independence and individuality.

Second Major Life Cycle - The Birth Day: The birth day rules this cycle from approximately 30 to 60 years. Your birth day number is regarded as being highly individualised, therefore extremely personal. It requires time to nurture and develop the embryonic qualities and traits that it contains which are initially dominated by external people, conditions and laws until stages of maturation and independence are reached. That explains why it holds second position.

Third Major Life Cycle - The Birth Year: The birth year number is generic. Due to its universal nature, it settles in third or last place ruling this cycle from approximately 60, until death. Calculate the year number by adding all of the years' digits together eg 1971 = 18. 18 reverses to 81. Look up 18/81's interpretations from Appendix 1. Take out 18's Tarot Key and look up its interpretations. Apply your findings to your circumstances. Further insights can be gained from reducing 18 to 9 then accessing its interpretations as a number and as a Tarot Key. Then reverse 9 to 90 and do the same for it.

NB: If the LPN ranges from 2 - 9, the first major life-cycle governs for the LD's entire first life-cycle. For 10s and 11s, it governs for most of the LD's first life cycle. After that, the second major cycle governs for at least three, successive life cycles. Then the third major life cycle governs for the remainder of the life.

PERSONAL EXERCISE: *Write out your three Major Life Cycles in order.* Find the major cycle's number that is ruling you now. If it is compound, lay out its "present" and "hidden" or reversed Tarot Keys. For instance, if you were born on the 16th and currently experiencing your second major life cycle, your *primary* numbers would be 16 (present) and 61 (hidden or reversed). 16 also reduces to 7. So 7 and 70 would be your *ancillary* numbers. The Tarot Keys that they correspond to are The Tower (16), the 7 of Swords (61), The Chariot (7) and the 2 of Pentacles (70). Study them in relation to yourself and how your life is currently unfolding as these numbers make up an important part of your present field of life experience, too. They contain important signposts that help you to figure out how to reach your Life Purpose. (See the final chapter and the three Appendices for additional tips.)

OVERLOOKED NUMBERS: My research has shown convincing proof to support the fact that the actual year number i.e. if it is a '12, '45, '76, '99 or '07 *does* impress your nature and circumstances. Compound year numbers are very common. If the year is 19<u>96</u> its compound year number is '96 (reverses to 69) or if 19<u>75</u>, '75 is the actual year number (reverses to 57). If the year number goes beyond the Tarot, reduce it and lay out its subsidiary Keys like: '96/69 = 15/51 = 6/60 and '75/57 = 12/21 = 3/30. These highly relevant numbers have been overlooked in the past. Look up your actual year number and its Tarot Keys' interpretations, naturally excluding the 19 or 20 for the century. Consider them to be *your* personal numbers. Their presence alerts you to other significant, lifelong indications that are hidden in your birthdate.

Number-pairing techniques are introduced in the next chapter. It is an amazing technique that provides you with a surprising amount of personalised information to open up your pathways in life exponentially. This is truly self-revelatory work. So I recommend that you have pen and paper and a Tarot deck at the ready to work along with the instructions as they are given in this and subsequent chapters with a view to: **always apply what you uncover to yourself.**

Chapter 5 – Calculating SDLDs And Their Cycles

 HANDY TIPS

1. Make copies of the unworked worksheet to practice on.
2. Follow the steps provided to calculate your own SDLD.
3. Colour or highlight your current cycle so that you can pinpoint it in a flash.
4. DOUBLE CHECK YOUR CALCULATIONS
5. Place your numbers and rulers on the ESOTERIC SYMBOLS.
6. Neatly write the Tarot Keys' names below each number.
7. Use your CHECKLIST to record notable features.
8. Keep this copy of your SDLD for yourself.
9. MASTER EACH STEP AND TYPE OF LD BEFORE PROCEEDING TO THE NEXT.

EXAMPLE WORKSHEET

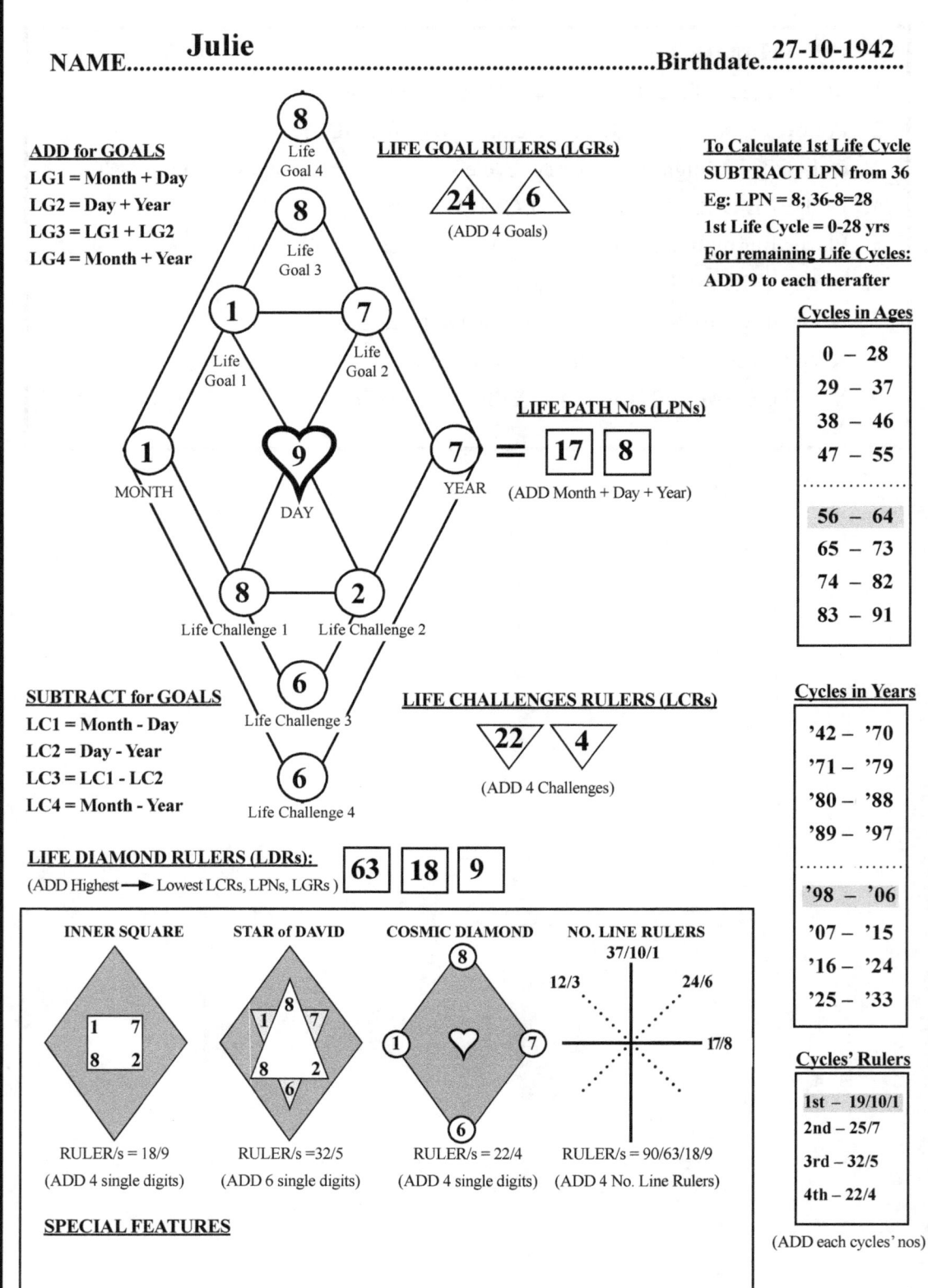

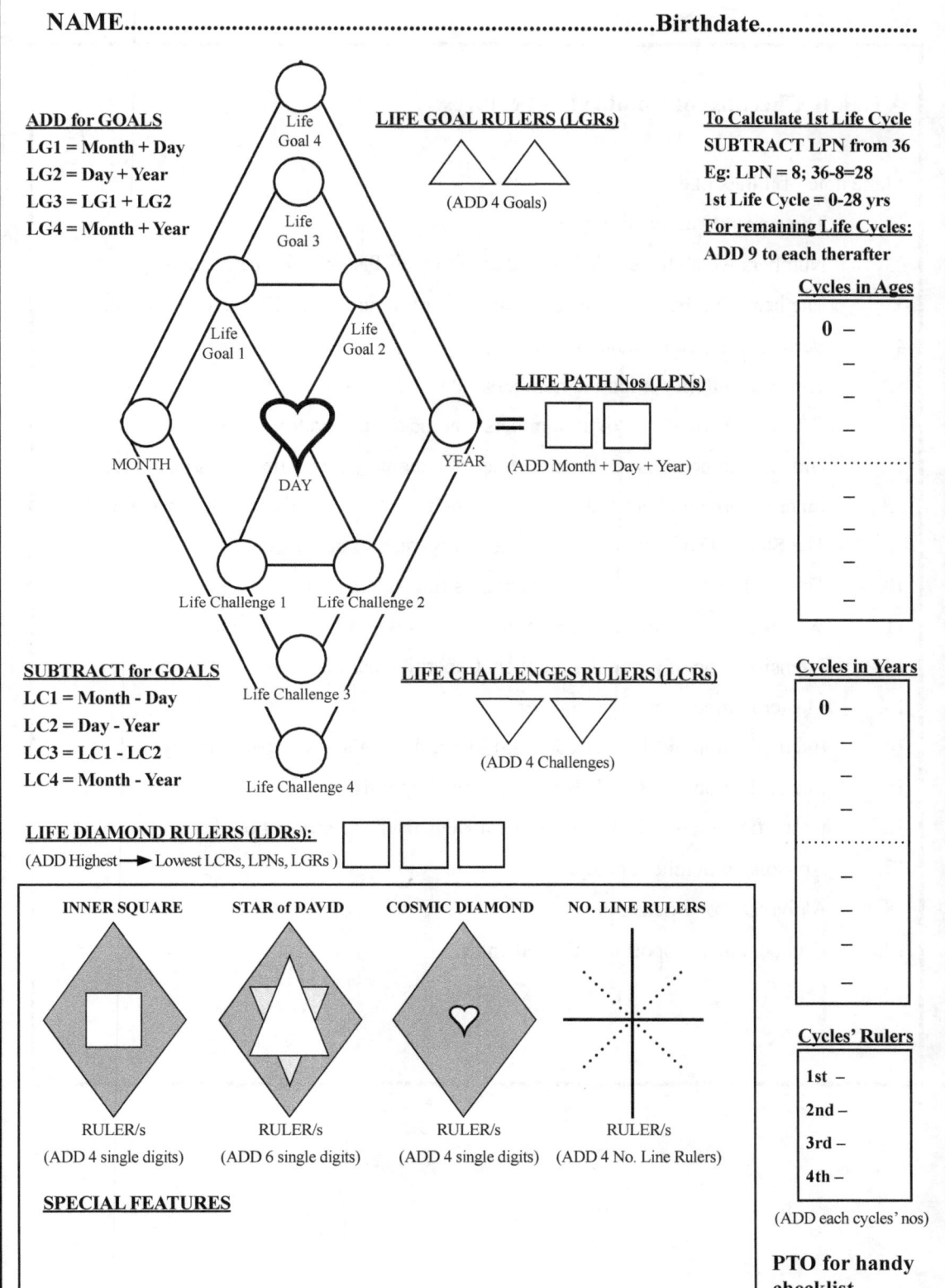

A Handy Checklist of Notable LD Features:

Make note of things like:

1. The currently active life cycle.
2. Numbers which have a definite relation to the LPN or major personal numbers.
3. The heart number (include compound and root number eg 27/9, then reverse).
4. Vertical core, compound numbers.
5. Top and Bottom compound numbers.
6. Cycle rulers (addition of all numbers that make up a cycle).
7. Hidden numbers (those that surround each diamond, triangle or magickal facet).
8. Inner square numbers and its rulers (remember to isolate them from the main LD).
9. The Star of David's numbers and its rulers (rulers same as for 3rd Cycle).
10. The Cosmic Diamond's numbers and its rulers.
11. Wheel of Life (number-lines, + and x crosses and Wheel's rulers).
12. Intensification of particular numbers (repetitive numbers).
13. Master numbers and tens numbers.
14. Intensification of Major Arcana and Minor Arcana Keys (repetitive Keys).
15. Intensification of "Royal" Keys and Aces (repetitive Keys).
16. Intensification of a Tarot suit (several Keys from the one suit or element).
17. An isolated number or Key.
18. A pivotal 9 or 1 personal year.
19. Numbers that support repetitive themes.
20. Other.

NUMBER-PAIRING TECHNIQUES

Abbreviated Terms used in this Chapter:
- ❖ LD = Life Diamond
- ❖ SD = Single Digit
- ❖ SDLD = Single Digit Life Diamond
- ❖ LG = Life Goal
- ❖ LC = Life Challenge
- ❖ LG/C = A Life Goal, Life Challenge combineation
- ❖ LPN = Life Path Number

CHAPTER 6

NUMBER-PAIRING TECHNIQUES

INTRODUCING NUMBER-PAIRING AS A NUMEROLOGICAL TECHNIQUE

Your knowledge and understanding of the ways in which your LD's numbers work in conjunction with their Tarot Keys, plus, how well versed you are at interpreting their symbology *and* placements, determines how much self-direction you can obtain from them.

Now that you have learned how to construct a SDLD and define its magickal symbols, you are ready to begin learning how to use number-pairing techniques. This chapter focuses on their introduction as a means to gain additional information from the single digits without compromising their numerological integrity. Number-pairing techniques originate from the *Numeroscope* (Book 4) as they are intrinsic to its delineation. They will become one of the most important tools that you can learn to use in order to gain access to copious amounts of previously inaccessible information that is secreted in your numbers.

Consequently, the introduction of this technique will prove to be the greatest boon to numerology since its inception! It is extremely versatile and can be applied to most single digit combinations within a numerological configuration. The compound numbers that it produces pave the way for bringing to light precious insights, especially when coupled with the Tarot.

Hence, number-pairing techniques radically transform the traditional LD from being quite ordinary into one that is highly sophisticated, extremely informative, categorically accurate and self-enlightening. In comparison, age-old methods pale to insignificance. They produce overly generalised, repetitive guidelines instead of definitive ones that address our multidimensional natures and infinite range of possibilities. Number-pairing unerringly addresses this shortfall.

Only single digits are used for number-pairing techniques. Tens and master numbers are never used. The paradox is that although number-pairing techniques work with the barest minimum, they produce maximum results. Apart from that, the really good news is that they are very quick and easy to learn. The following two points sum up all that is required:

Chapter 6 – Number-pairing Techniques

- Number-pairing techniques produce compound numbers from single digits.
- Four simple rules with four exceptions are all that is necessary to learn this technique.

To give you an idea of just how easy number-pairing is, once a SDLD is constructed, you can begin applying its techniques to it immediately. For instance, if 4 and 7 appear as *adjacent* numbers *anywhere* in the LG/Cs they can be combined and paired to read as 47. But that is not all! 47 can then be *reversed* to create yet another compound number – 74! Basically, you are employing two simultaneous procedures when using this technique. First you create a compound number by pairing two SDs and then you immediately reverse that number to create its mirror opposite. As you can imagine, this technique has the potential to more than double the amount of information to be found in a LD. (Created master numbers from single digits such as 11, 22, 33, etc. are exceptions; they cannot be reversed.) Magick happens when you combine corresponding Tarot delineations to these numbers! You will be truly amazed by what these extremely elementary procedures are able to generate – their end results are profound.

Tarot interpretations broaden the scope of LD's immeasurably by addressing a greatly increased range of individualised traits that traditional methods fail to address. This becomes all too apparent in LDs that produce single digits (SDs) only, making it extremely difficult for the numerologist to pinpoint positive and negative tendencies and to give an accurate, comprehensive assessment of their indications.

With the advent of the new millennium, many LDs will be comprised of SDs only, for instance a baby born on 5-4-2001. In such cases, the importance of the child's name, numeroscope and horoscope cannot be overstated. However, number-pairing techniques become invaluable in these instances. The compound numbers derived from them open up these LDs by uncovering insights that the SDs, on their own, simply cannot. Number-pairing techniques can be relied upon to make up for this deficit in most instances, but in rare cases they can also be severely limited by the LD's array of numbers. Regardless of the nature of any LD, you are about to discover that number-pairing when linked to the Tarot, significantly enhances your skill at uncovering your life directions.

Bill Clinton's LD gave you a taste of what can be done with the LGs and LCs when utilising number-pairing. You saw that specific, hidden details became exposed due to this technique. Although extremely valuable and not to be devalued, one can see how restrictive and generalised his SDs were in describing his life – Bill's potential for greatness is too well obscured by them. A more comprehensive analysis of his LD comes later.

Besides learning number-pairing techniques you will also be shown how to calculate other hidden numbers that belong to each LD's cycle. Not only that, you will learn how to apply number-pairing techniques to each mystickal symbol. Those who only wish to do exoteric delineations, ignore the steps covering them. At this stage, the emphasis is upon number-pairing techniques and not so much upon the inclusion of the Tarot. It will be gradually introduced as more and more advanced techniques are presented.

The Life Diamond

> **HANDY TIPS**
>
> **Suggestion: DO THIS FOR EACH CASE STUDY THAT FOLLOWS**
>
> On a separate piece of paper, write the person's name and birthdate on it. Then copy each LD and isolate or highlight the life cycles as per instructions. Keep your copy at your side. This saves you the trouble of flipping back to the examples over and over to check what is being brought to your attention. Once you have finished with the case study, keep your copy safely tucked in your book.

CASE STUDY: JULIE

For this introductory exercise, Julie's SDLD will be used specifically as a platform for calculation purposes. Each of her life cycles will be treated in turn. Tarot inclusions will mainly be held in reserve to simplify the mathematical procedures. However, it is anticipated that you will lay out the corresponding Tarot Keys for the compound numbers as they are revealed which would benefit your studies greatly. Refer to Appendix 2 to find their correspondences.

To begin, work along with the calculations as you go. Start by reducing any compound numbers, master or tens numbers from Julie's birthdate to their root digits. Position them on the baseline keeping this LD entirely composed of SDs except for its LPNs.

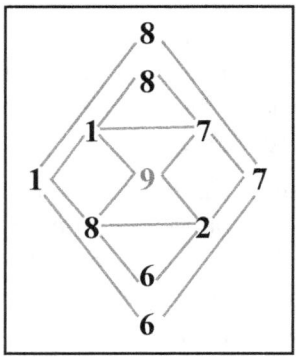

Julie: 27-10-1942 = LPNs: 17/8 (9+1+7= LPNs: 17/8)

Once calculated, commence by mentally breaking up the LD into two inner mini-diamonds, two opposing triangles and one large outer diamond. The three diamonds rule the first, second and fourth life cycles with the opposing triangles ruling the third life cycle. Both the opposing triangles and the cosmic diamond break the number-pairing rules. These exceptions are explained in the steps that follow. Draw connecting lines (pathways) to the numbers to help you define the life cycles within the LD.

No matter how expert you become, once you have constructed a LD, always **check your calculations, highlight the current life cycle and scan the LD** before commencing its analysis. Do this now to Julie's LD. The first helps you to correct possible errors, the second pinpoints the current cycle and the third gives you an intuitive feel for the initial impact that certain LD characteristics impress on your mind before you attempt to dissect and interpret it. Take notice of your intuition. Rely on it to sense things that may not yet be obvious but could prove to be very important as your analysis unfolds.

Doing these preliminary steps not only prepares you for more detailed work to follow but more importantly impresses any special features within a LD's structure on your mind which you might wish to note at the bottom of your worksheet. You may observe a strong placement, emphasis or similarities between certain numbers. Themes may be formulating in your mind as you take in repetitive numbers and numbers that share parallel traits. Remember that *all* numbers are intrinsic to *Julie's* nature, whether compound or single, so they should be noted *separately* and *collectively* as they form an integral part of *her* make-up for *her* life. Having done this initial yet extremely important exercise, you are ready to begin decoding Julie's LD in detail. Take your time in doing this, as it is not only essential for the development of your intuition but also for learning to synthesise the many directions held together within her map to life that determine major probabilities to be encountered in this lifetime.

Bearing in mind the above, what immediately captures your attention about Julie's LD? Were you quick to notice her repetitious 1, 6, 7 and 8s? Can you see that they can be paired to make several master numbers? What is this telling you? Do you sense that she may be multi-talented and/or has the potential to excel in certain areas of her life? What else is your intuition telling you? Listen to it. When you have finished this cursory exercise, you are ready to pair its numbers.

HOW TO APPLY NUMBER-PAIRING RULES TO A LD

The rules for number-pairing are easy. To begin with, you need to isolate from the main framework of the LD which of its facets you wish to decode. You are either dealing with one of the diamonds or the two triangles or a magickal facet. Once you have chosen which facet to decipher, do the same as you did for the entire LD – run your eyes over your selection mentally noting any outstanding features. When you have done that, you are ready to pair the SDs to create their compound numbers then consult their delineations and make notes. Hopefully you will find numbers similar to yours in the case studies which will help you to analyse your own LD's potential and follow its guidelines.

When number-pairing, you must work horizontally, vertically and diagonally just one step at a time to pair the single digits and create their compound numbers. You can never jump numbers to create compound numbers except in four instances….

Four Times When You Break the Rules

1. The first is when you are working on the third cycle's two opposing triangles and you need to pair the third goal with its third challenge; Step 3.
2. The second time is when you are decoding the cosmic diamond and need to pair the fourth goal with its fourth challenge; Step 4.
3. For the third instance, isolate the inner square from the LD. Pair its diagonals by ignoring the heart number; Step 7.
4. For the fourth occasion, isolate the Star of David from the LD. In order to pair each triangle's numbers, ignore in-between numbers; Step 8.

The Life Diamond

In a diamond, you can only pair numbers horizontally and vertically once – diagonally four times. Just visualise a diamond with a vertical cross inside it which helps to explain the one vertical and one horizontal axis within its four diagonals. The next diagram, using Julie's numbers from her first mini-diamond, demonstrates this procedure. For the inner square you get two horizontals, two verticals and two diagonals. For a triangle you get one horizontal and two diagonals.

In esoteric terms, the vertical axis of a cross symbolises spiritual aspiration, whilst its horizontal axis symbolises things of an earthly or everyday nature. Apply these distinctions to the numbers that appear on these axes. They will help you to gain deeper insights into the esoteric significance and meaning of the *placements* of these numbers and where to assign spiritual and mundane emphasis in their delineations.

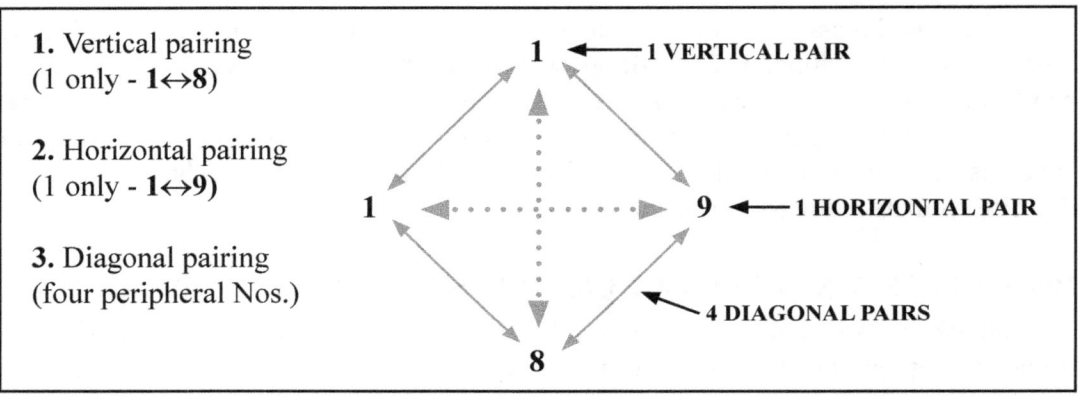

Because the aim of this book is to cater to numerologists at different levels, Julie's LD will be covered fully, beginning with her first life cycle. From there, successive life cycles will be systematically isolated and treated in sequence. When they are dealt with, the magickal facets will be introduced for advanced students in Steps 4, 7, 8 and 9.

STEP 1: NUMBER-PAIRING within the FIRST CYCLE

To begin, select the four numbers that make up the first mini-diamond. They stem from Julie's birth *month* and birth *day* numbers. When added and subtracted from each other, they make up the first mini-diamond and produce the first LG/C pair: LG1 and LC8. So 1, 9, 1 and 8 are the four basic numbers that you begin pairing together following the rules of number-pairing as given in the diagram above. As a reminder, when a compound number is derived in this way, it can immediately be reversed to create its opposite number.

Chapter 6 – Number-pairing Techniques

a) Start at the baseline. 1 and 9 are paired and reversed horizontally to become 19/91. You can also reduce 19/91 to make 10/1 thus obtaining more data.

b) Now pair the LG1 with its LC8 vertically to create 18/81. Reduce 18/81 to 9 for further insights. You have now dealt with the internal "vertical or spiritual axis".

c) The next step is to pair the month number 1 with its LG1 diagonally. 1 and LG1 become 11, then 2.

d) Then pair the 9, which is the birth day number, with the LG1 diagonally and you get a repeat of 91/19, then 10/1. Repetition intensifies these numbers.

e) Now pair and reverse the month number diagonally with its LC. 1 and LC8 become 18/81 then 9, the same as in b) above. Intensification more often than not inclines towards negative tendencies.

f) Now pair the day number with its LC diagonally; 9 and LC8 = 98/89. These numbers go beyond the range of the Tarot. When this situation arises consult the 0 to 99 Appendix. Also, add these numbers together; 8+9 and you get 17/71 then 8. They provide you with other numbers to include in your delineations. These numbers fall within the Tarot range giving you important information that can be relied upon to provide added, accurate data that is relevant to Julie's life (repeat this procedure whenever you find that numbers go beyond the Tarot range).

g) *Hidden* compound numbers and SDs can be extrapolated from the mini-diamond's numbers by adding the *sides* of the diagonals together and the vertical and horizontal axes, as shown below. Whether single or compound, these six hidden numbers increase your data bank. If you get a compound number, include its root digit. You may not wish to include this step but if you do, repeat it for all cycles – it is often worth doing!

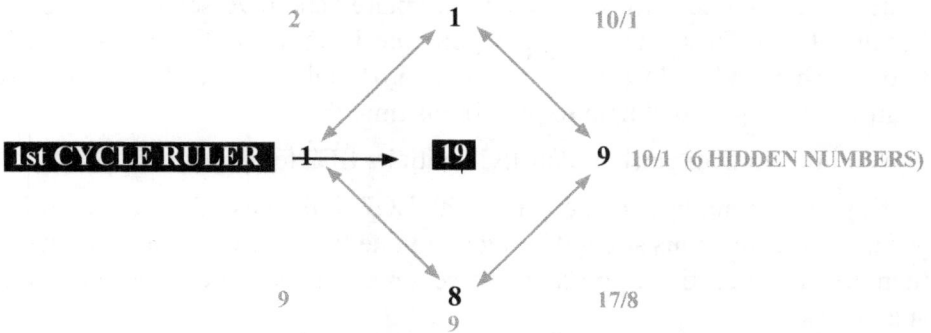

h) To find the first cycle's ruling numbers, add its four SDs together. 1+9+1+8 = 19/10/1. Ruling 19 has been positioned in the centre of the mini-diamond above Cycle Rulers are very important. Never leave them out of your calculations. Reverse 19 to make 91 for further insights. (Pop 19/91/10/1 next to No. 1 in the Cycle Rulers' box on your LD worksheet.)

i) Finally, link all numbers that you have created from this mini-diamond to their Tarot counterparts. Also refer to the final chapter and the appendices for guidelines on working with compound numbers and their suggested delineations.

The Life Diamond

The above steps form the basis for decoding all diamonds and will soon become second nature to you. Use this format as a prototype for their delineations. Begin by analysing numbers separately, then collectively looking for repetitive themes and numbers that work in harmony or against one another. To save restating repetitious steps for each life cycle, they will not be included in the following, but you must use Step1 as a prototype and follow all of its steps, remembering to include those that may be omitted below.

NB: IMPORTANT POINTS REGARDING the LENGTH of the FIRST CYCLE

For some people, this cycle can last for more than three decades. To help with its interpretation and timing, calculate Yearly Diamonds (Book 2) to obtain specific directions within much shorter time frames.

STEP2: NUMBER-PAIRING within the SECOND CYCLE

Use the birth *day* number 9, and the birth *year* number 7, from the LD's baseline. It produces the second LG/C pair. The four numbers in this mini-diamond are 9, 7, LG7 and LC2. They are active for 9 years. Repeating the steps outlined above you get:

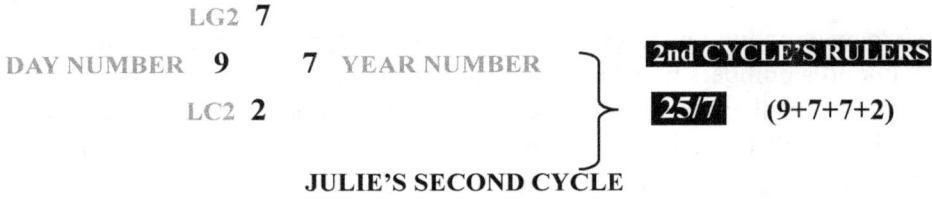

JULIE'S SECOND CYCLE

a) Start at the baseline. Day 9 and year 7 are paired and reversed horizontally to become 97/79. These numbers go beyond the Tarot range. Consult appendix 0 to 99. Then add 9+7 together, = 16/61. 16/61 and their root 7 provide extra, significant insights that help to plumb this time frame.

b) Now do the vertical pairing. Pair LG7 with its LC2 to become 72/27 = 9.

c) Next, pair year number 9 diagonally with LG7. It repeats 97/79 and their 16/61 = 7 as in a) above thus strengthening them due to repetition. This may incline them towards negative or more intense expression and experiences or, honing of specific skills.

d) Diagonally pair the year number 7, with its LG7 to become 77. 77 cannot be reversed but it can be reduced to 14/41 = 5.

e) Now diagonally pair the day 9, with its LC2 to become 92/29. Reduce to 11/2.

f) Then, diagonally pair the year 7, with its LC2 to become 72/27 = 9, which intensifies b) above.

g) Follow g) in Step 1 above.

h) Finally, add all SDs 9+7+7+2 to uncover the Cycle Rulers, 25/52 =7. Write 25/52/7 next to No. 2 in the Cycle Rulers' box on the LD worksheet.

i) Several of the compound numbers so far created in this mini-diamond can be added together to spawn yet another compound number, eg 29=11=2/20. These additional numbers expand and enrich the information concealed in this cycle.

STEP 3: NUMBER-PAIRING within the THIRD CYCLE

This step is a little tricky to begin with at first. Once you grasp the concept that you are dealing with an upper and a lower triangle instead of a diamond, you should find the going easy. So for this step, you need to single out the two opposing triangles that make up the third LG and LC within Julie's LD then prepare yourself for breaking the number-pairing rule for the first time. The third LG8 is derived from adding the first and second LGs (LG1 + LG7) which form its mini-triangle's baseline. The third LC6 is derived from subtracting the first and second LCs (LC8 - LC2) that form its mini-triangle's baseline. Six, not four, numbers are involved in this step. Repetitive procedures from the mini-diamonds worked on above, should be applied where applicable.

Certain, important points need to be made concerning the third LG/C's numbers. They require special attention because they are the aggregate of the addition and subtraction of the whole birthdate. This fact has to increase their personal nature. Apart from that, their *positions* are also important – this pair of LG/Cs sits on the spiritual axis on either side of the LD's core. Close proximity to the core adds to their potency.

Another important thing to consider about this cycle is its age range. Julie would be entering her mature years when activating this cycle for 9 years. Acknowledging this would lead you to anticipate that if Julie is becoming spiritually awakened or so inclined, these numbers and this life cycle could mark the tangible emergence of such qualities both intrinsically and extrinsically. If nothing else, this LG/C pair can be seen as a "maturity marker". Being on the spiritual axis, their compound numbers can be relied upon to provide you with pertinent, interpretive clues that describe Julie's aspirations. For Julie, these numbers are 86/68. From them we may anticipate mastery (8) of skills (6) in trade (6) and business areas (8). 86 may describe a family (6) business (8) that provides domestic services (6 - plumbing). Harsh (8) family (6) conditions may continue to prevail. Another aspect of 86 is the honing of creative talents. As 68, the Page of Pentacles, we can anticipate the beginning of an enterprise or hobby or spiritual leanings. Also, commercial and financial interests are likely to manifest.

NB: Esoterically, the same six numbers that make up this cycle also produce the Star of David.

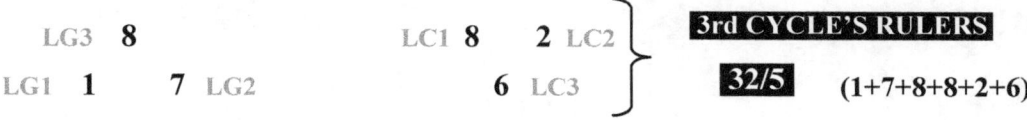

```
      LG3  8                    LC1 8    2 LC2  ⎫   3rd CYCLE'S RULERS
   LG1  1      7  LG2              6 LC3        ⎬    32/5   (1+7+8+8+2+6)
                                                ⎭
JULIE'S THIRD CYCLE'S LG TRIANGLE     JULIE'S THIRD CYCLE'S LC TRIANGLE
```

The Life Diamond

For the LIFE GOALS:

a) Pair and reverse the LG's baseline numbers LG1 and LG7 = 17/71 = 8.
b) Pair and reverse LG1 and LG8 = 18/81 = 9.
c) Pair and reverse LG7 and LG8 = 78/87 = 15/51 = 6.

For the LIFE CHALLENGES: -

a) Pair and reverse the LC's baseline numbers LC8 and LC2 = 82/28 = 10 = 1.
b) Pair and reverse LC8 and LC6 = 86/68 = 14/41 = 5.
c) Pair and reverse LC2 and LC6 = 26/62 = 8.
d) Pair and reverse LG8 with its LC6 = 86/68 = 14/41 = 5. This LG/C are a pair even though there are other numbers between them. Exceptions to the rules need to be made to jump over numbers in order to pair them. Follow g) in Step 1 above.
e) Add the *six* SDs from the two sets of triangles: 1+7+8+8+2+6=32/23 = 5 which uncovers this cycle's rulers. Place 32/23/5 beside No. 3 in the Cycle Rulers' box on the LD worksheet.
f) Repeat these steps for the third life cycle in any LD.

STEP 4: NUMBER-PAIRING within the FOURTH CYCLE (COSMIC DIAMOND)

For the final step, select the four peripheral numbers that make up the cosmic diamond (classified as one of the LD's magickal facets). The cosmic diamond is the large diamond which appears to represent your cosmic connections, as opposed to the very personal nature of the third life cycle. This is due to its founding numbers being universal in make-up. Prepare yourself for breaking the number pairing rules for the second time in this step.

1 and 7 are the two numbers that make up the cosmic diamond's baseline. It is activated during mature or senior years, depending upon the length of the first cycle. This diamond seems "unattached" from all other numbers only when you isolate it. In reality it is linked to the heart number. The cosmic diamond is active for 9 years (refer to Chapter 12).

JULIE'S FOURTH CYCLE

Chapter 6 – Number-pairing Techniques

a) Go back to the LD's baseline. Pair the *month* number 1 with the *year* number 7 to create 17/71 = 8.

b) To make LG compound numbers, pair and reverse 1 and LG8 to become 18/81 = 9.

c) Also pair and reverse 7 and LG8 to become 78/87 = 15/51 = 6.

d) To make LC compound numbers, pair and reverse 1 and LC6 to become 16/61 = 7.

e) Also pair and reverse 7 and LC6 to become 76/67 = 13/31 = 4.

f) Pair and reverse the top LG8 with its bottom LC6; 86/68 = 14/41 = 5. This is the second time that you break the rules by jumping over numbers in order to link the goal with its challenge to create their compound number. Make a mental note that 86/68 repeat and reinforce the third LG/C pairing. Follow g) in Step 1 above.

g) Add the mini-diamond's four numbers; 1+7+LG8+LC6 = 22/4 and you will uncover the hidden Cycle's Rulers. Even though its LGs and LCs are the same as the third life cycle, amazingly this cycle's rulers differ from it, which you only discover once they are calculated! A different number for this cycle clearly indicates and explains why *new and different conditions and experiences will definitely manifest here* when comparing it to Julie's *previous* cycle. This is what makes this work so fascinating. Fine details such as this bring forth the variables that ensure accurate forecasts and directions. Jot 22/4 beside No. 4 in the Cycle Ruler's box on the LD worksheet.

 **HANDY TIP**

When you have calculated the ruling numbers for each cycle place them in their "Cycle Rulers Box" (see worked LD Worksheet).

STEP 5: PAIRING the TWO TOP AND BOTTOM LGs and LCs

Step 5 through to Step 9 is where we really break with tradition by uncovering and introducing new facets to be found concealed in LDs. They open up previously unexplored dimensions of a LD which add extra depth and meaning to our lives. This step works with two aspects of Julie's LD that are apart from, yet intrinsically connected to her life and its cycles. What it does is to provide us with further insights about Julie by allowing us to access two strategic compound numbers derived from her spiritual axis. They form the upper and lower points of the Star of David linking them to the cosmic diamond (soul to spirit). Linking these pairs of numbers creates a bridge from the Star to the cosmic diamond. (The birthday number forms the bridge from the earth axis to the cosmic diamond.)

Julie's third and fourth LG/Cs are adjacent to each other, so they fall within the rules for number-pairing. They pair to produce 88 and 66, govern the entire life span and may

The Life Diamond

signify spiritual influences. These notions add an esoteric slant to their delineations when they are perceived as potential bridges to higher consciousness. Both master numbers may be further reduced thus; 88/16/61/7 and 66/12/21/3. Exoterically they offer Julie extra possibilities, gifts, traits and life experiences; traits that would be overlooked using traditional methods. NB: *These numbers are not cyclic but bring a foreground/background influence to any time span being examined.*

PAIRING TOP AND BOTTOM LGs and LCs   VERTICAL CORE NUMBERS

STEP 6: PAIRING the TWO VERTICAL CORE NUMBERS

For this step, delve deeply into the LD's heart to open up another two unexplored aspects of a LD. Nestled at its core are two sets of compound numbers that you can create with the heart number on the spiritual axis. Like the two compound numbers in Step 5, they are adjacent to each other thereby falling within number-pairing rules. They are intrinsic to Julie's life and nature and must not be overlooked. These pairs of numbers are also not governed by time similar to those in Step 5. 9, being Julie's most pivotal number connects to what I consider to be two extremely potent numbers because of their make-up and positions. Combined, they constitute exceptionally personal numbers that create the two *core* compound numbers on Julie's spiritual axis.

To create these numbers, firstly pair heart 9 with LG8 = 98/89, then reduce to 17/71, then 8. Secondly, pair heart 9 with LC6 = 96/69 and reduce to 15/51, then 6. Make a mental note of these numbers, knowing that being at the core of the LD and part of its spiritual axis *and* earth axis helps Julie to get in touch with numbers that exemplify spiritualising earthly work. This aspect of these two numbers (really four when reversed) makes them pivotal to Julie's spiritual objectives if she chooses to walk the spiritual Path. Vital clues pertaining to ways that she has at her disposal to merge virtuous qualities with mundane qualities can be ascertained from them. Their potency is due to their *make up and positions* in the LD thereby guaranteeing that their imprint reveals aspects of her authentic self. As you can imagine, powerful spiritual leanings may be obtained from these numbers.

NB: *These numbers are not cyclic but bring a foreground/background influence to any time span being examined.*

Chapter 6 – Number-pairing Techniques

Personal Exercise: Now take note of your own top, bottom and vertical core compound numbers. Look up their meanings. Take out their Tarot Keys. Closely study their interpretations and images and make jottings.

STEP 7: The INNER SQUARE

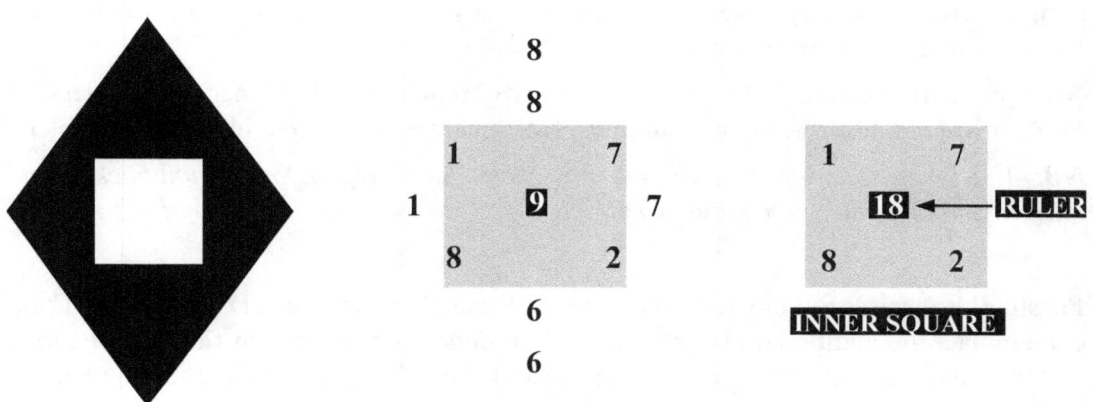

1. PAIR the HORIZONTAL LIFE GOAL NUMBERS
2. PAIR the HORIZONTAL LIFE CHALLENGE NUMBERS
3. PAIR the "SIDES" of THESE NUMBERS to FORM the INNER SQUARE

Step 7 has its own specialities. It draws your attention to four numbers within Julie's LD, when linked together, create an exceptionally dynamic square. These numbers are 1, 7, 8 and 2. They symbolise Julie's *inner square* a magickal facet that surrounds her heart number. From this square, you will uncover several extremely powerful compound numbers which can be generated from them. Because of their remarkable power, separate and study this square's constituent parts in isolation; first as single digits (as shown above) and then as paired numbers. All numbers from this square are unequivocally pivotal to the LD because they have a profound influence upon the individual and the tenor of their life. Their strength and dynamism is similar to the vertical core compound numbers in the previous step; they also enjoy lifelong influences. Chapter 4 explained the square's esoteric make-up.

Horizontals and Verticals: Having isolated the square's four SDs, pair the horizontal LG and LC numbers (from above and below the baseline). 17/71 and 82/28 form the top and the bottom of the inner square. Now link each LG/C pair, vertically, and join together 18/81 and 72/27 to complete the sides to the inner square. They can be triggered into action at any time.

Diagonals: Next, pair the square's diagonals and note how these numbers also strongly imprint their attributes on the character and life. This is the third time that you break the rule of not jumping numbers by ignoring the fact that the heart number is central to the

The Life Diamond

inner square. In this case you can get 12/21 and 78/87. Altogether you now have twelve compound numbers from Julie's inner square – in other instances you can get as few as two.

New Numbers: Sometimes the inner square can introduce new numbers to the LD. These additional numbers add vital insights to your growing pool of data. Although Julie's inner square did not bring to light any new numbers, it does intensify those it repeats. Its numbers are particularly beneficial to Julie in many respects bringing some relief to her LD's potentially, severe aspects.

Rulers: Finally, add the four single digits 1+7+8+2 together. Julie's inner square rulers are 18/81/9 which intensify existing numbers. Her square is interpreted in the next chapter.

NB: *The inner square's numbers are not cyclic but bring a foreground/background influence to any time span being examined.*

Personal Exercise: Fill in your "Inner Square Ruler Box" on your LD Worksheet. Then, contemplate the additional insights that your numbers impart to you first as SDs, then as compound numbers and finally as Tarot Keys. See if they intensify other numbers or Keys or bring new numbers to your LD. Use the square's guidelines given in the previous chapter to help you to interpret its meaning for you in relation to your everyday life and works.

STEP 8: The STAR of DAVID

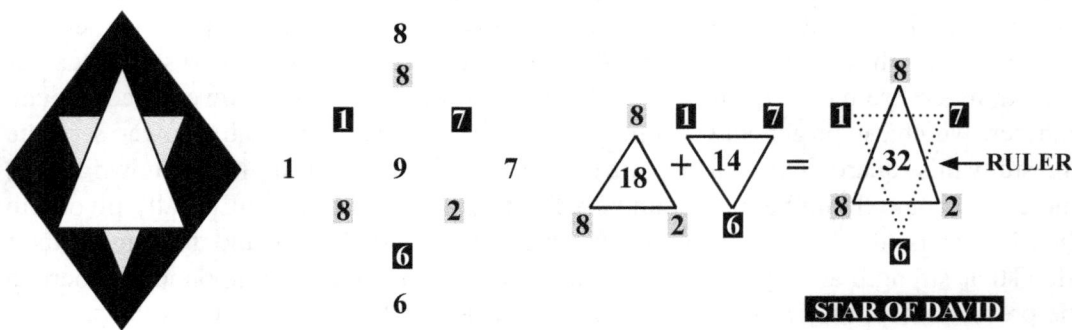

In this step, you are working with the *same* numbers from Step 3 but in an *esoteric* way (refer to chapters 2, 3 and 4). Step 3 keeps its triangles separated except for when you combine the third LG with its challenge. So for this step you use exactly the same numbers to create a very special, esoteric symbol that unites these two triangles. Isolating its numbers helps to distinguish the Star's composition without other numbers getting in the way. Once you have isolated the six numbers that make up the Star, highlight its two triangles using blue for the downward pointing triangle and red for the upward pointing triangle. Imagine the red triangle as your personality reaching towards your soul and then imagine the blue triangle as your Soul reaching towards your Personality. See these two triangles and the Star as a trilogy of symbols each with their own illuminating features that help you to extract ideas that relate to what you perceive to be your Soul's work.

Scan each triangle and note the paradox within their formation. See how their goals and challenges penetrate each other's field by binding the past and the present/future together in this configuration. Can you appreciate the deep personal nature of these triangles due to the potency of their numbers? If you are fortunate enough to get new numbers from pairing their diagonals or calculating their rulers, they will verify important facets of your inner work. If you are spiritually inclined, their appearance will be most helpful by bestowing additional gifts and lessons upon you.

To begin to interpret the significance and meaning contained in your Star, study its SDs and their Tarot Keys. Isolate each of the Star's triangles, write their numbers on their corners and calculate their individual rulers. Place each triangle's ruler in its centre and study them in the light of providing distinct clues about your spiritual work. Their combined total, i.e., the Star's ruler, is always the same as Step 3's ruler. Note that the red triangles ruler/s is the same as your inner square ruler or that it belongs to the same number-family. If you get new numbers in the other two ruler positions, they will be quite illuminating in relation to your spiritual aspirations.

Now pair each triangle's SDs by ignoring the heart number and breaking the number-pairing rules for the fourth time. Lay out the Tarot Keys for these numbers. Do the same for the rulers. Did you find anything new? Do not include the compound numbers from each triangle's base as an intensification factor because this will over intensify them as you have already dealt with them in the square – do not exclude them though, but note what they bring to each triangle just the same. You either get new numbers or intensification of existing numbers or a mixture of both from the Star. Whichever occurs helps you to gain spiritual perspectives about yourself.

For those on the Path, the Star must be interpreted esoterically *and* exoterically as it signifies the mixture of soul and personality aspects within the self. Apply the keywords integration, union, duality and opposites when decoding them. Other keywords such as struggle, hardship, tests, trials and triumphs can also be applied to the Star. They directly relate to deliberate efforts that aim at increasing and instilling enduring, spiritual qualities. Refer to the Star in the previous chapter.

NB: *The Star's numbers are not cyclic but bring a foreground/background influence to any time span being examined.*

Personal Exercise: Now fill in your Star of David on your LD Worksheet. Separate its two triangles so that you can distinguish between Personality and Soul indications. Take special notice of their rulers and decide what they mean for you. Decipher your Star according to the suggested guidelines given for it in the previous chapter, not forgetting to add your own insights.

The Life Diamond

STEP 9: The WHEEL of LIFE'S NUMBER-LINE RULERS

Finally, adding the four number-lines within the LD then calculating their rulers opens up the Wheel of Life magickal facet of the LD (refer to chapters 3 and 4). Doing this step often provides you with extremely insightful information. Sometimes, the number-line rulers reveal other very relevant dimensions of your make-up that may not appear elsewhere in your numbers. Steve Irwin (Stephen Robert Irwin: 22-2-1962 = 42/6; died tragically, on 4-9-2006). He was better known as the "Crocodile Hunter" or "Wildlife Warrior", provides us with one of the best examples of this phenomenon.

Having calculated his numbers after hearing of his death, shivers literally went through me when I had calculated his number-line ruler. It was 57, the 3 of Swords, which depicts three swords penetrating a heart. *Steve's death was caused by the barb of a stingray that directly pierced his heart!* But here comes the most revealing piece of information; neither 57 nor 75 appeared anywhere else in his SDLD's numbers! This makes 57's appearance and its imprint on Steve's nature and life that much more significant. On another level, 57 represented Steve's unbridled passion and empathy and deep commitment towards his family and children, patriotism for his country and a deep-seated concern for animals. 75, the 7 of Pentacles exemplified his generosity; Steve was happy to donate a large part of his earnings to protect wildlife. His LDs are well worth practising on.

To find the number-line ruler, you need to distinguish the four number-lines that make up the "skeletal framework" of a LD as shown below. This framework forms the axes of the LD's vertical (+) and diagonal (X) crosses. Add the numbers contained in each and place their totals near its number-line in a different colour or just circle them. Then add the four totals together to find their ruling number. Apply this information to the subject. Number-line totals can be abstruse in some cases and extremely illuminating like in Steve's case. They have a lifetime influence. As well as this, they can be activated at any moment during the life when the right conditions manifest. Remember to view the number-line rulers as "constellations" that constantly transmit their special qualities into and through the LD at all times.

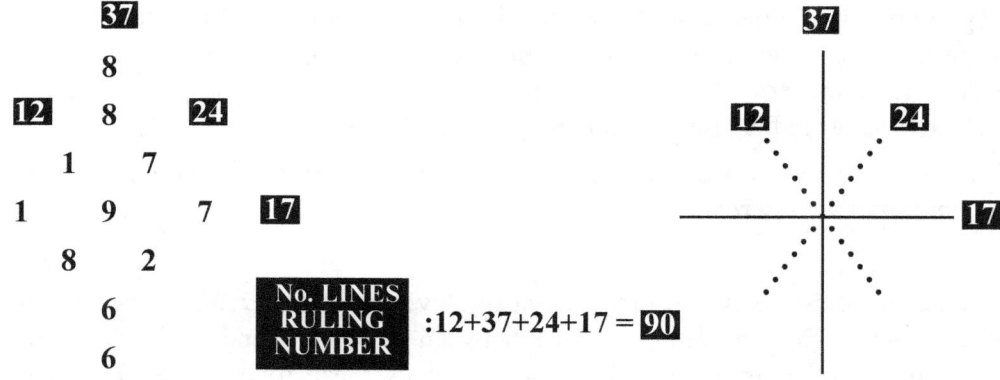

NB: *The Wheel's numbers are not cyclic but bring a foreground/background influence to any time span being examined.*

Personal Exercise: Add up each arm of the LD. Put their number-line rulers on your worksheet. Then add up the two arms of the vertical cross and the two arms of the diagonal cross. Get a total for each. Write them down. View the vertical cross ruler as applying to everyday life and the diagonal cross ruler as applying to your spiritual life or things that you hope to become successful at. Finally, add the two cross's rulers to obtain the over-all Wheel of Life ruler. Do any of these rulers produce new numbers? Do they intensify any numbers? If so, which ones? For any new numbers, take out their Tarot Keys and study them with reference to your Life Path.

Now that you are aware of how much can be extrapolated from a LD, it is recommended that an intensification list is compiled. Note anything on the LD worksheet that appears outstanding for whatever reason. You may centre your attention upon things like those listed below. NB: This list appears on the back of the blank worksheet.

A Handy Checklist of Notable LD Features:

Make note of things like:
1. The currently active life cycle.
2. Numbers which have a definite relation to the LPN or major personal numbers.
3. The heart number (include compound and root number eg 27/9, then reverse).
4. Vertical core, compound numbers.
5. Top and Bottom compound numbers.
6. Cycle rulers (addition of all numbers that make up a cycle).
7. Hidden numbers (those that surround each diamond, triangle or magickal facet).
8. Inner square numbers and its rulers (remember to isolate them from the main LD).
9. The Star of David's numbers and its rulers (rulers same as for 3rd Cycle).
10. The Cosmic Diamond's numbers and its rulers.
11. Wheel of Life (number-lines, + and x crosses and Wheel's rulers).
12. Intensification of particular numbers (repetitive numbers).
13. Master numbers and tens numbers.
14. Intensification of Major Arcana and Minor Arcana Keys (repetitive Keys).
15. Intensification of "Royal" Keys and Aces (repetitive Keys).
16. Intensification of a Tarot suit (several Keys from the one suit or element).
17. An isolated number or Key (like Steve Irwin's 57).
18. A pivotal 9 or 1 personal year.
19. Numbers that support repetitive themes.
20. Other.

LIFE DIAMOND WORKSHEET

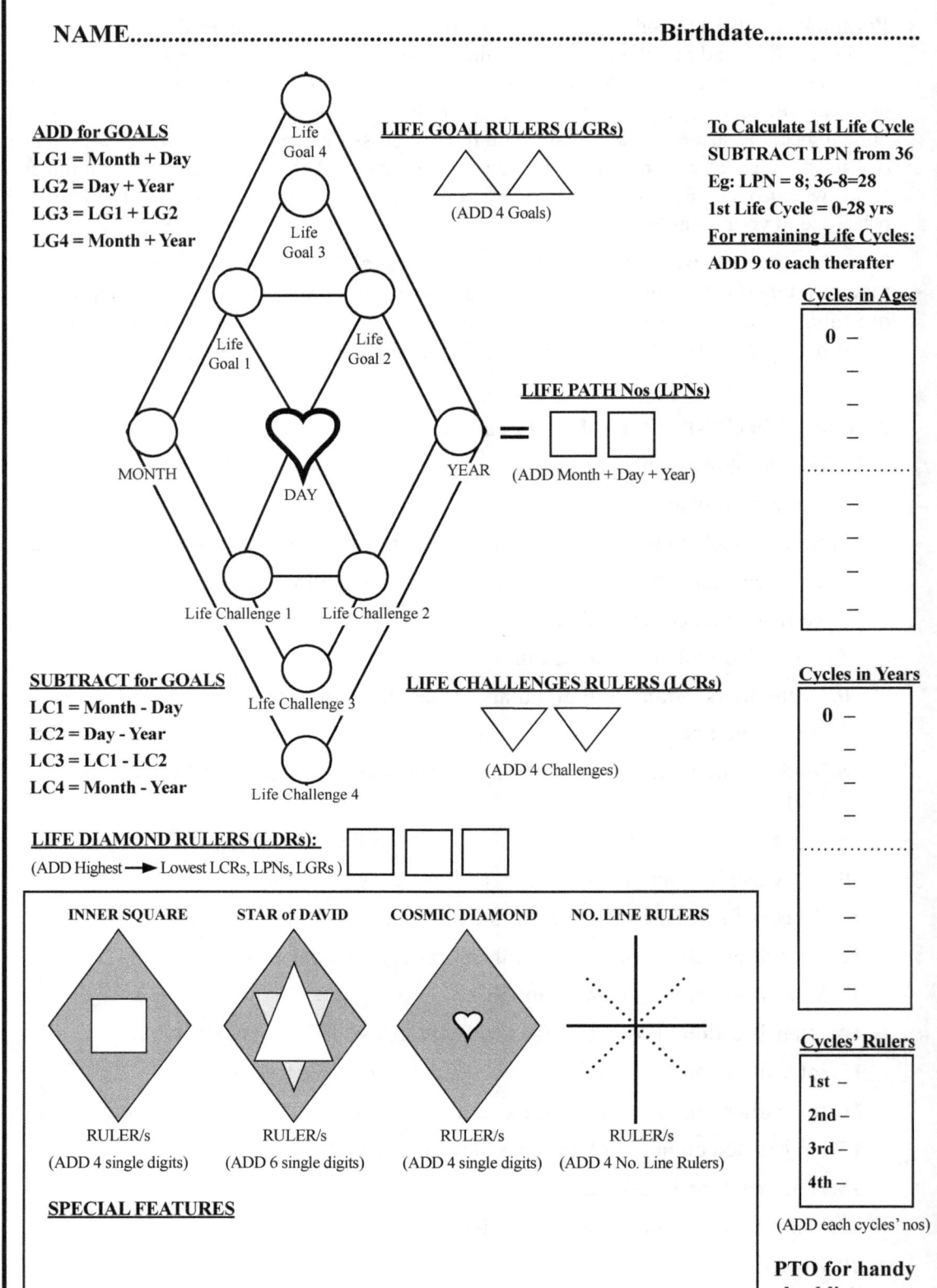

INTERPRETATION GUIDELINES

Abbreviated Terms used in this Chapter:

- ⬥ LD = Life Diamond
- ⬥ SD = Single Digit
- ⬥ SDLD = Single Digit Life Diamond
- ⬥ LG = Life Goal
- ⬥ LC = Life Challenge
- ⬥ LG/C = A Life Goal, Life Challenge combineation
- ⬥ LPN = Life Path Number

CHAPTER 7
INTERPRETATION GUIDELINES

In this chapter, you are being introduced to two basic ways in which to interpret a LD. To attempt an over-all impression of the LD or to focus on the current life cycle are good starting points. This and the following chapter address these two common approaches using Julie's LD as the main teaching tool. To begin, an interpretation of a life cycle which forms the basis for interpreting all life cycles is covered first. It is followed by an interpretation of Julie's LD which includes a basic format from which esoteric symbols and number-line rulers can be analysed along with the current cycle. These interpretations cover a very broad platform upon which more specific interpretations can be formulated. Look for numbers and configurations in the interpretations that are similar to your own. Use the way that they are handled and presented to help you to interpret your own LD. You will either follow them to the letter or devise your own methods. Your own LD is your best teaching-tool. Use it as your foundation from which to learn to interpret others.

A most important point needs to be brought to your attention before you begin your interpretations. LDs contain a plethora of information on many different levels. Because of this, several attempts at interpreting them is often necessary as *all is not revealed at once*. This is owing to LDs containing layers of information which are exposed and brought to your attention *at the fitting time*. That time will be when you are ready to receive and comprehend its information (like a child cannot read until ready). This phenomenon is attributable to working with a tool which is designed to reveal progressive stages of sequential growth. Where you are now is not where you will be at in the next moment, day, year or decade. You bring to the interpretation of your LD all of your expertise and all that you are at this moment. As you grow and evolve, further dimensions within your LD will open up to you to work with as you bring to it a renewed reality earned from hard won experiences and honed skills. Hold firm in the belief that what you need to know *now* is always revealed.

When reaching the interpreting stage, your approach hinges upon how much you want to know and what is being sought as to how deep you wish to delve. You can do a quick, cursory interpretation which is governed by time restrictions or one that is unhurried and in-depth. The most common approach is to seek Life Path directions as this is what the

LD was originally intended for. They can be interpreted exoterically or esoterically. For those on the Path, spiritual directions receive top priority. If this is the case, both mundane and esoteric indications need to be combined to give the best results. Future prospects are also highly sought after, often determining another way that the interpretations may be handled. No matter which of these approaches is chosen, it is always essential to locate, and then decipher the current life cycle's indications.

HOW TO DECODE A LG/C CYCLE

First, select the cycle for interpretation. Then obtain an intuitive grasp of it by scanning its numbers, hidden numbers and cycle rulers. Scrutinise them firstly upon their own merits, then in relation to other numbers within the cycle and finally, in relation to the LD as a whole. Next, seek links and triggers to the LD's extensions (which are introduced in the next chapter) and major personal numbers and other branches of numerology. How far you go with this step depends upon what and how much you are seeking. Build your picture as you go. Do all of this *keeping whoever is being analysed uppermost in your mind.*

1. **Life Cycle for Analysis**

    Calculate the *age-range* of the particular life cycle being examined and pinpoint which year is being activated in the cycle. This is *the* vital factor that determines exactly which phase of the LD is being analysed. Julie's first (really fifth) life cycle will be examined for this exercise since this is where she is currently at, as she is activating it for the *second* time (see Chapter 12). The next most important points to bear in mind when interpreting any part of a LD is to factor in the gender, character, status, inclinations and prevailing conditions surrounding whoever is being examined.

2. **Single Digits**

    Scan the first life cycle's SDs. Absorb their meanings and essence. Think of their basic attributes and note their placements. Notice any thing at all that stands out in their placement and nature. For example, all of Julie's SDs in her first/fifth mini-diamond share similar qualities that depict intelligence, leadership, power, drive and strength. It is an unusually strong group of numbers which can incline her towards rebellion and wilfulness, or being severely dominated, restricted and limited by those who wield any form of authority over her. The latter happened to be the dominating factor until senior years.

3. **Paired Compound Numbers**

    Create compound numbers from the single digits using number-pairing techniques. This step produces many numbers and Tarot Keys to weigh and consider. Because there are so many, it may help to list them and make jottings of what you consider to be fitting for the case in hand. Ponder likely outcomes while considering the over-all nature of the LD against the person's age, sex, character, inclinations and background. This will help to put together distinct possibilities about what the specific life cycle is depicting.

While engaged in this initial phase, common or parallel themes often begin to leap out at you as you develop and collate your data. Having prior knowledge of Julie's circumstances will help to choose the way in which you feel her directions are heading. If prior knowledge is not available to you, you must use your intuition and expertise, the numbers at hand and any peculiarities about them for guidance, especially if they are multiple or link to and reinforce other major personal numbers. Each compound number not only adds further insights and understanding but also provides *more definition* to the cycle's directions. Take especial notice of those that hold prominent positions in the LD. Consult Appendix 1.

4. **Corresponding Tarot Keys**

    Find the Tarot Keys that correspond to the numbers and lay them out before you. Decide on what you can extract from them. Make notes. Consult Appendices 2 and 3 and your personal Tarot books.

5. **The Ruling Numbers of a Life Cycle**

    This is the hidden or esoteric number that rules a particular life span. It supplies you with extremely important information that helps you determine the predilection of a life cycle. Do not leave it out of your calculations. Julie's first/fifth cycle's ruling number is a powerful 19 which is intensified because it repeats the two 19s already present in this cycle. Repetition often inclines to the negative. Because of this, you would lean towards negative connotations being dominant during this cycle. This is exactly what Julie experienced during its first activation. She was completely dominated and over-ridden by her mother. This resulted in identity damage, victim issues, learning difficulties and an early marriage. However, two good outcomes emerged from this – one is that such a strong emphasis more often than not provides a breeding-ground for special characteristics and gifts to emerge, as it did for her. The second is that if you are unable to make the most of your first cycle the first time around, you get a *second chance* when you *reactivate* it for the second time around with maturity, wisdom and experience on your side! Julie is exercising a role reversal in her marriage during this cycle's reactivation. She is reclaiming her power which one would hope to see under those 19s. (Life cycle reactivation is introduced in Chapters 10 and 12.)

6. **Hidden Numbers**

    Calculate the cycle's or symbols' "hidden" numbers for more insights. Their inclusion helps you to be more confident in your forecasting. When judged against the period you are examining, these numbers shed further insights and leads about its directions; especially if new numbers appear among them.

7. **Magickal Facets**

A magickal facet may form part of your analysis. Advanced students will be challenged by them as they are abstruse and tenuous making them difficult to apply to the life. Follow the same basic guidelines as for life cycles to isolate their numbers. Persist with them as they do provide definite soul-based guidelines. Do not forget that they have a lifelong, background influence.

8. **Final Analysis**

Once you have collated your data regarding a particular life cycle, magickal facet or overall Life Purpose, it is time to piece everything together and reach carefully considered conclusions. Always attempt to emphasise and build on the positives, and highlight strengths. Whenever confronted with what appears to be apparent negatives and difficulties, seek corroboration from other branches of numerology to confirm your findings especially if the indications are very auspicious or unfavourable. Suggest alternate solutions and/or strategies that provide positive means to overcome, offset or lessen the negatives. The antidote to negative outcomes, as simple as it may sound, is often found in the positive attributes of the "offending" number or a change in attitude. Paradoxically, we learn best from our mistakes! So have faith in the numbers and let them guide you. Ask them what their specific message is for you.

INTERPRETATION BEGINNINGS

This interpretation of Julie's LD gives a broad outline of its outstanding features which produce an over-all synopsis of what it generally depicts. To attempt to interpret every aspect of a LD would cover volumes.

General Impressions: This is the stage when you gather general impressions whilst calculating and scanning the LD and make jottings on the worksheet of any salient features that you find. By way of illustration, you will learn to recognise that some numbers literally jump out at you because they are either notoriously positive or negative. Take the number 57 for example. If it appears via number-pairing or as a *whole* number (whole numbers are dealt with in Chapter 9) in the LG region, there would be no doubt that unhappy experiences will eventuate, as 57 is commonly regarded as being a severe number even at the best of times. Even its reverse, 75 can be rather gloomy in some respects. Some numbers are like that – they are simply inherently negative by nature. No matter where they appear, one must be cautious in their interpretation. Because of 57's notoriety for unhappiness and loss, you may wish to highlight that it does have positive aspects; Steve Irwin's "57 number-line ruler" is a good case in point. It needs to be remembered that highly sought after qualities are won from the pain that a negative 57/75 combination inflicts. By comparison, positive numbers like the number 32 or 74 do have their down sides. If they happen to be situated in one of the LC positions, they lessen but not altogether counteract negative influences by indicating limited or temporary discomfort. These are important points to weigh and consider.

Having completed this cursory stage, which impressions from Julie's numbers captured your attention? Were you quick to note their repetitious nature and the appearance of several master numbers? Did you define what is causing this phenomenon? Did you notice that it stems from her *heart 9* at the centre of her LD? (9s always create repetitious numbers which then create master numbers when paired.) Having noted *frequency*, have you also taken your time to acknowledge *intensity* as well as the *positions* of her numbers? Do any of these numbers pick up on any of Julie's major numbers or the LD's number-line rulers, cycle rulers, etc? What is the make-up of Julie's esoteric symbols? Do they have any special features worthy of note? These are good familiarising points to begin with in getting to know her LD, learn from and then take any similarities from it to your own LD to deepen your understanding of how to interpret it.

Homing in on Major Themes: Getting down to specifics, Julie's SDs are so repetitive that they tend to oversimplify and generalise her LD concealing the actual promise and diversity that it contains. Do not be put off by this. When SDs repeat like hers, they supply several clues about where to lay emphasis. This idiosyncrasy gives you the interpreter, wonderful leads. Because there are fewer numbers to work with, you are more easily able to determine Julie's Life Path trends due to less deviation being present in her numbers. When numbers repeat and reinforce each other like in Julie's case, they can in an ideal sense lean towards being great motivators, such as having the determination to overcome adversity and hone specific talents, skills or develop noble traits; which she did. But in most cases, special talents or traits more often than not manifest as a result of sacrifice, privation and struggle.

In most instances, intensification of a number due to repetition more than likely inclines it towards manifesting negative expression and outcomes until its lessons are transcended. This negative orientation seems to be due to the added emphasis which is placed on it making its effects appear more focused, severe or intense. However, the presence of several master numbers and tens numbers tends to have the same effect, but these numbers produce their own specific effects, such as signifying the potential for multi gifts and talents – also often at a price! Julie's LD contains both types of intensification. It has intensification by repetition and by its several tens and master numbers.

Julie's paired compound numbers are a great help for getting to know her potential. They provide strong indications as to what else the single digits might be representing for *her*, thereby narrowing in many instances, generalised and speculative interpretations. Judging by the nature, frequency and position of her numbers, Julie's LD heralds much promise of success which is displayed more by its compound numbers, such as 17, 19, 27, 69 and 78, and her master numbers.

Although several of Julie's compound numbers indicate success, others most definitely forecast an onerous life. From this perspective, you would anticipate that any success would be hard won. As it happened, Julie experienced a most repressive childhood, being brought up by a domineering, harsh and manipulative mother (24, 66 and three 8s, not to mention prevalent 18s!). Following the pattern set by the mother, her husband mirrored Julie's mother in many ways. Julie and her husband worked extremely hard, starting from humble beginnings to become millionaires (78s and top 88). If Julie had not "starred" so well (central horizontal goal, 17 and LPN17, the Star Key) in her business and organisational skills (three 8s and a LPN 8 plus 78s and 88), I would expect her to have become very well known for one of her talents because of her prominent 17s, 18/81 and 27/72, that combine to suggest making a name for oneself in some way only for her restricted upbringing and overbearing, sometimes tyrannical husband.

This strong domination theme brings us to examining LC82/28. They are holding a strategic position firstly as challenges and then as forming part of her inner square and Star. 28 strongly indicates business and organisational abilities but it also indicates the strong possibility of "unfinished business" (I am using another perception of the term "business" thinking of it as what we "busy" ourselves with) in relationships as a carry over from past lives. Such a strong 28 helps you to not only understand why Julie had gifts in business and trade but also why she had to learn to find herself through the pain of the constant power struggles she endured first with her mother, then with her husband. Power plays and reversals in close relationships and money used as power have been a big factor in Julie's life, so far.

To return to Julie's entrepreneurial aspect, let us consider 96 and 98 which are core, vertical compound numbers. They reinforce this theme. 96 can be interpreted as representing Julie's family business and running it from home. Its reversal 69 links to the Ace of Pentacles. On its own, it signifies a penchant for money-making enterprises (especially when supported by 27s and 78s), property dealings and accumulation of assets. 98/89, her other central compound numbers also depict money making potential. These numbers, plus so many 8s, over all, point to almost guaranteeing financial success and attaining a secure retirement (multiple 78s).

1	7
8	2

Julie's Inner Square: Now we shall concentrate on Julie's inner square due to its revelatory aspects. When you isolate Julie's inner square can you see positive connotations within its negatives? Favourable indications can be drawn from pairing the 2 to the 7 of her 17. This creates a 27 which increases the imaginative component of the 17 because 27 is very inspirational, innovative and self-directed. The same goes for the 8. It increases 17's potential to become masterful by pairing 8 to 17's 1, to make 18. A central combination of 17 and 18 strongly indicates metaphysical leanings as does 87 from one of the inner square's diagonals. Stress factors are also evident in the square's SDs and should not be overlooked. The inner square's rulers are: 18/81/9. They intensify the 18 and the "hidden" 9s in the square's numbers. These rulers increase Julie's potential for developing psychic tendencies and metaphysical interests as well as experiencing the dark side of The Moon (Julie's mother) which is 18's Tarot Key.

18's root ruler 9, however, intensifies her "heart 9" endowing her with multi talents and extremist tendencies when the elements of her inner square are synthesised.

Because several of the inner square's numbers contain beneficial qualities they help to alleviate some of the oppressiveness that Julie's LD depicts. Do all that you can to find a LD's redeeming factors when it appears grim at first glance like Julie's, or you might miss the promise it contains if efforts to synthesise the LD's numbers give way to fragmenting them which is much easier of the two to do. Remember to criss-cross the inner square's numbers to create 78/87 and 12/21 and utilise them, too. 78 intensifies Julie's other two 78s which equate to the 10 of Pentacles; they are often beneficial Keys signifying wealth and material security. 12 and 21 intensify Julie's 12/21 from her left, horizontal number-line and 66. 12 in particular, accounts for Julie's different approach to life, personality eccentricities and tastes (12, The Hanged Man). It is further reinforced by her 7s which can also indicate unusual tendencies. 21, on the other hand corresponds to The World. This Tarot Key provides Julie with the potential to raise herself to higher levels of mundane and/or spiritual attainment. It works extremely well with her 17 and 18.

Volumes could be written on these numbers, alone. What I suggest is that you extend the leads given in all case studies that follow, by exploring aspects not being selected for attention. For this exercise, I have intentionally dwelt upon the inner square's numbers because they are vital to opening up any LD and should be considered after the heart number has been thoroughly examined in the way that it and the inner square set the *general* tone of the LD. For instance, Julie's heart 9 magnifies each of its paired compound numbers that it creates. Simply by its nature, it adds intensity and multifaceted potential to each.

Julie's Star of David: In Julie's case, no new numbers appear within her Star. It serves to intensify existing numbers making its indications easier to determine. However, more information pertaining specifically to spiritual inclinations can be gleaned from finding the rulers of each separate triangle in the Star by simply adding their numbers together. Julie's red triangle adds to 18 and her blue triangle adds to 14. Her Star's overall ruler is 32.

Esoterically, ruling 18 and 14 provide you with clues that relate to Julie's active struggle to develop and integrate Personality and Soul aspects and to resolve whatever conflicts with this. This is so because this triangle depicts the Personality aspect reaching towards the Soul aspect. It connects her challenge sector to her most potent goal on the spiritual axis. By using her numbers as tools and guides, Julie can work out how to facilitate soul growth. Armed with this knowledge, she has the power to initiate whatever is required to "elevate' herself because 12, 17, 18 and 21 represent spiritual attainment via self-correctional development.

In the blue triangle, we have the Soul aspect reaching earthwards towards the Personality aspect of the self. It lets Julie know how her soul is assisting her process by giving her direct guidelines from its numbers, Tarot Keys and symbolic representations from the Star itself as well as from the links it makes to other symbolic correspondences. Both 14 and 18 are extremely enlightening in that they basically inform Julie that she has the capability for synthesising (14) disparate or conflicting aspects of herself by implementing *voluntary* change (18). They form a major part of her spiritual work by providing Julie with definite indications that she is being given the opportunity to evolve spiritually via *self*-imposed change, and having the courage to tread the "thorny path".

32 as the Star's ruler, suggests that she can be successful at increasing spiritual awarenesses and attributes if that is her conscious desire and she does the "Work" of the Star. Its hidden numbers such as 10, 13 and 16 provide further pertinent clues. 10 teaches via *imposed* change that has a "forcing" effect which expands Julie's self-awareness from the lessons it brings. 13 facilitates the use of discriminatory powers that teach her to eliminate whatever inhibits her soul growth. Its reverse 31 warns of being distracted from her Path by insignificant things and that the Way forward will not be made easy. 16 is the "awakener" which helps her to see through illusion and make sound choices. Its reverse, 61, warns she may have to "discard" in order to have what she wants. The presence of 16, 17, 18, 19 and 32 strongly warn of a fall from Grace if Julie strays from her Truth.

Julie's Cosmic Diamond: Julie has already had the experience of her cosmic diamond. It is made up of 1 and 9 across and 8 and 6 from top to bottom. Its ruler is 24 and its SDs pair to make 18/81, 78/87, 16/61 and 76/67. The esoteric nature of 16, 18 and 78/87 very nicely facilitated a 9-year-period when Julie was able to overtly pursue spiritual directions in conjunction with everyday concerns. 76 signified that during this time, Julie put her back into the hard work involved and reaped rewards (78) according to her labours. 67 signalled a gradual process of unfoldment and consolidation and that gains on all levels were steadily accumulating.

Julie's Wheel of Life: Julie's number-line totals provide strong lifelong indications that help us to understand certain aspects of her nature better. 12 intensifies the 12 within her inner square and master 66. It alerts you to expect something "different" about her. 37 bestows commanding, artistic and psychic qualities and a taste for the good things in life. 24 reinforces the love of gardening, holidaying and travel and devotion to her family. In Julie's case, it also signifies family difficulties like dominance issues between her parents, in her marriage and, consequently, in her own family. 17/71 add developing skills as well as strengthening her penchant for occult interests.

90 as the number-line ruler is a very powerful number. It can signify limitless potential or greatness. Because of its magnitude, 90's attributes must be carefully weighed and measured against Julie's abilities, circumstances and level of evolution. This must be done in an effort to ascertain its correct level of application to her. You need to always be mindful of the fact that every number embodies infinite levels of skill and attainment in order to accommodate the vast ranges of human ability and development. Always consider the innate potential of any number in relation to its subject – especially when you are dealing with such a high tens number like in this case. 90's root 9 provides strong clues about Julie's Path. From 9's keywords it can be surmised that some of her main lessons centre upon the cultivation of sympathy, compassion and empathy for others, to render unconditional service and give wise counsel.

Julie's Current Life Cycle: Having made cursory observations of the features outlined above, the next step would be to concentrate upon the currently active life cycle. Presently, Julie is *reactivating* her first life cycle. This means that she has completed a first round of her LD's cycles and has begun the second round. This is a new area of study that is introduced in Chapter 12. It puts forward the proposition that we do not remain on the fourth LG/C for the remainder of our lives and uses recurring major life events to verify that we definitely start our cycles over again. For example, Julie's baby sister died during her first life cycle when she was 11 and her father passed away near the end of '05 when she was 63, while *re-experiencing this cycle for the second time*. This shows similar events being repeated when the cycle is reactivated (Chapter 12). However, the numbers of the cycle must concur with the events. In Julie's case, 19, active in this cycle, as well as 19 being its ruler, were strong indicators of the possibility of a loss of a family member. What is so interesting is the fact that Julie experienced a close family member's death during each cycle which is one of 19's possible outcomes.

To address Julie's directions in her present cycle, she has two 1s, an 8 and a 9 which pair to make an 11, two 18s and a two 19s. The cycle ruler is another 19. Importantly, this cycle stems from the earth axis. Because of this, it would normally mean that everyday concerns would attract the main focus of attention. However, at this juncture in her life, Julie has reached her senior years. This means that she has had time to develop spiritual aspects within herself. So, we would need to combine both esoteric and exoteric connotations in our interpretations because Julie would be conjointly attending to her everyday affairs and furthering her spiritual aspirations at the same time. We would anticipate that whatever this cycle's numbers indicate, Julie would be continuing her everyday and spiritual development according to their nature.

For example, from the presence of two 1s, a 19 and two hidden 10s, you would expect Julie to unfold further independent, assertive sides to her nature by actively taking her power back and gaining more control over her life. Hopefully, she will have learned from dominance issues (8) in the past how to reclaim her power (19) and not play the victim (11's root 2). Her numbers are "tailored" to help her to accomplish this; it all depends upon how well she has learned from her past mistakes and how much she is in touch with her true self.

In this cycle she has 1 intensified and two hidden 10s that will constantly challenge her ego and circumstances, thereby testing her mettle. Through constant change new and repeat lessons are experienced from which she can learn and grow. 18 works particularly well with them from the perspective that it bestows upon Julie the ability to instigate voluntary change. 11 beautifully facilitates such a process. She can use it to educate herself and right any injustices or imbalances and learn to attract more equilibrium (11) and harmony (11's root 2) into her life. Justice's sword (Key 11) will help her to cut away whatever she is aware of that hinders her from maintaining balance in her life. The numbers in this cycle provide Julie with a wonderful opportunity to refine and totally revamp herself and/or initiate a new phase or path.

Prevailing Indications: The most exciting feature in beginning her life cycles over again is that Julie has reached a point in her life when she can consolidate and improve upon past works. For instance, she can draw on her heart 9, a powerful prevailing influence, to further develop her artistic and spiritual attributes and shine her light for others. She can use her 1s, 11 and 19 to initiate new learning and develop a sunny rather than a gloomy outlook on life. The need for education is part of her Life Path which is being strongly stimulated and reinforced by these numbers, especially during this life cycle. She now has a golden opportunity from which to capitalise on them.

This concludes setting out a framework from which an over-all impression of a LD and its current cycle can be gleaned. The next chapter advances your studies further. It introduces additional techniques that greatly enhance all LDs – especially for those, like Julie's, which have few numbers with which to work. In all cases, you will find the extra information that these techniques disclose to be extremely helpful and illuminating.

 **HANDY TIPS**

NB: LD's cycles operate within long time frames. In order to obtain much more specific guidelines, Yearly Diamonds (Book 2) should be employed to step down the LD's current cycles into yearly time spans. They hone accuracy in forecasting and timing of events.

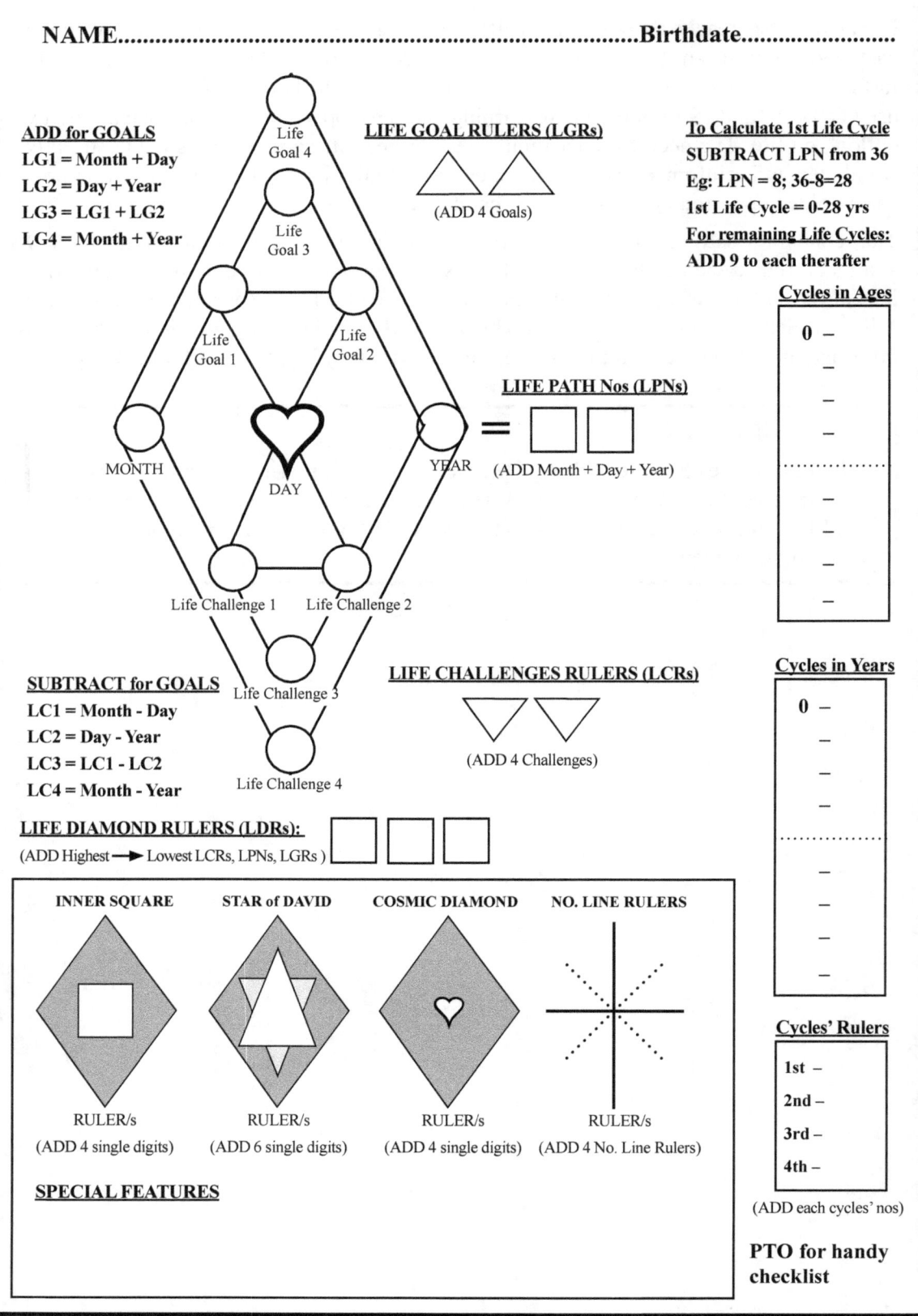

LIFE DIAMOND EXTENSIONS

Abbreviated Terms used in this Chapter:
- ❖ LD = Life Diamond
- ❖ SD = Single Digit
- ❖ SDLD = Single Digit Life Diamond
- ❖ LG = Life Goal
- ❖ LGR = Life Goal Ruler
- ❖ LC = Life Challenge
- ❖ LCR = Life Challenge Ruler
- ❖ LG/C = A Life Goal, Life Challenge combination
- ❖ LDR = Life Diamond Ruler
- ❖ LPN = Life Path Number

CHAPTER 8
LIFE DIAMOND EXTENSIONS

INTRODUCING LIFE GOAL RULERS (LGRs), LIFE CHALLENGE RULERS (LCRs) AND LIFE DIAMOND RULERS (LDRs)

This chapter opens up the possibilities of a LD further by adding three extra dimensions to it to create goal, challenge and LD rulers. What these three ruling numbers do, is to provide you with the final demarcation of the LD in conjunction with its number-line rulers. When you have calculated all of its rulers, which naturally include all LPNs, you have before you the completed emblematic field of experience that represents your mini map to life.

The full titles and definitions of the three ruling constellations' numbers follow:

1. **LIFE GOAL RULER (LGR)**

The Life Goal Rulers (LGRs) are the totals of the four LGs when added together.

2. **LIFE CHALLENGE RULER (LCR)**

The Life Challenge Rulers (LCRs) are the totals of the four LCs when added together.

3. **LIFE DIAMOND RULER (LDR)**

The Life Diamond Rulers (LDRs) are the sum total of the LCRs+ **LPNs**+ LGRs.

Note number **3,** above. This is where LPNs fit into the calculations and why they must be included as an extension of each LD's baseline. Not only do they supply vital information but also form an integral part of the LDR equation. LD rulers often share amazing correspondences with the LGs and LCs and other major personal numbers. SDLDs composed of a limited range of numbers are particularly enriched and enhanced by the inclusion of LD rulers. In such cases the rulers literally come into their own by providing sorely needed information that proves to be most helpful in the final analysis. They add much deeper insights that turn out to be exceptionally useful due to their high degree of relevance thereby giving the LD's guidelines much more definition and accuracy.

LGRs, LCRs and LDRs can be comprised of groups or single ruling numbers which influence the LD above and beyond the cosmic diamond somewhat like the zodiac's constellations do for the astrological chart. Stretching the imagination, they may be perceived as constellations to the LD in a similar fashion. They have a life-long, background influence and can be activated at any time. The LGR is interpreted as ruling the LGs and the LCR as ruling the LCs. The LDRs rule the entire SDLD. LGRs, LCRs and LDRs often present more than one number which represent different aspects of a *personalised family* of numbers. For example in Julie's LD, her three LDRs are based upon a family of nines (63/18/9); Bill Clinton's are based upon a family of twos (47/11/2). Other SDLDs can throw up four or five LDRs within its range of numbers. The emergence of any new numbers in these positions never fails to describe additional personal traits and life possibilities with a high degree of accuracy.

Once the LGRs, LCRs and LDRs are calculated, be confident that they will have a definite bearing on the person's innate potential, temperament, inclinations and outward expression. To avoid distractions and to assist you in concentrating upon the new material that they introduce, they provide the main focus for this chapter. In particular, note that their compound numbers are retained in their "ruler" and LPN positions. By not reducing the rulers to their root digits, you are able to access their "parent" Tarot Keys to embellish your findings.

The case studies of Julie, Bill Clinton, Nicole Kidman, Wallis Simpson, The Dalai Lama and Gandhi are all used to illustrate the inclusion of LD rulers. Both Julie and Bill Clinton's SDLDs are used to introduce the main teaching steps.

Julie's LGRs, LCRs and LDRs bring to notice two things. The first is that new numbers have emerged; the second is that, by their very nature, they do little to alleviate the stress in her SDLD. This is to be anticipated. You cannot have a SDLD signifying a life of struggle and its LGRs, LCRs and LDRs depicting something otherwise. What they do is to confirm your impressions by providing you with rock solid information that is highly relevant about the subject's potential and the way that the life is lived.

HOW TO CALCULATE THE LGRs, LCRs and LDRs

CASE STUDY

JULIE: 27-10-1942 = 53/8 (using root numbers you get: **9+1+7= LPN17/8**)

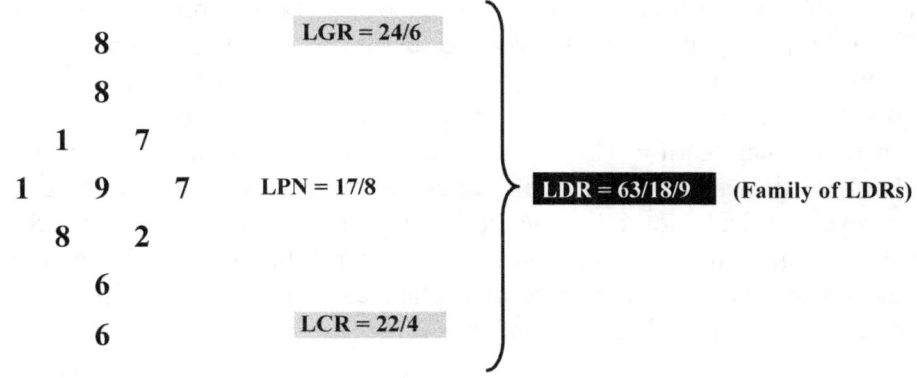

The Life Diamond

1. ADD all four LGs together (1+7+8+8) to obtain the Life Goal Rulers (LGR24/6).
2. ADD all four LCs together (8+2+6+6) to obtain the Life Challenge Rulers (LCR22/4).
3. ADD the LGR and LCR totals to the LPNs (17/8) to create the Life Diamond Rulers (LDRs). Always add the *highest* bracket of numbers together first, to obtain the highest LDR possible, then the next highest and so on, depending on how many there are. For example:
   a) First, add Julie's LCR22+LPN17+LGR24 to get her highest LDR which is 63.
   b) Next, add the single digit totals of these numbers together: LCR4+LPN8+LGR6. They create the second highest LDR18.
   c) Now LDR18 can be reduced to its root digit LDR9.
   d) 63, 18, and 9 make up Julie's LDR family as shown above.

LDRs can be tricky to calculate especially when you are presented with uneven sets of numbers. There can be wide variations in them so you need to work with what you have in a logical manner. You can have a single LCR with two LPNs and three LGRs. In this instance, you would use the SD LCR *three* times in your calculations. You would add it to the highest numbers in the other two sets, then the next highest and finally add all SDs. Also in this example you would add the LPN's higher number to the LGRs highest then next highest numbers. It would be used *twice* in your calculations. It is straightforward when you have even sets of rulers to work with as in Julie's case.

NB: Reverse ruler extensions to obtain further insights eg 63 to 36.

Now, let us see what these new techniques have created.

Firstly, Julie's SDLD contains several repetitive numbers which severely limit its scope. Fortunately, her LGRs, LCRs and LDRs make her LD much more comprehensive and informative due to their inclusions. Julie's LGR24 and LDR63 bring new numbers to her SDLD. They confirm that she is likely to experience many difficulties during her life. These distinctive numbers provide added information that reveals very strong clues about her nature, world and Destiny.

For example, LDR63 is a difficult number at best. Being the LD ruler gives it extra power. It does little to alleviate the harsh, yet successful life Julie has led up until now. 63 equates to the 9 of Swords. The image on this card clearly depicts that things will not be easy this lifetime until Julie can come to grips with her situation and learn why it is the way it is and then learn ways to relieve the stressful conditions she continually faces. Her LDR18 indicates emotional woundedness and that the study of psychology or being open to psychological counselling would be of great benefit to equip her with the necessary skills to deal with stress related situations. When Julie discovers her authentic self and becomes proactive in making appropriate changes to herself and her life, she can transcend the negative potential in these numbers.

36, LDR63's reversal depicts struggling to become successful and bring several things to fruition. 36's Tarot Key is the 10 of Wands showing a figure weighed down by a heavy burden which describes the oppressive nature of much of Julie's life. But, its many wands also depict the potential to achieve numerous accomplishments and successes in several areas of her life. She has. This is its positive angle.

LGR24, without its addition, would not intensify the following aspects of Julie's nature and life. For instance, gardening skills, one of its delineations, shows in her exquisite garden. Julie adores flowers and in May '06, she actually travelled overseas to enjoy a gardens' tour! This is a nice blend of a love of gardening and long-distance travel as travel is also an aspect of 24. Pets or a love of animals is another which makes 24 special when, Julie actually paints lovely dog portraits.

LGR24 equates to a "queen" Tarot Key; the Queen of Wands. It helps to confirm the dark side of Julie's mother. When operating in negative mode, this queen can depict a tyrannical woman/wife/mother resorting to jealousy, domination and emotional blackmail to get her own way. She can turn on others without cause and damage their sense of self to maintain power over them. This perfectly describes Julie's mother. Now, Julie needs to overcome her mother's negative legacy and reclaim her power. If she is unable to do that, she will continue to succumb to her husband's oppressive domination tactics thereby continuing this theme in her marriage (42, 24's reversal).

LGR42 depicts the many difficulties Julie has experienced in relationships even though it is a Goal Ruler. It bears out my feeling that the "shadow number", i.e., the hidden, reversed number, seems to have difficulty in finding a positive avenue for its expression. It appears to have to go through a "struggle" to manifest its positive qualities. 42's Tarot Key is the 2 of Cups; a very lovely card, depicting a happy union which, in all likelihood, represents a deep yearning on Julie's part to have a happy marriage (42) and home life (42's root 6).

Invariably, these extensions reinforce whatever is indicated in the LD. In fact, if you are at all unsure of how things will transpire the inclusion of these numbers will provide you with very accurate guidelines that not only help you to decipher what the LD is representing but also support your summations. Subsequently, they boost your confidence and forecasting skills. For instance, Julie's LDR63 beautifully illustrates this point. It bears out the SD and inner square ruler signs that Julie will most likely experience life as largely being tense, harsh, disappointing and even cruel in many but never in all ways. To alleviate disheartening prospects such as this, find those that endow her with particular strengths and gifts, like others in her inner square do to counterbalance them. Find the *redeeming factors*! Probably one of the most important tasks facing any practitioner of numerology is to find favourable aspects to offset those that appear discouraging at first.

Next, Bill Clinton's LD is treated on a more advanced level that shows you how to find numbers that have similar themes or incline towards a certain theme when found in certain groups. Tarot Keys are included to highlight certain features.

The Life Diamond

CASE STUDY
BILL CLINTON: 19-8-1946 = LPN 47/11/2

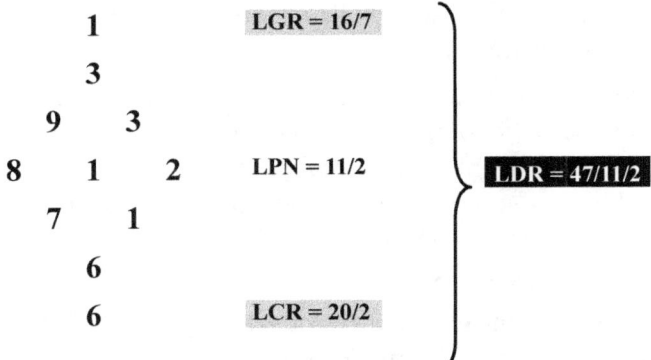

1. Add all of Bill's LGs together (9+3+3+1); their total creates his LGR16/7.
2. ADD his four LCs (7+1+6+6) to create his LCR20/2.
3. ADD the LGR and LCR totals to his LPN (11/2), to create his LDRs. For example:
   a) Add Bill's LCR20+LPN11+LGR16 to get his highest LDR which is 47.
   b) Next, add the SD totals together: LCR2+LPN2+LGR7 create LDR11.
   c) Bill's LDR11 can be further reduced to create LDR2.
   d) 47, 11 and 2 make up Bill's LDR family above.

   NB: Ruler extensions can be reversed to obtain further insights.

The addition of Bill's three sets of ruling numbers, above, has presented us with a rarity. It is seldom that a LDR family actually reproduces the LPN family! More commonly, you find different numbers holding these positions. However, all is not lost, as this situation serves to provide a useful example of a situation when a person's LPN is being *reinforced*. This actually helps to make the analysis of the SDLD simpler, in the sense that the Life Path of that particular individual is clearly laid out – there are few deviations! The value in this is that it provides the numerologist with a strong indication of where to lay emphasis.

Repetitious numbers generally add to the strength of the virtues and vices that they represent. Therefore the tendencies are that the person with repetitive numbers is given the capability to express his or her positives and negatives more overtly. Hence they tend to be markedly positive or negative. Unfortunately for most people, the negative inclination seems to be more commonly expressed until awareness dawns and conscious steps are taken to temper or transform compulsive/obsessive and/or negative tendencies.

For those who are searching for purpose and meaning, LDRs repeating LPNs would be of great assistance as they hone life directions by clearly signposting how their destiny may be reached. They would also be more aware of their strengths and shortcomings thereby developing greater confidence in their decision-making processes by knowing that 47 represents a number of *right* choice. Being able to achieve their destiny is largely dependent upon whether or not right intent and right choices were made initially.

INTERPRETING BILL'S LGRs: Bill's SDLD is similar to Julie's in that its few numbers are greatly enriched by the addition of his LGR, LCR and LDR numbers. It is also a very good example of intensification due to the presence of several repetitive SDs and compound numbers. As a result you would be on the lookout for special gifts, idiosyncrasies, clear guidelines and specific, repetitive lessons.

To begin with, Bill's LGR16/7 intensifies The Tower, found in his LCs and cosmic diamond. But, like his LDRs, it does act as a reinforcer, having definite value from this standpoint. As repetitive numbers lead the analyst towards more accurate interpretations, LGR16 strongly indicates a rise to great heights (the tall Tower). It is reinforced by his inner square 79 (which also reduces to a "hidden" 16). As 79 is the number of the "hero", it makes a nice combination. With 16 intensified, he will enjoy fame and fortune and a life full of surprises, reversals and disruptive influences. A "fall from Grace" is very predictable at some point in this case because 16/7 is repeated in his LCs which is one of The Tower's possible outcomes *no matter its position*. Intensified 16, combined with two LC17s, often inclines them towards negative expression. If so, a sudden fall from Grace definitely becomes a strong likelihood, because negative 17s can attract defamation if Bill ever loses control (16's root 7, The Chariot) or makes careless choices in the way that he conducts himself (LDR and LPN 47, the 7 of Cups).

The value that can be seen in the repetitive 16s is that you can expect their traits to be up front in Bill's character as well as being operative in his circumstances. Some of 16's attributes indicate that he is very prone to deception in matters of love, sudden infatuations, and misunderstandings in sexual expression and so on. (Because of the self-indulgent or narcissistic tendencies of his two 39s, you can see how the nature of several 16s, plus the scandal factor and sexual deviance that is inherent in the 17s and 39s, could all merge to become a very real threat to his reputation, 71 and 81 (17 and 18's reverse), if he ever succumbs to inappropriate behaviours – then the downfall dynamic would be triggered. 16 in the powerful LGR position gives a clear warning of a "Humpty Dumpty syndrome" especially when linked to two LC17s, The Star Key. By being aware of highly precarious combinations such as these, one can take note of their negative possibilities and put appropriate strategies in place with a view to moderating or completely transcending them.

LGR16's root 7 corresponds to The Chariot. This Key depicts either being in full command of things or careering out of control. We have clearly seen these traits in Bill's character and actions as it is the LGR and first LC in his SDLD. We have also seen his ability to surmount his problems in order to achieve his ambitions and the ability to turn things to his own advantage (61s and 2s!). When up against it, Bill can fully exploit his talents and ride roughshod over others to serve his own needs especially when multiple 61s are coupled to the 66, Queen of Pentacles and the self-indulgent aspects of his Knight of Cups (39s). These traits are fanned by the LCR2 and LPN2. Negative 2s can indicate divorce, separation, loss, disagreement, trouble, misery, strife, unhappiness and ruin, destruction and hate, and war and peace – not to mention being extremely manipulative as well!

If nothing else, this is a particularly good example of a Goal Ruler behaving in positive and negative ways.

INTERPRETING BILL'S LCRs: The LCR20, reinforces Bill's year number (1946 = 20) and inner square ruler. So it is not new, but adds another dimension to Bill's family of LPNs and LDR2s. 20 is often found in the charts of people who require an enormous amount of stamina and fortitude in order to perform their life's work. It would be a great asset to have this number if your heart was set on attaining a goal that required great demands, abundant energy and unstinting endurance. 20 also gives Bill the determination to hang in there when the going gets tough. It provides great strength and resolute will to be able to cope with the huge pressures that this number can represent. It clearly depicts the colossal workload and responsibility Bill has chosen for his Path in this incarnation. These are its positive aspects; its redeeming factors.

20 equates to Judgement. We all saw 20 negatively in action when Bill was at the brunt of probably the most publicised and notorious court case in history – he certainly met his "Judgement Day". Its root 2, mirrors and strengthens his LPN2. It equates to The High Priestess. However, this is Bill's LCR2! It strongly emphasises "brought over" skills in arbitrative, diplomatic abilities as well as his propensity to be mysterious and deceptive. Being the ruler of his LCs, it also represents the stark opposites in his personality, behaviour and actions and difficulties within personal relationships. These positive and negative 20 and 2 traits are nestled in the karmic realm of past-life works concealed within his SDLD clearly indicating personality flaws to be corrected in this lifetime.

Having dealt with the salient features of Bill's LGRs and LCRs, we shall turn our attention to his LDRs, beginning with the highest and finishing with the lowest.

INTERPRETING BILL'S LDRs: Bill's LDRs belong to the 2s family. As mentioned previously, they are an exact replication of his LPN family. The highest LDR is 47, corresponding to the 7 of Cups. This card clearly depicts a figure in its foreground endeavouring to decide which cup to select from seven - it has to be the *right* cup otherwise things go awry. Each cup but one symbolises wishful things in life that seduce the bearer of 47 into making the wrong choice and losing sight of the cup that represents the main goal or right choice. True intent can get lost unless the right choices are made. However, 47s have a wonderful capacity to manifest their dreams. As you can imagine, being faced with having to make decisions amidst a barrage of options would immensely challenge a person who held the Presidency of America, let alone an ordinary individual. This Key in particular, teaches the result of consequences for one's actions being all about cause and effect! The trick is to make the right choice and stay on target. 74, being 47's reversal equates to the 6 of Pentacles which puts one in a position of being able to assist others as well as being the recipient of assistance and many benefits from others; 74 is a handy number for a politician to have.

Only for the digressions along his path, one cannot help wondering what Bill could have achieved when you reverse his 16 and 47 to make 61 and 74 and compare them with those in the SDLD of the Dalai Lama. The Dalai Lama uses his 74 as a great spiritual leader and protector of his race and their religion (the Dalai Lama's case study features in the four that follow). The suggestion here is: as he has the capacity to make a difference, will Bill contribute more greatly to humanity in some way in the future? He certainly has the numbers to do so.

Chapter 8 – Life Diamond Extensions

 HANDY TIPS

The main point of including LGRs, LCRs and LDRs to a SDLD is to be ever watchful for numbers that add outstanding information, intensify existing numbers or, pose a threat in some way. The hardest thing to achieve is to learn to synthesise the SDLD's array of numbers and weave its story together as demonstrated above. Once the total SDLD is constructed, tie its numbers to other major, personal numbers in an effort to reach accurate conclusions. Seek those numbers within and without a SDLD that relate to and reinforce each other. Especially seek those that present parallel themes; jot them on your checklist of notable features. To further these suggestions, consider Bill's LGR7 with his LPN47 and you will note a correlation between the two. Both numbers contain the element of being in charge as a consequence of making right choices. His LCR20 and LDR11 also have strong links to each other. They stand for great strength and courage, right morals and ethics, the law and being just and fair, otherwise one must pay the price – the Monica Lewinski trial! Bill's 11s (plus two behind the 47s) and 39s emphasise justice, unselfishness, understanding and empathy for those who are less fortunate. The latter is to be striven for in his 47's reversal, 74. Never underestimate the power that the LGRs, LPNs, LCRs and LDRs contain.

Four fascinating case studies follow to highlight how LGRs, LCRs and LDRs add more depth and meaning to a SDLD. Tarot inclusions enrich each analysis.

CASE STUDIES:

WALLIS SIMPSON:
19-6-1896 = 49/13/4

```
                3         LGR = 22/4
                5
            7   7
        6   1   6         LPN = 13/4
            5   5
                0
                0         LCR = 10/1
         LDR = 45/9
```

NICOLE KIDMAN:
20-6-1967 = 49/13/4

```
                2         LGR = 23/5
                6
            8   7
        6   2   5         LPN = 13/4
            4   3
                1
                1         LCR = 9
         LDR = 45/18/9
```

The Life Diamond

NICOLE and WALLIS

Here are two examples where the addition of LGRs, LCRs and LDRs helps to provide significant information by presenting several new numbers for consideration. It is not so much that these ladies share fame and fortune and have the same LPNs but, are/were they happy? That is the burning LDR9 question! Their LDRs, that they basically share, can answer that because these numbers are so powerful. They never fail to provide instant clues.

What led me to do Nicole's numbers was to see if she could ever find the love and happiness for which she so much yearns. Her LDR45/18/9 family brings new compound numbers to her LD. Unfortunately for Nicole; they are not fortunate numbers to have as LD rulers. When I saw them I felt sad – especially on seeing 18, The Moon, supporting a gloomy 45, the 5 of Cups. At worst, heartache and tragedy will strike Nicole when you combine them with a 57, the 3 of Swords in her SDLD. LDRs 45/18/9 linked to her LCR9 and paired 57 signify grief, shock and sadness, like her tragic (18) miscarriage and divorce – central 42, 43 combination – from Tom Cruise which brought untold grief, disappointment and sorrow to her. True inner peace and happiness will not come easily to Nicole with these LDRs having other numbers in the LD, itself, to bolster them.

LDR9's family reveals Nicole's many talents, but more so her very high ideals and standards that may fail to measure up to the reality of her situation (LPN4). Someone or something may dampen them.

It is fascinating to compare Wallis's chart with Nicole's and to note that they not only shared the same LPNs, but the same LDRs as well which makes one wonder how much hope Nicole has of achieving true happiness. As with Nicole, Wallis's LDR family of 9s introduced new numbers to her LD that failed to add fortunate trends to it. She neither became queen nor was she accepted by English society which must have been a huge disappointment to her (LDR45). The promise was there in the 66, the Queen of Pentacles, which becomes a compound number in the cosmic diamond. This can be a self-serving woman seeking money and power, especially when fanned by her central horizontal 77, the 9 of Pentacles, and 55, the Ace of Swords! Also note the two, central 17s which not only put her in the spotlight but also defamed her. Hers is a daunting inner square.

77 depicts a woman who has every material luxury yet lives in confinement or feels lonely and alone even among others. It is the only redeeming number in Wallis' inner square but from a material sense. The other numbers in her LD are very intimidating. Her six 75s in the 7 of Pentacles signifies disappointing results and her six 57s, the 3 of Swords, add up to extreme heartache. 55, the Ace of Swords, and multiple tens numbers in the challenge area, do not lift this LD. LCR10, the Wheel of Fortune signifying wealth and/or poverty, intensifies her challenge core 10 so the "wheel" is likely to turn against her at some stage. 10s, 16s, 17s, 55, six 57s, 30, 50s and 60s all combine to warn that regardless of the amount of scheming (third cycle ruler adds to 29 – an untrustworthy person, if negative) and hard work (75) that has been put in, everything that has been built up (LGR22) can all come crashing down if they manifest negatively. The inclusion of her LPN13, Death,

Chapter 8 – Life Diamond Extensions

and LGR22, The Fool, send out a clear warning to watch one's step! LGR22 also heralds public notoriety (global due to the LDR9, in this instance) but not necessarily that which would be pleasing to Wallis (LDR45)! Her LD is an excellent example of intensification when you consider so many repetitious numbers in it.

Returning to Nicole, her numbers are not as severe as Wallis'. They contain redeeming factors like her two 23s, the King of Wands, which can be reversed to expose two fortunate 32s, the 6 of Wands – the number of success. One is hidden in the enviable position of LGR. The other is in her LC area. (Many would love to have just one in their numbers!). Nicole's 32 is visible when she graces the red carpet, cheered on by her adoring fans. As an aside, Nicole's three 62s, the 8 of Swords, are interesting from the perspective of confinement. Tom Cruise certainly held Nicole "captive" until he was finished with her – 43, the 3 of Cups, in the LC area (often depicts infidelity) and adjacent compound 73, the 5 of Pentacles, as being abandoned. 28 indicates definite power struggles in relationships. Finally, 28, 41, 68, 78 and 9s combination are exciting indicators of the potential to become very wealthy but will Nicole find true happiness?

CASE STUDY:
14TH DALAI LAMA: 6-7-1935 = 31/4

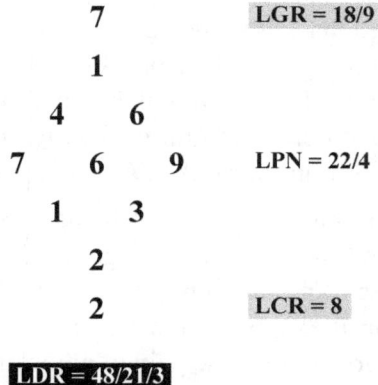

The 14th DALAI LAMA

Despite being exiled in India, the Dalai Lama is still regarded as being the spiritual leader of Tibet. Repetitious numbers abound in his SDLD. Its paired numbers clearly depict the enormous struggle that he has endured, especially in the make-up of his inner square and the Star of David. Note 31s in the inner square and the Star. 31 corresponds to the 5 of Wands which graphically depicts struggle. It is the red triangle of the Star which is the more "active" and apparent of the two in everyday life. 46/64 also part of the square and the Star depict family crises (his people) and the betrayals and the very real threat to his life. 12, 13, 16 and LPN22, which intensifies the 22 at the bottom of his LD, all signify a type of forced change whereas 61 signifies a self-imposed change in that the Dalai Lama had it in his power to initiate the time when he would leave Tibet rather than be imprisoned (16, The Tower) and safely continue to lead his people (LPN4, The Emperor) from India. Core 62 on the spiritual axis adds to the precarious nature of the Dalai Lama's predicament which depicts a figure being bound for a time to distressing conditions and having to hold his tongue (26). 63 supports this most difficult period by depicting excessive worry and sleepless nights (9 of Swords) due to pressing demands (36, the 10 of Wands). 61, 62, 63 and 64 paired from the heart number provide an excellent example of being able to predict that the Dalai Lama is very likely to face extreme situations at some point in his life. Positively, SDLD17s indicate fame and fortune. Negatively, the slander aspect came forth in the bad press (now include 39) he received from the Chinese who are infamous for their biased propaganda against Tibet and the Dalai Lama.

Significant information wells up when LD rulers are added to the mix. The LDRs in this SDLD provide an excellent example of when their inclusion adds vital data that assists in interpreting a person's destiny. LDR48, a new number to the SDLD, is a classic example. It clearly depicts the heartbreak caused by the Chinese invasion. 48 is the 8 of Cups, depicting the Dalai Lama actually leaving his cherished homeland (24 in the blue triangle of his Star of David). LGR18 links to this, presaging deception, tragic circumstances and emotional turmoil and LCR8 indicates possible cruelty and brutality. Unexpectedly, the powerful root LDR3 tells the story in both its positive and negative aspects! Positive 3 represents harmony and action, perfect love, tenderness and soul force, plenty, fruitfulness and exertion. *But* 3's little known negative connotations can be horrific. In its extreme negative expression, it can manifest its worst side through the "Infernal Sphere", where 3 represents the "Three Degrees of the Damned", the "Three Infernal Judges" and the "Three Infernal Furies", all of which characterise the atrocities committed by the Chinese upon the Tibetans. For a long time, negative situations dominated the Dalai Lama's life.

However, all is not lost. LDR48 symbolises, despite the heartbreak of being forced to leave his beloved homeland and all that is known and familiar with meagre possessions (intensified 61s), that new horizons hold the promise of moving on to something better, even greater. The second LDR21 and LPN22 support the 48/61 theme, by indicating the end of an era or phase as well as having the courage to embrace the pain of adjustment in order to improve one's lot.

Note the paired 74, the 6 of Pentacles, in this SDLD. It is the number of a great benefactor and protector when used at its highest level. 74 also reduces to 11 which intensifies the 11 to be found in the red triangle of the Star; in this case, they denote a great teacher. Add to this the paired 27s, the Ace of Wands, the 29, the 3 of Wands and the 79 all from the cosmic diamond, and you get an inspirational, intelligent, enterprising leader (27) who is an idealist (29) and the people's hero (79).

CASE STUDY:
GANDHI: 2-10-1869 = 36/9

```
            7            LGR = 20/2
            2
         3     8
       1    2    6       LPN = 9
         1     4
            3
            5            LCR = 13/4

      LDR = 42/15/6
```

GANDHI

Gandhi, a political leader who thought nothing of voluntarily sacrificing himself (12's, Hanged Man) for his cause (bottom 53, a dashing Knight of Swords), was a great reformer (four 13s, Death, and a 14 Temperance) and an immeasurable inspiration (top 27) to his people (top LG7 and central 22), no matter what the personal cost (12s and 75 from pairing top LG with bottom LG) and tireless work involved (31s, LPN36 and 76, 8 of Pentacles – cosmic diamond). He saw his life mission as being to regain independence from British rule and to abolish the caste system in India using the media as one of his major weapons (central horizontal compound numbers 14, seeking a unified nation, 24 plus LDR6, and 38, the media). Nothing could deter him from achieving these goals even if it meant starving himself to death (LCR13/4, Death/Emperor) from severe fasting (paired 34, the 8 of Wands and 14, Temperance, can take things to extremes). He struggled (31s) to sway the nation (central 22, LDR6, G7 and 24) to bring it round to his way of universal, visionary thinking (LPN9, 26 and 27). LDR15, The Devil, backed up by his LCR13, Death, represents two powerful numbers working in harmony (past life and the present life) aiming towards the removal of British rule (13) as well as severing India's own political and social fetters (15) in order to bring about great social reform (LGR20 and 14, base of inner square and red triangle). LDR6 represents working from the Soul to create peace and harmony.

LDR42 gave Gandhi an ability to know the heart (root 6) of his people. LDR15 gave him the gift of seeing through and beyond illusory belief systems and materiality to the Truth. LDR6 added discrimination and incisiveness which led to making right choices (6, The Lovers) His struggle against the odds and ultimate triumph after a great battle is depicted in his four 31s and LGR2. 27 and two 28s depict uncanny fund-raising abilities. Ghandi raised vast amounts of money, LPN9, yet took nothing for himself (dedicated voluntary worker from 12, 33 in Star, LPN36, 75 and 76).

Gandhi's paired 11 clearly shows his love of the law and equality and his remarkable teaching qualities – qualities that he taught by example. It shows the sword of Justice and the passing of new laws as he laboured to right the scales in India's favour and bring equal status to the "untouchables" in his country (renewal aspect of LGR20). Gandhi's LGR2 accents his day 2 which gave him diplomatic and statesmanlike status as he fought for cooperation and solidarity (positive 14) among the opposing viewpoints and warring factions (negative 2) of his people. Gandhi's day number 2 and his LDR6 demonstrate how he beautifully combined them to orchestrate a *non-violent revolution* and achieve his purpose via peaceful, harmonious means! The Tarot depictions of the scythe, dagger and sword (three 13s plus LCR13 = scythe, and the dagger or sword of Zain, the Lovers' Hebrew letter, and the mighty sword of Justice) conjure up dramatic images of the awesome power that Gandhi had within his grasp to right the scales of unfair discrimination (11s and 6s) in the people's favour (LDR6, 42/24 and 46/64 all similar aspects of a family or nation). He could also use his other sword (LDR's 51, the King of Swords) to cut the bonds of the caste system (15, The Devil) and lay bare the truth that the caste system needed elimination (13s), as it only promoted inequality and dissent (31s). He was also able to provide the bare bones upon which a new political system (LGR20 and vertical 22) could be rebuilt and established (LCR4, The Emperor). He did this by example. He gave up his worldly possessions signified by 48 and 75. 48 is also the total of his LD's number lines which powerfully reinforces his ability to abandon that which he perceived as inappropriate, unnecessary, archaic and useless.

This very brief overview of the LCR, LGR and LDR sets the foundation for revealing their interconnectedness within the SDLD. The tapestry they weave is truly fascinating. Hopefully, these brief synopses, and the case studies that follow, demonstrate that the inclusion of these numbers is most certainly useful for the additional and illuminating insights that their constellations reveal. Their inclusion personifies recognisable facets of the above personalities and their lives that have become public knowledge. I urge you to try these techniques on your own SDLD. I feel certain that you will not be disappointed with what you uncover about yourself and others.

To help to reinforce these claims, construct several LDs for people you know, as well as notable people who have achieved fame in different ways. For instance, I was astonished to find Annie Besant's (1-10-1847) SDLD to be an exact replica of Bill Gates'. She was a formidable figure who became head of the Theosophical Society in India. The similarity between Bill and Annie shows in their philanthropic tendencies. Bill is well known for extreme generosity regarding charitable work, whereas Annie was well known for her altruistic work. Their achievements were/are extraordinary to say the least.

For example Annie, as an Englishwoman in a foreign country, championed the cause for home rule in India. In so doing, she inadvertently prepared the political way for Gandhi to follow. Note that Annie has 47 in her year number, a number that she and Bill Clinton also have in common, sharing a humanitarian focus and the ability to manifest their dreams. 47 is often found in charts where people use their particular type of expertise to manifest something that, in some way, serves the "greater good" in its reversal, 74.

John F. Kennedy (29-5-1917), a social reformer, had 47s in both LDs (another technique for constructing a LD is revealed in the next chapter). When he was elected to the US Presidency at 43, his Yearly Diamond contained a 47 and its ruling number was also 47 thereby triggering his 47s to be found in his LD's challenges! Did being in the challenge section of his SDLD mean that his Presidency would be short-lived? JFK was assassinated on the 22nd November 1963. His LCR18 heralded deception and tragedy, which was supported by the threat of a sudden demise in his LPN16. Calculate his LD and see for yourself.

Before moving on, make sure that you have mastered the SDLD and its extensions.

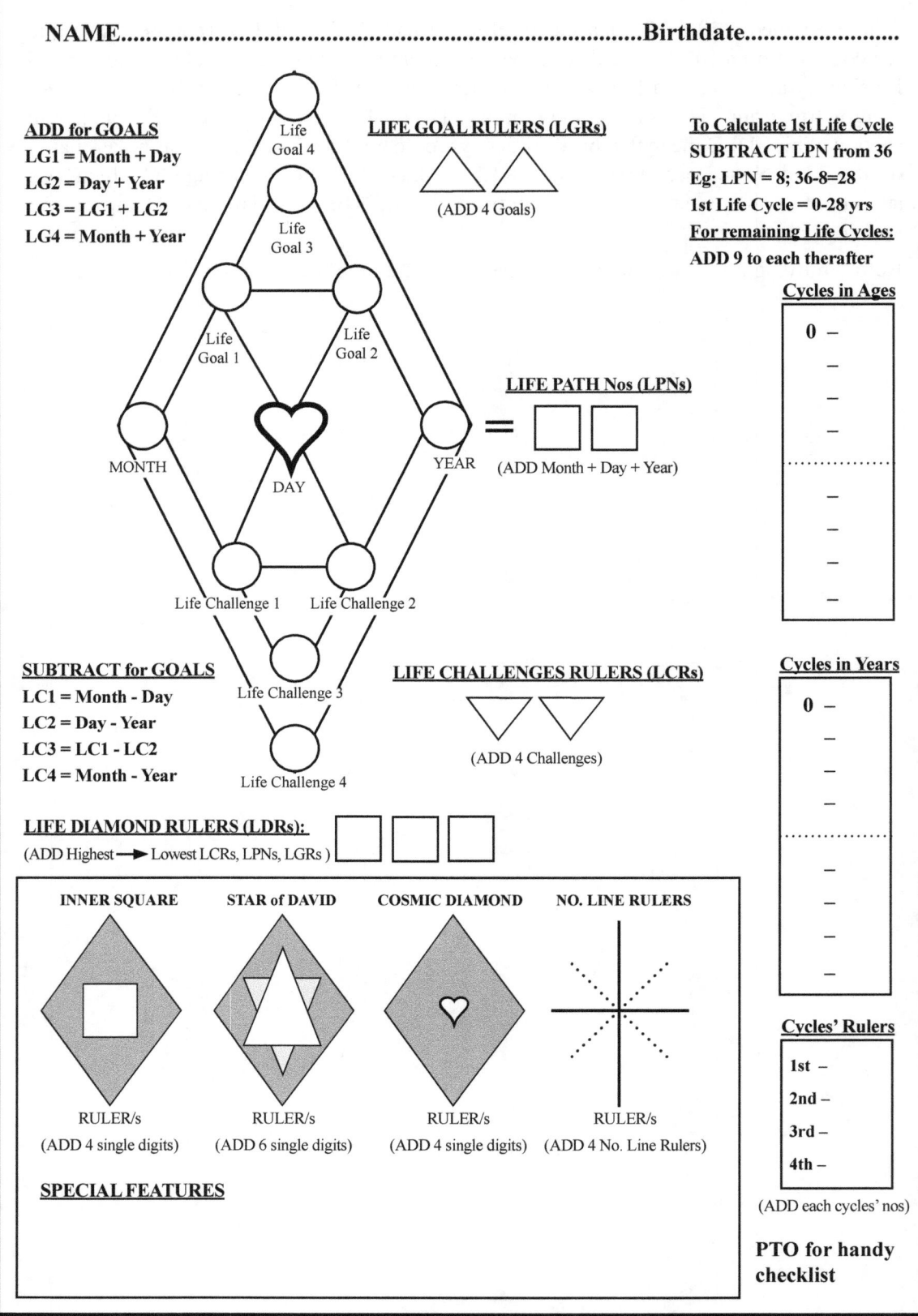

THE WHOLE NUMBER LIFE DIAMOND (WNLD)

Abbreviated Terms used for Single Digit Life Diamonds in this Chapter:
- LD = Life Diamond
- SD = Single Digit
- SDLD = Single Digit Life Diamond
- SDLG = Single Digit Life Goal
- SDLGR = Single Digit Life Goal Ruler
- SDLC = Single Digit Life Challenge
- SDLCR = Single Digit Life Challenge Ruler
- SDLDR = Single Digit Life Diamond Ruler
- SDLG/C = A Single Digit Life Goal, Life Challenge combination
- SDLPN = Single Digit Life Path Number

Abbreviated Terms used for Whole Number Life Diamonds in this Chapter:
- WN = Whole Number
- WNLD = Whole Number Life Diamond
- WNLG = Whole Number Life Goal
- WNLGR = Whole Number Life Goal Ruler
- WNLC = Whole Number Life Challenge
- WNLCR = Whole Number Life Challenge Ruler
- WNLDR = Whole Number Life Diamond Ruler
- WNLPN = Whole Number Life Path Number

CHAPTER 9
The WHOLE NUMBER LIFE DIAMOND (WNLD)

INTRODUCING THE WHOLE NUMBER LD – Using Your *TRUE* Numbers in a LD

The Whole Number LD, as its name implies, is based upon *non reduction of existing numbers in the birthdate,* therefore its *true* numbers. It evolved as a direct consequence of number-pairing techniques which opened the way for working with compound numbers and the Tarot. This meant that after aeons of being ignored, the birthdate's compound numbers could be brought into play. As a consequence, several new terms became necessary in order to differentiate between and separate the various components of the Single Digit LD (SDLD) from the Whole Number LD (WNLD). Their abbreviated terminology on the previous page, helps you to immediately distinguish between firstly the type, and then the separate facets of each LD.

You will find that WNLDs are excellent self-guidance tools. Like their companion SDLDs, they also contain extremely personalised information. Their baselines are comprised of exactly what is found in the birthdate. For instance, if the birthdate contains compound numbers like 10 for the month or 16 for the day or the year number is 18 (from 1971), these numbers are retained and placed in their respective positions on the baseline without reducing them to their root digits. Accordingly, this baseline gives rise to the Whole Number LD. It allows you to work with true numbers instead of working with numerically contrived substitutes.

True numbers establish a greater connection to your Life Path because they are your *authentic numbers – your "givens" at birth*. They represent the **unblemished essence concealed in your birthdate's numbers** which is unfortunately lost if the WN approach is not employed. The benefits gained from using WN methods are that you have sole ownership of the numbers that make up *your* WNLD's cycles, symbols and ruling numbers. Working with your true, given numbers at birth engenders confidence in being able to decipher them with greater accuracy.

Reduction practices erase infallible signs that lead to uncovering your authentic self. They ignore your "parent numbers" that "spawn" your single digits thereby obscuring especially tailored guidelines and objectives that your soul's precise *selection and positioning* of your birthdate's numbers is intended to achieve. This "Divine Engineering" greatly impacts on what emerges in the goal and challenge areas and their subsequent extensions. Do not dispense with your whole numbers as they provide you with explicit information that is intended for the comprehension of self, strict guidance and subsequent intelligent use. They are a symbolic representation of something deeper, providing you with unique insights that impart greater definition and clarity of self. Consequently, you move closer and closer to realising your true birth potential as WNLDs bring your chosen Life Path *alive*.

You will find that the same basic methods for SDLDs calculation, construction and interpretation are required for WNLD's. Because only whole numbers (whether compound or single) are worked with, they sometimes exclude the need for number-pairing. Naturally, this depends upon the composition of the numbers in the birthdate. Exceptions arise when WNLDs' numbers are a mixture of single digits and whole numbers necessitating combining single digit, number-pairing and whole number techniques in the one LD. Others are when certain birthdate's numbers are so low that they can only produce single digit LDs.

Four WNLDs of Bill Gates the "Microsoft" magnate, Hugh Hefner of "Playboy" fame, Oprah Winfrey popular TV hostess and St Joan of Arc, France's saviour, teach you the WNLD's techniques. They also illustrate the complementary and contrasting aspects that exist between SDLDs and their WNLDs by displaying them side by side.

Each case study produces an extremely ordinary looking SDLD that contains few variations due to several repetitive numbers. Not one of these SDLDs addresses the high level of achievement that each individual chosen for study attained because their extremely limited number range, coupled with the use of traditional methods, masks each LD's potential as well as curtailing its interpretive capacity. Traditional methods, in such cases, leave much to chance, placing the numerologist in a predicament as so few variables cause prognostications to lean heavily towards over-generalisation. However, number-pairing, the Tarot and WN methods end this by uncovering hidden potential and guidelines that traditional methods obscure.

There is nothing difficult about constructing WNLDs. You simply place whole numbers exactly as they are found in a birthdate and as they appear in the life goals and challenge positions. *Never reduce* any addition or subtraction totals if they yield compound numbers. Sometimes SDs appear in the goal sector. More frequently however, SDs and zeros appear in the challenges. Amazingly though, you will often see the zero LCs in the SDLD *disappear* in the WNLD. The next chapter is entirely devoted to this phenomenon.

One of the most exciting things about WNLDs is that new numbers may appear in them that convey further insights and dimensions about you or about whoever is being studied. More often than not, these numbers can turn out to be absolute gems because of the insights they reveal. Whether new or not, what you are able to glean from your whole numbers' positions and guidelines are precious, especially when you know that you are dealing with your authentic numbers.

A particular study comes to mind that elucidates these points. A WNLD revealed a salient feature that distinguished the major difference occurring in one individual when compared with another who had matching inclinations, a different birthdate but an *identical* SDLD.

The two people being studied were PAUL FOSTER CASE (3OCT1884) and ALEISTER CROWLEY (12OCT1875). Only when their WNLDs were calculated did the differences between the two master magicians become clear. I was fascinated by the fact that three of Aleister's WN goals were master numbers with his potent third goal being 55 and that Paul had no master numbers in his WNLD at all. 55 was particularly enlightening for two reasons; one was that it often signifies a radical change to one's life direction and the other explained why Aleister succumbed to evil forces because 55 corresponds to invoking force for good or evil. Aleister gravitated towards black magic as his powers grew whereas Paul steadfastly remained a white magician.

Without the added information that Aleister's WNLD provided, you would be hard pressed to numerologically substantiate the potential for attracting or being attracted to evil from his SDLD's numbers. Both Paul and Aleister's LDs provide a truly outstanding example of what WNLDs can reveal when you have what became two diametrically opposed individuals presenting identical SDLDs. This is a major illustration of what makes WNLDs so useful. It would be well worth your while to calculate and study Paul and Aleisters' LDs as they present a most interesting example on which to practise.

Another feature that often occurs in WNLDs is that totally different challenge numbers come to light. When they do, they either remain true to their SD number family or produce a challenge that belongs to *a completely different number family*. If the latter occurs, you will discover that you essentially have the SDLD's challenges and their rulers representing one thing and the WNLD's challenges and their rulers, representing something else. Check to see if this type of contradiction has occurred between the SD and WN challenge families. Observe that goals *never* alter number families; this phenomenon provides you with a handy way of proving your calculations.

This checking process is very important because it means that you might get different numerical fields emerging due to WNs being preserved. WN challenges that change number families have strong implications. The main one being that new traits and possibilities can be accounted for that would normally be numerically inexplicable. Another is the flow-on effect that alters WNLCR and WNLDR number families. When variances between LDs' challenges and extensions occur, carefully consider how they might impact upon you or the subject. The simplest solution is to perceive them as additional traits and then find how well this works.

WNLDs present you with much larger numbers which may necessitate the use of a calculator. Do not be daunted by their appearance as I have uncovered an easy way of decoding numbers that go beyond one hundred which you are soon to discover.

Because this is a new area for study, a more formal analysis is applied to the first case study which lays the foundations for interpreting all WNLDs. The other three are interpreted using various slants with the underlying aim being to demonstrate different ways of interpreting each in the hope that they may assist in developing your own methods.

Chapter 9 – The Whole Number Life Diamond (WNLD)

HANDY TIPS

DO THIS FOR EACH CASE STUDY THAT FOLLOWS

As the work advances, becomes more complicated and moves to higher levels of expertise, copy each case study onto separate pieces of paper. Use them to study the instructions and references to each to save flipping back over and over again to check, understand and verify the special features being brought to your attention.

HOW TO CALCULATE WNLDs

Bill Gates' LDs will be used to introduce the basic steps that systematically teach you how to calculate, construct and interpret WNLDs. Starting points to this approach are briefly summarised as a handy checklist below. It provides a suggested outline to follow that can be used to combine all methods introduced so far in order for you to begin to appreciate the best that each LD has to offer.

1. First, construct a fully completed SDLD.
2. Second, apply number-pairing techniques and Tarot Keys to it.
3. Third, fully construct a WNLD with its respective components:
   a) Set up the baseline with *unaltered* month, day and year numbers
   b) Add the baseline to get the *whole number* LPN family
   c) Create *whole number* LGs by addition
   d) Create *whole number* LCs by subtraction
   e) Create *whole number* LGRs, LCRs and LDRs by addition
   f) Do not forget to reverse whole numbers when summarising
   g) When delineating, refer to the appendices and personal resources
   h) Create a Tarot Key WNLD (see front cover)
   i) Use Tarot Keys for numbers greater than 78 by either reversing the number and/or reducing it to the next successive lower digit e.g. 86 = 68, the Page of Pentacles when reversed or 14, Temperance; 41 the Ace of Cups and finally 5, The Hierophant with 50, the 10 of Cups.
   j) Consult *Appendix 1* for all numbers from 0 to 99
   k) Apply number-pairing techniques to ruling numbers exceeding 100.

The Life Diamond

CASE STUDY: BILL GATES
BILL GATES: 28-10-1955 = 58/13/4   (Bill's *whole* year number from 1+9+5+5 = **20**)

	3	SDLGRs = 13/4			30		WNLGRs = 202/4	
	5				86			
2	3				38	48		
1	1	2	= SDLPN:4	10	28	20	= WNLPNs: 58/13/4	
0	1				**18**	8		
1					10			
1		SDLCR= 3			10		WNLCRs= 46/10/1	

SDLDRs = 20/11/2   WNLDRs = 306/225/9
TRADITIONAL METHOD – (SDLD)   **WHOLE NUMBER METHOD – (WNLD)**

DO THIS FOR ALL WNLDs:
- ✧ Copy out Bill's LDs and double-check your calculations before moving on.
- ✧ Make sure that the LPNs, LGs and LGRs in particular, remain true to their number families that appear in their companion SDLD – if they do not, then an error has occurred.
- ✧ Challenges often change number families but not always. If they change, then the WN challenge and WNLD rulers produce a different number family. If they remain true to their SD number families, then the WNLDRs remain true to theirs. Looking at Bill's WNLD you can see that his WNLPNs and WNLGRs stay true to their SD "four" number families but his WNLCs, WNLCRs and WNLDRs do not due to the major changes occurring in his WN challenge area, namely WNLC18 and WNLC8.
- ✧ Write the Tarot Keys' names beneath their numbers.
- ✧ Construct a pictorial image of his WNLD.
- ✧ Stop.
- ✧ Survey what you have before you comparing both LDs.
- ✧ Check for any new numbers and outstanding features – highlight them.
- ✧ Absorb. Reflect. Listen to your intuition.
- ✧ Go.

In their own unique ways, each LD will reveal precise aspects and dimensions about the person being studied. This is what you are looking for – things that jump out at you – so immediately scan each LD for anything significant that stands out from the other.

Absorb these outstanding features before you begin to attempt to analyse them. Make jottings about them or mark where they occur using highlighters or colours. Put together an intensification list (similar to the one on the back of your worksheet). Keep any peculiarities in mind as you begin to unravel the guidelines. Build on that intuitive feel for what you sense each LD is portraying, first as separate entities, then as a combination. Get out corresponding Tarot Keys to boost your mental picture and cement impressions. Make paper Keys for those that are multiple or duplicated. Place reduced Tarot Keys on their "parent" keys. See them as *additional layers* of the personality and life.

Now find where one LD bears the other out by looking for repetitive and/or supportive themes. They often verify the intuitive impressions that you are sensing and acknowledging. Doing this quick overview helps you to test your theories when your analysis yields corroboration or contradiction of your first, intuitive perceptions. Do not forget to include all LD extensions in your initial survey. They should reinforce their LG/Cs and LPNs, either by providing you with entirely new pieces of information that are relevant to what you are able to sense or by repetition which intensifies and reinforces what you are beginning to accept as high probabilities. Double-check your calculations while you do this. Then take special note of the numbers and Keys that replace any zeros. Having done this preliminary work, you are ready to begin your interpretive analysis.

(I seldom add WN magickal facets due to their large numbers unless for special reasons. This is a choice you make according to what you are seeking. If you need to work with them, use number-pairing techniques on the large numbers to extrapolate from them what you need to know. Instructions on how to do this are given in Point 3, of Bill's WNLD: sub-step e) below).

Bill's LDs present an excellent example of stark differences that appear between them. When you cast your eyes over his SDLD, you should find it quite extraordinary. This is because Bill's SDLD not only boasts five 1s but basically, no new numbers are introduced via its extensions. That is most unusual. You are virtually given no extra hints about his potential for genius and high levels of greatness. By contrast, the whole or true number LD is awesome in comparison with so many 8s and 10s appearing in it. The 8s and 10s literally emanate leadership, power, stamina, wealth and solidarity. Other points to note are the first appearance of numbers exceeding 100 in his WNLD's extensions, cycle rulers, inner square and Star. Having taken in a cursory view of each LD, formulating hypotheses as you go, you are now ready to begin a much closer analysis of each in which to verify your intuitive impressions. We shall now begin with a brief outline of Bill's traditional SDLD.

1. BILL'S SDLD

Having advanced to this point, an in-depth study of Bill's traditional SDLD should not be required as you are capable of doing this yourself. When you ponder its numbers, you will notice that they do not reveal the huge potential that he innately possesses. Their limited range makes it difficult to predict his amazing success story. However take from its SDs what you can as they do provide salient information.

2. NUMBER- PAIRING Bill's SDs

Normally number-pairing techniques break open SDLDs into a veritable cascade of highly prized information. But in Bill's case, his SDLD is so repetitive that the compound numbers produced from number-pairing are severely limited. Even so, they provide information that is extremely relevant to him and his life. The repetitive nature of the single digits in his LG/Cs creates no less than five 11s with another nestled in his family of SDLDRs. This gives rise to a very interesting phenomenon, making *six* 11s in all. It has to mean something particularly significant and very special about Bill with so much emphasis on the one number.

Other number-pairs that help to detail Bill's story follow. Bill has three energetic knights and two powerful kings in the goal area of his SDLD. Two 53s, equate to the Knight of Swords (one crowning his spiritual axis) and 25 equates to the Knight of Wands. These knights are about travel, are highly focussed, "on a mission", have abundant energy, incisiveness and an ability to pioneer new fields of science and technology (especially when combined with 4s). Therefore, with little variation in his numbers these Keys focus upon what can turn out to be a passionate force to prompt change (especially when you include SDLG5 and three paired 13s). 53's reversal, 35 equates to the 9 of Wands. Some of its relevant keywords are strength, courage, productive schemes, recognition and money *and* that there is always something else to accomplish no matter what has already been achieved. This suggests that Bill will always have more to achieve.

Kings represent being in a position of authority. His two kings are 23, the King of Wands (tripled) and 51, the King of Swords (doubled) – neither of these kings suffers fools gladly. They are very inspirational, incisive kings who have powerful leadership qualities, a relentless driving force and creative, inventive minds. The King of Wands has the disposition to be a staunch family man with a penchant for looking after the underdog, the sick and the needy which are evident in his enterprising, philanthropic tendencies. Bill has demonstrated these virtues time and time again not only by encouraging his employees to own shares in his companies and become very rich themselves but also by the enormously generous donations that he gifts to medical research and other worthy charitable organisations. Triple 32s from the 23s provide strong indications of success.

Five 21s from the horizontal axis and the inner square all link to The World. They indicate a willingness to try new ideas, bring things to completion and keep raising oneself to higher and higher levels of improved character and competence. 21 also facilitates scientific pursuits that can eventually lead after much struggle (four 31s) to accomplishment on a large scale. As 21 is The World, Bill could literally have the world at his feet with such a strong emphasis on 21 or, has he brought the world to him! Has any man before him touched the lives of so many throughout the world via his productiveness? (Oprah also has dominant 21s which she has used in a different, yet similar fashion.) The 21s reverse to make 12s, which endow Bill with the ability to view or approach things differently or have a knack for unusual creative expression and/or communication. Esoterically, 12, The Hanged Man, has very spiritual qualities which Bill may materialise.

Bill's three 13s and one in his LGR13 will test his ability to dismantle, reorganise and reconstruct whatever has become redundant to allow for constant revision and improvement as 13 is the Death Key (it more often operates in these ways rather than focusing on the word "death" and living in constant fear of a death occurring either to you or someone close. It is more of a "finishing off, clearing out and let's move on" kind of thing). 13 is often a *"transition"* Tarot Key or number which works extremely well with 20 (renewal and rebirth aspects) and 21 (ending phases and changing levels). Mind you, for some, the actual dismantling and rebuilding process can be painful as most transitions tend to be.

13's root digit, 4 reinforces Bill's LPN4, which is known as the number of applied science and pure mathematics, finances and health – areas of great interest to him. Fundamentally, 4 is about being organised, practical, efficient and responsible, productive and accomplished. It links to the Emperor Tarot Key which is a powerful card representing father figures or influential individuals. They often display leadership qualities and high ethics with the innate ability of basing all of their judgements on sound reasoning and logic. These inherent qualities denote that Bill's 4s are a great asset to him.

Now we can understand the presence of a SDLDR20 to support Bill's other two 20s (inner square and year number). This emphasis helps him to withstand the enormous pressure and onerous responsibilities placed on him due to the vast empire that he has created and developed. An intensified 20 endows Bill with the ability to withstand constant pressure and stress which would be required to handle such a large corporation as his. Presently, Bill is shifting his emphasis to philanthropic works. Does this major shift from a corporate, material focus to an altruistic focus expose the spiritual potential latent in 12, 20 and 21?

3. BILL'S WNLD

Bill's grand WNLD which can be seen to be displaying its mighty whole numbers seems to make his SDLD, to its left, pale into insignificance! Constructing both LDs side-by-side helps to demonstrate the stark differences between the two. Mentally acquaint yourself with their similarities and differences, strengths and weaknesses. After due consideration, begin your analysis. Especially note that the SD zero challenge, SDLC0 has now become a WNLC18, revealing Bill's *true* challenge via this method which bestows upon him reorganisation capabilities which is a wonderful trait for him to have. The appearance of these numbers provide definite guidelines to follow.

This is one of the most exciting facets about using this approach, as numbers more often than not take up the traditionally held zero positions. When they do, having a number replacing a zero significantly helps to define the actual Life Path, as there is really not a lot that you can get from a zero – no tangible direction in many ways because it offers endless possibilities! Getting a number in their place is a revelation in itself. It is much easier to work under the direction of a number than play guessing games with zeros which know no bounds. The focus of the following chapter is on "zero replacement" in WNLDs because this interchange and exchange of energies between LDs is so fascinating, it requires its own chapter.

a) HOW TO CALCULATE WHOLE NUMBER LCs (WNLCs)

To break from the usual format, Bill's WNLCs will be studied first, as this is where dramatic changes are more likely to occur. Place the birth date numbers, 10, 28 and 20 exactly as they are in their predetermined positions on the baseline still using *subtraction* to obtain WNLCs. *Do not reduce the totals if a compound number is the result!* The four WNLCs you get in order of appearance by using this method are 18, 8, 10 and 10. Their appearance demonstrates that radical changes have occurred in *all* of his WNLC positions which is not uncommon with this method.

Challenge number families often change like this, so do not anticipate that their numbers will continue to stay within their particular number family's range. In most instances, be prepared for an entirely new number that belongs to a different number family to emerge. As a direct result of WNLC family changes, WNLDR families also change to another number family, thereby bringing new numbers to this position. This happens in Bill's WNLD – we see an entirely new WNLDR range of numbers appear because his WNLCs have changed number families.

WNLC18: The appearance of different number families in the WNLD actually adds quite significantly to personality traits, life situations and directions which explain obvious characteristics that cannot be accounted for in the SDLD. In Bill's WNLCs, you get this happening. His 0 is replaced by 18 and his second WNLC becomes an 8! These two numbers belong to different number families from those in his SDLD therefore; they *define different aspects of his nature and potential*. I regard the WNLCs as being Bill's true challenges and the SDs as being a substitute for them. Knowing Bill's true challenges paves the way for greater accuracy when delineating his life directions.

For Bill, his first "new" WNLC18 links to The Moon in the Tarot. It indicates a penchant for reorganisation, a vivid imagination, scientific writing (in this case, the computer field) and acute mental and intuitive faculties. From this you can see that WNLC18 tells you that his SDLC0 is concealing vital information which helps you to define *specifically exclusive* characteristics and pathways that naturally reach more accurate findings. Look up your favourite numerology and Tarot books and refer to the appendixes at the end of this book to get a feel for what an 18 and its reversal 81 offers in Bill's case. Take out 18's Key and reflect on its pictorial image and what it represents. Add to this what you think Bill brought into this life through 18 and 81, as numbers, and what their potential lessons might be. Are they signifying a scientific background, emotional depths, compassion and empathy developed in past lives? Will his 18 denote tragedy at some juncture or a rise in status as an 81 in this life?

WNLC'S ROOT 9: WNLC18 reduces to WNLC9. 9 supplies you with even more information. It can mean that Bill has learnt a lot in past lives, bringing over entrepreneurial skills, knowledge and wisdom. It also suggests tying off loose ends and/or completing past life works. Apart from its traditional delineations as a number, 9 equates to The Hermit in the Tarot. Negatively, it could translate as aloofness, being a "know all" and feeling more superior to others. Or, Bill's Path may be to become that of a protector and a wayshower for those less wise or fortunate than himself. The latter seems to be the case.

WNLC8: The second SDLC1 is replaced by WNLC8. Both LCs are powerful numbers, but the WNLC8 points more towards Bill's money-making, management skills and business acumen rather than with the emphasis focusing upon personal development as the 1 would normally do. 8 personifies the potential for honing innate or brought over skills until they reach higher levels of excellence, become specialised, then completely mastered (working well with his 21s and 9 from 18/81, above). It hints at certain degrees of mastery having been attained in related fields in past lives. 8 is common in charts of people who require higher energy levels for their chosen path, so Bill has this gift at his disposal which will bolster his 20s. 8 equates to the Strength Key; another great asset! Negatively, Bill could be influenced by his power and wealth and focus purely on materialism. Positively, he may gravitate towards spiritual pursuits, defend the helpless (add his Knights here), maintain his integrity (Kings and Queens) and possibly master a past life aspect (8).

WNLC10s: Two powerful WNLC10s replace the SDLC1s, subsequently remaining in the same number family. This is where ruling cycle numbers come to the fore when you have the same numbers appearing in the goal or challenge positions. In Bill's case, his third and fourth cycle rulers give clearer indications as to how these repetitive numbers work. Cycle three is ruled by 208 and cycle four is ruled by 70 – two totally different numbers. (See (e) below for ways to use 208). Their explicit qualities and likelihoods give you specific guidelines about what is ruling these two 10s. These rulers tell us that Bill is under the influence of markedly different energy fields for these two cycles. The same thing happened to Julie for her third and fourth cycles giving her the opportunity to develop different aspects of herself and to enjoy different life experiences – the same can be applied to Bill.

Getting back to Bill's 10s, they have lifted his 1s to a higher octave, indicating cycles of culmination mixed with beginnings. Similar to his 9, they indicate finishing off past life works so that the way is made clear for new works to begin. The 10s also step up the vibrational rate, giving the potential of taking one's leadership, creative and inventive capabilities to more superior levels (linking to his WNLC8 and 21s). They imply making or losing a fortune as they equate to The Wheel of Fortune Key in the Tarot. We know that Bill has made it to become a multibillionaire with good fortune favouring him (accumulation of gains). He was engaged in a very expensive lawsuit that ran into millions so bad fortune has also taken its turn at manifesting losses. But it is more fascinating to see the Wheel operating as "wealth" being used to benefit those in "poverty", which to me stems from using the 14 from Bill's WNLG86 to *blend opposites to produce something new* from them (his 1s, 10s, 13s, 20s and 21s!).

Having dealt briefly with the WNLCs, we shall now turn our attention to Bill's true WNLGs. Unlike the WNLCs, the new numbers appearing in the WNLGs positions **always retain their single digit number family**. This means that they consistently reduce to the same root digit as their SDLGs – you will not find maverick numbers here. Because root numbers never alter, it presents a good way to check your calculations.

The Life Diamond

b) HOW TO CALCULATE WHOLE NUMBER LGs (WNLGs)

From adding the baseline's three numbers, 10, 28 and 20, in the traditional ways, Bill's four *authentic* WNLGs of 38, 48, 86 and 30 emerge. They expose the real nature of Bill's SDLGs by making known what kind of a 2, 3, 5 and 3 each one represents. As you can see from the additions of the whole numbers, his two SDLG3s are derived from a *different* parent number. To be aware of this is extremely important because, when you notice that two SDLGs are the same number, the next thing that you need to know is: do they also share the same *parent* numbers? If they do, then this would intensify that particular number's qualities, gifts, tests and outcomes. They may be expected to bring about repetitious or paralleling themes during each activation. If they do not, then anticipate the addition of entirely new themes coming in at the time of activation. Different parent numbers facilitate greater diversity and possibilities. As in this instance, the parent numbers actually distinguish Bill's two SDLG3s as being different from each other. Now you can confidently predict that not only different life experiences will definitely occur when each of their cycles become active but also that *different character traits, skills and directions will also develop under them*. This phenomenon is invaluable in assisting you to become more confident in your work and more accurate in your prognoses.

Bill's first WNLG38: The important point to stress is that there are many 2s in the 2 family, but for Bill, his happens to be a WN38, 2 making it *unique to him*. This is the purpose behind this approach – to uncover the **authentic numbers that are especial to each person** as well as **uncovering what that particular number represents for them**. In Bill's case, 38 offers its singular gifts, opportunities and lessons that can only belong to it/him. This is another most important point because you need to remember that this is how to treat each number wherever it appears. View it and its qualities as always being unique to that person.

Like 38, many compound numbers will appear in the WNLGs that can be further reduced, thereby creating yet another compound number. Use whatever comes forward to enrich and broaden your scope of analysis. That is what makes working with the WNs so exciting – they expose their own particular set of numbers within a number family for you to utilise. What you do is to treat Bill's WNLG firstly as a 38, then as an 11 and finally as a 2. (Place Justice and The High Priestess and its reverse, Judgement, on top of or adjacent to the Queen of Cups Key in your pictorial WNLD. Do this for all numbers that can be reduced. This practice enables you to uncover the different dimensions and possibilities within each number.) A brief analysis follows.

38 is a queen, Cups number. It will heighten Bill's intuitive, psychic, imaginative and emotive faculties which are reciprocated in his 11 and 2/20. 11, 2 and 20 have already received much coverage. Because 38 is the Queen of Cups, it gives Bill the potential to become top in his chosen field (as a Queen has already risen to the top) and fraternise with people of high rank or authority. Publishing and the ability to commercialise one's creative talents are related to this Queen which we have seen an abundance of under the title of "Microsoft" (3 represents creative, communicative abilities and 8 the corporate

world - the birth (3) of an enterprise (8)!). Bill would have a very keen business sense and a "nose" for what people want. This Queen can also represent the kinds of women Bill attracts or is attracted to. The latter infers that he is not always the initiator of his life events. This is a fundamental point that needs mentioning when considering a number or Key's possibilities.

Bill's second WNLG48: What does WNLG48 bring to Bill's life? It links to the 8 of Cups which shows a figure in a red cape turning his/her back on what is known and accomplished to take a new path that holds greater promise. Yet taking this action may well be tinged with certain regrets and emotional pain (remember the 48 in the Dalai Lama's LD?). It can also represent the ability to show much courage and determination, especially if a radical, emotionally charged situation arises that requires an about face or assertive action. 48 decrees that radical change and sacrifices are required in order to have what you want, do what you must do or feel forced to do. 48 often demands that something has to be abandoned or sacrificed in the letting-go process which is often linked to nostalgia or tinges of pain if something unpleasant or close to the heart needs to be abandoned. The negative side to this would be to ignore the need to change direction or focus and sacrifice the greater for the lesser or, it might be that you are caught up in a situation that you feel you must remain in for whatever reason. The latter's "sacrifice" aspect stems from 48's 12. (Bill recently announced that he is gradually handing over the reins of his company in order to devote his time to charity organisations.)

48 is similar to Bill's SDLGR13. It signifies the need to eliminate the outworn, to open the way for a new stimulus, project, career, house or direction. But, 48 is different. It tends to signify being put in a position in which something is relinquished in order to gain something of greater value. Sometimes there is a kind of "reckless abandonment" associated with it. To quote several instances from *Yearly* Diamonds, a female client at 38 sold up everything to move interstate so that she could become a mature-age student and study anthropology – something that she had always yearned to do. She instigated this under her 48, which was the YDRN in her Yearly Diamond that year. A female friend with 48 in her family of YDRNs sold her home and bought a caravan to finance her books while she travelled the eastern seaboard of Australia to promote them. Yet another sold her home and gave up her livelihood to move to a warmer climate and begin again. Her 48 was also her YDRN. A 24 year-old young man resigned to travel overseas under a 48. Pope John Paul II died leaving the earthly realm behind when his YD contained multiple 48s. Also under a 48, a father, for the sake of peace, let go monies lent to his daughter and a woman gave up fighting for monies that were rightfully hers, due to poor health. Short-term sacrifices for long-term gains are often 48's motivating force.

Bill's five 21s from his SDLD, plus his 48 and 13 help him to know or sense when something ceases to be useful and it is time to let go and turn towards the call of something higher or new which holds more promise; its rewards may be more intrinsic than materialistic. One can see that happening as he prepares to increase his focus upon humanitarian work. WNLG48 reduces to 12, The Hanged Man, which operates like a different version of the 48 and 13. It offers a further dimension to them, bringing forth parallels that link these numbers when viewed from a certain angle. They all require courage, strength, sacrifice and determination in the face of change and they also have a very strong spiritual component to them. (48 and 12 seem to produce a sterner, more reserved 3 as its root number.)

Bill's third WNLG86: Powerful 86 occupies the third WNLG – a number that can be used for great good or evil or self-aggrandisement. It puts an entirely different complexion on the SDLG5, which pales into insignificance by comparison. 86 is making its statement, thereby providing specific directions, overtones and undertones to count on when it becomes active. I have not found 86 common to WNLDs. However, it can be found in the SDLDs of Joan of Arc, Gandhi, Tony Blair, Carl Jung, Walt Disney, Jackie Kennedy, Charles Chaplin, Christopher Reeve and Barry Humphries and Hitler when number-pairing.

How interesting to compare the stark opposites of this number's expression against its subjects! Here we have Gandhi and Hitler expressing 86 at its best and worst – Gandhi, through unconditional love, care and service to the greater good and upliftment and liberation of his race and Hitler with megalomania, hatred, abject cruelty and being hell-bent on the destruction, incarceration and annihilation of a race. Then you have Barry Humphries using his two 86s as a satiric comedian. Judging by these great personalities, 86 is not a number to be treated lightly! Bill seems to be turning in a similar direction to Gandhi in that he wishes to invest his energy and wealth into helping to overcome impoverished conditions in Africa and India.

John Nash (the mathematics genius depicted in the movie *A Brilliant Mind*) has eight 86s in his Numeroscope. As a further aside, when 86/68 came up in their Yearly Diamonds, Mary Shelley eloped, Sarah Ferguson married Prince Andrew, Christopher Reeve broke his neck and was consequently severely paralysed and O. J. Simpson was charged with the murder of his ex wife and her lover. From these examples, it can be deduced that 86 is indeed a very powerful number signifying greatness, perversity and life-altering events.

Returning to Bill, we are looking at a combination of numbers that give him exceptional possibilities and faculties – his 86 in particular. It can be interpreted as suggesting hard won mastery (8) of a particular thing and striving for perfection (6). In Bill's case, the 8-6, combination points to a powerful enterprise (8) that reaches into the homes of millions (6). He also cares for the welfare of his employees and humanity at large; the latter being a direction that has growing appeal for him. Furthermore, 86 suggests exceptional expertise in the fields of commerce, trade, banking and financial markets. 68, (86 reversed), links to the Knight of Pentacles giving Bill yet another knight in his numbers. This knight carefully weighs and considers before carrying out money-making plans and decisions. He also depicts the ability to painstakingly manifest material things.

86/68 reduces to 14. 14 corresponds to Temperance. Two of Temperance's keywords are "artful synthesis" and "moderation" – both wonderful assets for Bill to have to draw upon. 14 can be substituted for 86 as 86 goes beyond the Tarot but 86 better represents the potential for developing a global enterprise (reinforced by his WNLDR9 family) and supporting health organisations (6) with huge donations of money (8). 14 reducing to 5, The Hierophant endows knowledge, wisdom and power gained from a willingness to explore and experiment. 5 equates to charity and welfare organisations of which Bill is a major sponsor. It is interesting to see how 5 and The Hierophant are becoming so prominent in Bill's life. Is this because of its commanding position on the spiritual axis and being the apex of the red triangle in his Star?

Bill's fourth WNLG30: WNLG30 is holding a commanding position at the apex of the WNLD. As a number, it ranks as one of high achievement after extensive effort. 30 supports an unfolding success theme that is developing with the support of Bill's WNs: 28, 38 and 86 plus the 32s paired from his SDs. You will find 30 in the LDs of Winston Churchill, Adolf Hitler, and Osama Bin Laden, Leonardo da Vinci (WNLCR30), Helena Blavatsky, Annie Besant, Margaret Thatcher, Germaine Greer and Bob Hope. It correlates to the 4 of Wands which holds the promise of bringing one's work or enterprise to a successful conclusion accompanied by a sense of celebration, contentment and joy. Greater accomplishment can be expected from 30 as it is a ten's number which raises its root 3 to a much higher octave.

3 has so many traits that it is difficult to intuit which of them best suits Bill's circumstances and potential. However, herein lies the beauty of the whole number method – 30 not only narrows down the speculative field which encompasses its root 3 but also differentiates the fourth WNLG from the second WNLG, which also spawns a root 3 from its parent 48. 30 specifically points to the culmination of success that choosing the right path (48) reaps. Definite lines of direction stem from this 3's parent number. Having this clear differentiation between a 48/3 and a 30/3 greatly enhances the chance of making accurate delineations. For instance, the 3 from 30 would be uplifting and joyous contrasting with 48's 3 that tends to be a tad austere. 3 equates to the Empress – often called the card of "abundance". Bill's 3 from 30 has manifested as a luxurious family life, the birth of a highly lucrative creative enterprise, publication and recognition, travel, joy and fulfilment, ie, "abundance".

c) HOW TO CALCULATE WHOLE NUMBER LPNs

This method exposes the specific family of WNLPNs that is uniquely tailored to suit Bill's Life Purpose. Obtaining his exclusive set of LPNs cannot be more important in cases like Bill's when only a SDLPN can be obtained from his SD baseline. The WNLD uncovers the other LPNs that his SDLPN4 veils. Its calculation lays bare Bill's series of WNLPNs that belong to *his* "four" family. By adding Bill's WN baseline as it is, you reach the highest LPN that it can produce, i.e. 10+28+20 = LPN58. 58 is then reduced to 13 and further reduced to 4. So 58, 13 and 4 are Bill's true "four" LPN family. Their now *individualised* set of directions is fundamental to Bill giving him firm guidelines to follow.

Bill's highest WNLPN58, the 4 of Swords, distinguishes Bill's true pathway from all other fours, providing inclinations and details that unlock specific aspects of his Destiny. It reveals *his* hidden directions and trends by providing explicit indicators and bearings. For instance, 58 often appears in charts of high achievers – people who set themselves high standards and goals. Their objectives are often hard-won as 58 tends to suggest a specific kind of impediment, illness or restriction of some kind that must be liberated or overcome in the bid to be successful, as with dyslexia in Sir Richard Branson's case. So 58 endows Bill with the innate ability to strive hard for whatever he wishes to accomplish despite his unique types of "setbacks". This often means putting up with some form of encumbrance or confinement until projects or goals reach fruition. These hindrances can be self-imposed; even happily undertaken. (Did you pick up that 58 depicts yet another knight? – a quiet achieving knight?)

Other "58 people" are: Joan of Arc, Leonardo da Vinci (highest LPN85), Mary Shelley, Albert Einstein, Margaret Thatcher, Amelia Earhart, Carl Jung, Walt Disney, Elvis Presley, Richard Branson, Jack Nicholson, Tony Blair and Hugh Hefner. Dedication and perseverance seem to be their common theme.

WNLPN58 further reduces to 13, Death and 31, the Five of Wands and finally, 4, The Emperor. They have received ample explanation.

d) HOW TO CALCULATE WHOLE NUMBER LGRs, LCRs and LDRs

WNLCRs: Add Bill's four WNLCs: 18+8+10+10 = 46/10/1. Here we have a new set of challenge rulers. This is common to WNLDs. His SDLCR3 has changed to a powerful, tens family of WNLCR46/10/1 (46 reverses to 64). It is very interesting how the WNLD maintains the emphasis on the SD "ones" through its three 10's and WNLCRs. The 10s strongly hint at innate strengths but also a struggle to develop a sense of self – Bill may have suffered from an identity crisis at one stage. 46 is what I call a reciprocal number in that one receives kindnesses, gifts and pleasantries and/or gives them. 64 hints at having to remain forever vigilant due to possible betrayals or pressing health issues. (46/64 featured in Gandhi's numbers which also bore out these possibilities.)

WNLGRs: Add Bill's four WNLGs: 38+48+86+30 = WNLGRs202/4. (See (e) below)

WNLDRs: To find Bill's highest WNLDR, add 46+58+202 = 306. To find Bill's next highest WNLDR, add 10+13+202 = 225. To find Bill's lowest WNLDR, add 1+4+4 = 9. This completes Bill's set of WNLDRs which are: 306, 225 and 9. (See (e) below)

e) NUMBER-PAIRING LARGE, WHOLE NUMBER LGRs and LDRs

As WNLDs, WNLGRs and WNLDRs often go into the hundreds; the following methods propose ways to work with them. Given time, they may prove their worth.

WNLGRs: Having obtained WNLGR202, simply break it up into number pairs like this: 202 = 20 and 02. The numbers that you can work with are 20 and 2. Having isolated these numbers, the next thing to do is to run your eyes over each LD, birthdate and other major personal numbers to see if you can find them elsewhere. As it happens, 20 and 2 are present in both LDs and Bill's *year number* which is 19**20**. Therefore, they can be viewed as fortifying Bill's Life Path requirements. Expect to see these numbers strongly and visibly at work in his life and nature due to their intensification. In a case where no other 20s are present in the overall chart, I have found that the individual *is* exhibiting 20 and 2 traits simply because they are "present" in their numbers.

WNLDRs: Bill's WNLDRs produce a family of 9s. This is very exciting because they introduce new number fields and sets of influences into his numbers. These 9s are especially significant from the standpoint that they help to explain the high degree of universal impact that Bill has had on the world. They reinforce his dynamic drive for attainment and his global effect on humanity. Bill's WNLC18, which also reduces to a 9, links to and reinforces this number family adding publicity (18) and public acclaim (81) to it.

The highest WNLDR is 306. Split 306 into 30 and 06. You will find that 30 reinforces the fourth WNLG, thereby emphasising the probability of fulfilment, great achievement and success in a chosen field. 6 brings in a new number, however. It reinforces things such as; family, work and health codes, responsibilities, obligations and duties, trading and subordinates. 6 can also be linked to *extended families* i.e. Bill's entrepreneurial and humanitarian works. (Also reverse 30 to make 3 and reverse 06 to make 60. Add their possibilities to your analysis, like 60 equates to earned success and, I think, the masses!)

The next highest number, WNLDR225, is found from the addition of WNLGR202, WNLPN13 and WNLCR10. I use this way of obtaining the next highest ruler when uneven sets of numbers hold ruler positions. WNLDR225 brings its unique attributes to add to Bill's story, making it quite acceptable. It works well for him, reiterating his gifts for running a large enterprise and risk-taking (22) and especially, highlighting his crusading (25) and incisive qualities (52). Use your own discretion when calculating WNLDRs when you are faced with uneven sets of rulers. Always find what consistently works best.

Finally, this powerful family of 9s is a really important inclusion because it helps to explain Bill's illustrious achievements. Through an exalted 9, he has the aptitude to act as an instrument for Higher Powers.

This brings Bill's case study to an end. A less formal approach is applied to the following case studies assuming that you have mastered the 1, 2, and 3 format provided above. It has laid the foundations for more advanced techniques such as learning how to synthesise the diverse elements contained within SDLDs and their companion WNLDs. The process of employing different interpretive skills begins with quite a different entrepreneur; HUGH HEFNER.

The Life Diamond

CASE STUDY: HUGH HEFNER
HUGH HEFNER: 9-4-1926 = 31/4

```
                4         SDLGR = 21/3              22        WNLGR = 102/3
                4                                   40
            4       9                           13      27
        4       9       9   = SDLPN: 22/4    4      9       18   = WNLPN: 31/4
            5       0                            5       9
                5                                    4
                5         SDLCR = 15/6              14        WNLCR = 32/5

    SDLDR = 58/13/4                          WNLDRs = 165/12/3
  TRADITIONAL METHOD – (SDLD)            WHOLE NUMBER METHOD – (WNLD)
```

As you can see, Hugh's SDLD is comprised of only four different numbers having an extremely limited number range which greatly lends itself to number-pairing methods, cycle rulers, LD extensions and constructing a WNLD. Because his numbers are mostly sequentially repetitive, this phenomenon makes them even more restrictive than normal. Hugh's SDLD presents us with an outstanding example of how traditional methods are severely limiting. They can only deliver repetitive, stereotyped delineations in cases like this, presenting a dilemma for numerologists.

WNs Expose Precise Directions: Fortunately, the WN method divulges exactly what kind of a 4, 5, 9 and 0 Hugh's SDs truly represent, thereby providing specific guidelines as well as a much greater degree of latitude within which to delineate his SDLD's restrictive number range. Hugh's WNLD clearly shows that each SDLG4 is spawned from a different parent number (13, 40 and 22) thereby dispensing with broad, repetitive, non-specific interpretations. With the expanded knowledge that can be gained from the WN approach, not only are Hugh's possibilities broadened but specific qualities, character traits, directions and trends can be homed in on. This enables Hugh's unique traits to be exposed and extrapolated from each SD due to knowing the separate influences that each of its distinctive parent number represents. This is the main advantage of the WN method. It brings to light hidden, authentic, totally individualised aspects of the Life Path due to using whole numbers.

Inner Squares: Interestingly, neither Hugh's SD nor WN squares introduce new numbers as they can be found in either LD – especially the WNLD.

Stars of David: The same can be said for his Stars; they intensify existing numbers.

Cosmic Diamonds: Except for the appearance of WNs 14 and 18, no other new numbers make their appearance.

Importance of Cycle and Number-line rulers: In such a repetitious SDLD as this, calculate all Hugh's cycle and number-line rulers, to gather together as much data as you can. Work at uncovering anything that will assist you in making sense of a restrictive array of numbers such as inner squares and Stars, etc. Curiously, Hugh's SD cycle rulers are also repetitive with the first cycle ruler being 22, the second 27, the third 27 and the fourth 22. However, their WN cycle rulers shed much more light on the way that these cycles can be experienced as they are all different. Their sequential order of activation is: 31, 63, 98 and 58. Now we have excellent additional information with which to work. 31 shows his struggle to become a success; 63 the involvement of so many women in his life; 98 can augur public acclaim or disgrace and 58 points to eventual success from overcoming obstacles.

SD Number-Line Rulers: 22, 23, 27 and 13 = 85/13/4. Note that the number-line ruler intensifies Hugh's SDLDR58 and WN cosmic diamond ruler, except that it has reversed to 85. 85's keywords that can be applied to Hugh are the ability to overcome shortcomings and master strengths to achieve greatness; changes in lifestyle due to changes in financial situation; investing in a pioneering venture; business expansion and finally, trade and commercial practices and impulse spending. These 85 aspects actually summarize what his cycle and number-line rulers embody. See how 22, 27, 13 (31's reverse) and 85 (58's reverse) duplicate his cycle rulers. When combined, they endow him with enormous, inspirational (27s), imaginative, creative (13s) potential that can be channelled into a large enterprise (22s) which are analogous in many ways to what 85 typifies.

Themes of entrepreneurial success can be supported further in the following. As in Bill Gates' WNLD, Hugh's SDLDR58 suggests it was the overcoming of personal difficulties and obstacles that brought him wealth, fame and success (fanned by several 4s and 9s) from his "Playboy" magazines (38, publishing, elicited from the reversal of 83 as the first two letters of his name: "HU" (see Chapter 6: Book 3) and SDLPN22 = large enterprise). Often a 9 with 4s depicts unemployment and a reduced income but, in Hugh's case, he amassed a fortune and became famous for his eccentricities in the sex industry (triple 9s – sexual love and 5s, SDLCR15 and especially, WNLDR12, all combine to indicate a penchant for eccentric sexual tastes). As with Bill Gates' SDLD, Hugh's SDLD also beautifully typifies the force, focus and peculiar bent that several repetitious numbers can produce. Note the strength and solidarity in his SDLGs and the added strength that becomes apparent in the changes to them in the WNLD.

WNLGs: Hugh's WNLG's 13, 27, 40 and 22, suggest great power as they are all strong numbers. His top WNLG22, which duplicates his SDLPN22, strengthens his ability to build and oversee a large enterprise whose products can have widespread appeal, reach the masses and attract public attention. This happens when you combine his triple 9s and WNLCR32 with them. Unlike his SDLD the WNLD shows you at a glance just exactly what Hugh had at his disposal. The WNLPN31 supports its WNLGs of 13, 27, 40 and 22 and first WN cycle ruler 31, signifying that a struggle will be necessary to achieve personal dreams and goals and that a "never give up" attitude will help to sustain and fortify Hugh's aims. These traits are also evident in his SD inner square's 40, 50 and 90, SDLDR58 and number-line ruler 85.

Intensification by Multiple Numbers: The three 9s and several 4s in the SDLD, driven by freedom-loving triple SDLC5s suggest straying from traditional, totalitarian values. They signify that he, as a person, may be completely self-absorbed. This is also borne out in his final WNLC14 and four paired 49s in his SDLD and three in his WNLD which all combine to indicate a high degree of self-indulgence and insatiable appetites – temperance (14) being the antidote! The WNLCR32 suggests a high accent on success but it would tend to be more self-serving, tinged with unusual, behaviour – especially with so many SDLC5s, SDLCR15, paired 49s and WNLC14 plus a WNLDR12!

WNLG27 supported by other 27s as two cycle and one number-line ruler, suggests Hugh's enterprising capabilities are brimming with innovative ideas. His three SDLC5s pair to make two 55s – all are numbers in Tarot parlance that can be used for good and/or evil which indicates how his work is perceived – some see it as being good and others as evil. The two 50s, the 10 of Cups, also paired from these fives, signify how some view his magazines and life-style as being injurious to the moral fibre of the family (a negative 50 can represent the destruction of the family unit). The SDLC0 has become a WNLC9 in the WN method, making the second mini-diamond entirely comprised of a family of 9s. The four SD4s and three SD9s give him extraordinary talent, entrepreneurial skills, intellect and a penchant for luck, making money, possible eccentricity and a love of the dramatic. His third SDLC5 has changed number families to a WNLC4, which specifically points to business acumen and, at the same time, intensifies his SD fours. The final WNLC14 gives Hugh the gift of synthesis, which is an excellent tool for publishing and business organisation. Both WNLC14 and WNLCR32 can achieve success in respected or corrupt ways.

WNs that EXCEED 100: Experiment with Hugh's large numbers appearing in the WNLGR and WNLDR positions. As you have now learned, simply apply the number-pairing method to them. His WNLDR165 can be split up, paired and reversed to read as 16/61 and 65/56. This technique shows promise especially when you have few numbers to delineate in cases such as this.

WNLDR165: Consider what happens when Hugh's WNLDR165 is split to create 16/61 and 65/56. The Tower 16, can be extrapolated from 165, adding a new number to his make up. Taking Hugh's nature and life events into account, it may be interpreted as his heightened reputation and his obsession with sex with the "Tower" representing the phallic symbol that he built his empire upon. Dedication to his goals is evident in 61, the reversal of 16. Hugh's business empire is indicated in 165's 65; 65 equates to the King of Pentacles – a hard working, money-making King and, in Hugh's case, the lucrative empire he built up. Hugh saw himself as the epitome of maleness (repetitive SD4s) in his prime but impotence struck. Then Viagra and staged display (SD9s) were needed to sustain a masquerade in later years. 65, like the 16, adds a new number to Hugh's LDs, thereby introducing further personalised dimensions from which to obtain vital information.

Other traits surface when 65 reverses to 56. This can signify not being able to see or admit to the folly of one's ways, i.e. being blind to one's faults. 56 bestows the gift of intuiting what the public wants which suits Hugh's enterprising nature. 12 derived from the addition of 165 gives Hugh a different slant or focus on life. In his case, it strongly points to preoccupation with sex, stemming from the over emphasis on his LC5s fanned by his multiple 9s, indulgent 3s and paired 49s.

WNLGR102: Root 3s obtained from WNLGR102 and WNLDR165, strengthen Hugh's sexual appetites and those of striving for wealth, fame, luxury and success. 3 also boosts his creative talents in the publishing industry that targets a male audience (his strong 4s) based on sexual (heart 9 – sexual love) entertainment (3s). The 10 in 102 signifies Hugh's rags to riches story.

CASE STUDY: OPRAH WINFREY

OPRAH WINFREY: Oprah Gail Winfrey's rags to riches life story (note her WNLC10 and four paired 10s!) delightfully supports the propositions put forward in the previous case studies. Her LDs are more briefly summarised focussing on their outstanding features. Practise on those not treated.

Again, a freer, approach is used to synthesise the ways that each LD adds more depth and meaning to the other by integrating their complementary and divergent features. The continuing aim is to reveal more advanced techniques as each is learned and mastered to encourage the development of higher and higher levels of interpretive expertise while at the same time achieving a deeper understanding of each LD type's dynamics and the way they work in concert with one another.

OPRAH GAIL WINFREY: 29-1-1954 = 31/4 and 49/13/4

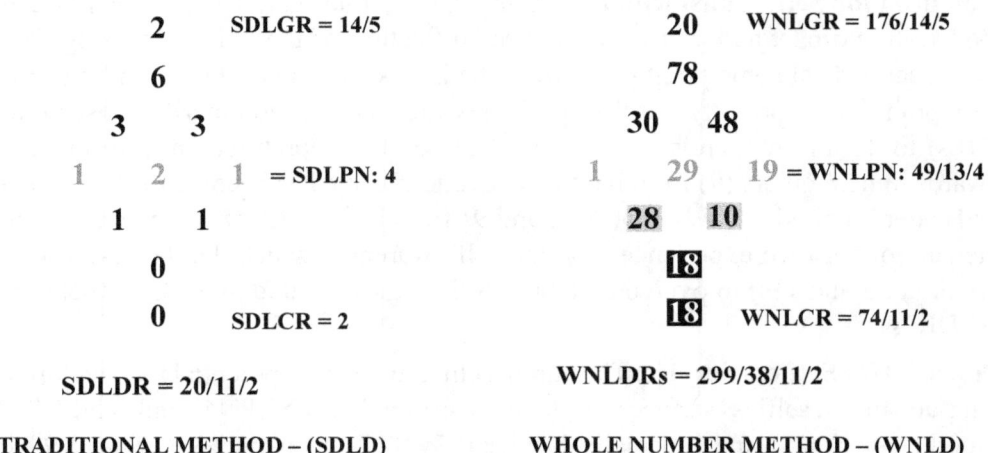

TRADITIONAL METHOD – (SDLD)   WHOLE NUMBER METHOD – (WNLD)

WNLD: The most interesting thing to note about this LD is the amount of new numbers it brings into play. Unlike Hugh's, Oprah's WNLD has many new numbers in it which give her a much wider range of possibilities and abilities. As a result, she may be categorised as being more flexible than and not as rigid as Hugh.

The Power Inherent in the Reversed Numbers: Oprah's numbers are as amazing as she is – especially those that appear in her WNLD backed up by those that can be created from pairing her SDs. Note how Oprah drew on her powerful, "hidden" WNLPN31 (Tarot Key "struggle" from WNLPN13's reversal) to find a way out of her oppressed conditions (two paired 62s). Oprah has seven 31s in total which help to appreciate how palpable the "struggle" aspect is in her life.

Viewing Oprah's two 62's reversals as 26s, we have a truly wonderful example of how the "present" number (62) and its "hidden" number (26) operate. At first, Oprah was unable to speak out against her molesters and persecutors – Key 62, the 8 of Swords. Then she summoned the courage (62's root 8) to find her voice and speak openly against cruelty (8) in whatever form against any human being. This is Oprah expressing her hidden 26 qualities. She has found her voice and uses it to "broadcast" (aspects of 26, the Page of Wands) her tale and share the wisdom (9) she has gained from her psychological damaging (WNLC18s). Combine her 62/26s and 13/31s with her 20s. See how she was endowed with the ability to break free from oppressive conditions (62) to transcend, renew and completely transform herself (20 and 13).

Oprah's WNLPN49 provides another such example. Its reverse, 94 signifies having difficulty in defining and keeping within certain boundaries eg. finding the self-discipline to control self-indulgence problems such as her persistent weight problem. It also signifies difficulties with males.

High Potential for Self-Transformation: Link Oprah's four paired 21s to her 13s, 20s, 31s, WNLG48 and 62s, and you have the personification of the "Phoenix rising from the ashes" occurring at some point in the life. The intensification of these numbers, plus 48, give Oprah the opportunity to self-transform which she has voluntarily chosen (two WNLC18s) to do. From exercising this aspect of her 18s, Oprah has moved forwards and upwards to help others (9) from her "woundedness". She has become the "Wounded Teacher/Healer" (paired 33, WN LDRN38 and 9s from her WNLC18s) – a person who, from the pain of her own experiences and the self-awareness which that brings, teaches others (paired 33 and 11s) to overcome their psychological wounding (18s) inflicted by others (LDR2s).

High Potential for Selfless Service: The numbers that support the potential for developing humanitarianism and selfless service are contained in Oprah's WNLPN49 and WNLCR74 (the "Good Samaritan") and especially her heart WN29 and paired 33. 29 and 99 in her highest WNLDR299 lean toward humanitarianism with 99 escalating this quality to reach grand proportions. To fortify this theme, Oprah's SD inner square's composition nicely supports the "Wounded Teacher/Healer" and selfless service themes. Its 33, 21s and 11s enfold her compassionate SD "heart 2", contributing to her becoming a world (21s) teacher (33, 11s and SDLGR5) through the medium of television WNLDR38! Her

SD square's ruler is 8. 8 signifies her earthly work such as overcoming weaknesses and mastering specific aspects and skills. The WN square's ruler is 116 that splits to create 11 and 16. 11 stands for education. 16 stands for being jolted out of false realities eg, "light bulb moments". This aspect of 16 can be used as a self-correction tool via awarenesses gained from the education aspect of the 11.

Earth and Spiritual Axes: Note how much of Oprah's mundane "Work" can be extrapolated from her SD earth axis. It has unfolded as wanting to share (heart 2) her life experiences with the world and provide an avenue for others to do the same with a view to making the world a better place. This innate need to improve oneself and "make a difference" basically stems from each axis' combined total of *six* paired 21s. She is using her 26s, as the Page of Wands, from her SD spiritual axis to literally share (heart 2, through WNLDR38's TV and magazine medium) her opinions and those of others, along similar veins, to the "World" (Key 21). Most importantly, for her viewing public, Oprah has demonstrated how one *can* successfully extricate oneself from seemingly impossible situations (those difficult numbers) and reinvent oneself (20s, Judgement) to become a better person (21s) and help others do the same (heart 2). In recent shows, spiritual traits emerge at times which are the higher aspect of her 20s and 21s.

The All-Powerful Third WNLG/C Pair: There is a strong "protector" element present in what Oprah has set herself to achieve. It probably stems from her wounding (WNLC18) which is expressed through her all-powerful WNLG78, the 10 of Pentacles. 78 is all-powerful because it represents the summation of her birthdate. Its opposing, equally powerful WNLC18, The Moon, beautifully supports this theme. It represents her keen interest in and use of psychology as a tool for understanding her personal nature as well as that of others – especially in respect to the abuse of women (WNLC18 relates to The Moon – women, and WNLDR38; a prominent female fighting for women's rights; Oprah using her powerful 2s – The High Priestess; as seen by her many fans).

WNLCR74: Although WNLCR74, the 6 of Pentacles, clearly supports the above themes. It also symbolises Oprah's challenge to *not* be greedy or seek the limelight for her role as a benefactor. What I have noticed is that people who set themselves up in this "78 sponsor role" often do not like to draw attention to their good deeds. Oprah basks in the glory that her generosity attracts but maybe a lot more goes on behind the scenes that we do not hear about.

When an Apparent Lack is Not So: Because themes of struggle and strife and the pain of adjustment are so prevalent in Oprah's life, you would expect to find several swords and/or fives dominating her numbers. Not being obvious at first, they can be found. But they need to be strongly positioned to account for such prevailing themes. Two paired 62s on Oprah's spiritual axis are the easiest to find. As the 8 of Swords they account for some of Oprah's constraints. Another is 58, the 4 of Swords which rules her fourth WN life cycle. It also signifies impediments. Yet another powerful sword is located in Justice's Key forming the base of Oprah's inner square and Star. Then *Zain,* the seventh letter in the Hebrew alphabet means a sword. Because Zain is allocated to The Lovers (Key 6), it forms a "sword" association with all of Oprah's 6s. One holds the powerful third, SD

The Life Diamond

goal position and two more rule her first and second life cycles. These swords confirm a strong presence which is otherwise hidden if her LD's are treated superficially. They are wonderful assets for attaining liberation in that they enable Oprah to sever the ties that bind and inhibit her as well as cut away the dross in her life.

Now to finding Oprah's 5s. They rule her third life cycle, her Star and her goals. Because they are holding prominent positions, this helps to make up for their apparent lack in the LD. These 5s facilitate the urge to change one's life for the better, due to the high degree of discomfort experienced.

Due to the introduction of many new ideas and approaches, it would be wrong for you to get the notion that the traditional method is losing its impact. On the contrary, Oprah's SDLD was purposefully favoured in the above analysis to demonstrate that it is not obsolete, especially when it contains its unique idiosyncrasies and precious types of information which is inordinately valuable to the numerologist. For instance, consider the four 1s, in her challenge area. On the one hand they point to a damaged sense of self; on the other they signify having the potential to single-handedly achieve something momentous which may be the product of the type of damaging that Oprah experienced. The *positioning* of SDs in a LD is so important. From their positions, they impart essential information that is vital to deciphering the Life Path thereby maintaining their value.

Where would we be if we did not have SDLDs to apply number-pairing to them and extrapolate their inner squares and Stars of David and know which numbers were on which axis? Bill's, Hugh's and Oprah's SDLDs are a testimony to that, as is Joan of Arc's that follows. The traditional method of constructing the SDLD has proven itself over the centuries – it is in using *new deciphering techniques to update outmoded methods* where the difference lies. Another reason that the traditional method continues to maintain its place is due to the fact that we have just moved into the 21st century which creates low numbered LDs.

Until this century's *year* numbers begin to increase, many new souls will have very low numbers in their birth dates, therefore SDLDs may be the only type of LD that you can get. Just think 1-1-2000 could spawn yet another great humanitarian as these numbers exactly replicate Bill Gates' and Annie Besant's SDLDs! And there will be others whose birth dates can only spawn SDLDs – their SDLD also being their WNLD!

CASE STUDY: St JOAN of ARC

St Joan's birthdate presents us with a rarity where the WNLD is only marginally altered with only two compound numbers emerging in its goals. This phenomenon makes her SDLD powerful. She seemed to draw from the essence of its SDs and what their pairs made. Her type of birthdate reflects many that the early stages of this millennium will produce.

St Joan of Arc (Jehanne or Jeanne d'Arc) was born on 6JAN1412 and burned at the stake at nineteen, on 30May1431. Her SD/WNLDs reveal a story of triumph and tragedy.

Number-pairing and extension techniques bring out their true meaning. They help to expose a wonderful story of an enlightened being who, at an early age, fulfilled her soul's purpose. Traditional techniques would fail miserably at unveiling this unique tapestry of life events, to relate St Joan's incredible story.

St JOAN of ARC: 6-1-1412 = LPN: 15/6   **BURNED at STAKE: 30MAY1431**

```
            9      SDLGR = 24/6                9       WNLGR = 51/6
            3                                  21
        7   5                               7  14
      1 6      8  SDLPN = 15/6           1  6      8  = WNLPN: 15/6
        5   2                               5   2
            3                                  3
            7      SDLCR = 17/8              7    WNLCR = 17/8
     SDLDR = 56/20/2                     WNLDR = 83/20/2
```

St Joan's SDLD is an extremely good example to use for many reasons. One is that it is rare to find a SDLD that depicts a person, at an early age, utilising the highest possible potential that their numbers imply. Although she died at the tender age of nineteen, her shortened life span demonstrated her advanced level of spiritual attainment. Through all that St Joan was, did, became and accomplished, one can easily see *all* of her numbers in action providing her with everything that she needed to live out her destiny during her brief stay on earth.

This brings us to another reason for studying St Joan's numbers. Anecdotes drawn from her life illustrate that she was not confined to only those numbers that made up her first mini-diamond which is traditionally seen as "exclusively ruling" her during its active time span. They clearly show that all of her LD's numbers other than her first LG/C cycle were concurrently expressed in her character, aspirations, activities and circumstances. Repeated, factual data such as that that follows, repudiates traditionally laid down time frames and principles.

LGR24: For instance, St Joan's LGR24 made an indelible impression on her entire life being plainly active throughout. It clearly epitomised that although a *country* girl, the major part of her destiny involved her *country*men ("country" is a strong 24 characteristic). She also travelled her *country*side during the well documented battles she led with "travel", especially country travel or long-distance travel or travel to another country, being other strong 24 traits.

The Life Diamond

Cosmic Diamond: Beneficent 17, 18 and 19 are found in each cosmic diamond. Their combination and their Tarot Keys provide strong indications that help to get a feel for what can be achieved during the lifetime. For young Joan, they represent the possibility of achieving honour (19), fame (17) and reputation (18). This is especially so in their "reversed" numbers as she aspires to achieve her earthly purpose. 89/98 also in the cosmic diamond supports this theme. Their applicable keywords follow: "immense talent in a given field; fame and fortune; public acclaim or disgrace; public lawsuit (when she was publicly acclaimed a heretic and sentenced to death); mediator for peace (she actually mediated between the instructions from her "Voices" and those in power with the goal of reinstating the Dauphin); an activist, lobbyist (she most certainly lobbied for France's freedom) and campaigner. Paired 78 and 18 from the cosmic diamond bestows upon her their "protector" aspects. St Joan activated them similarly to, but differently from, Oprah.

Spiritual Axis: Idealistic 39/93 at the SDLD's zenith strongly ignites St Joan's altruism and passion. 12 from them enabled her to willingly sacrifice herself for the Greater Good. Her two 36s (reversed 63s) that also appear on the spiritual axis strengthened her innate sense of obligations, duty and responsibility – she could shoulder onerous burdens that would ordinarily overwhelm others. This powerful positioning and intensification of hidden 36s on the spiritual axis made Joan all the stronger and more determined. Their actual 63's visibly revealed the depths of despair that she endured in seeing the plight of her beloved France. Her indomitable faith and strength may have wavered at times as she waited for the hour of her chilling death. Both from the spiritual axis, paired LG/C33 indicates selfless service and LG/C79, the people's champion. When these numbers are coupled to her LDR20, 89/98 and baseline paired, 16, they depict the tremendous effort that she put into regaining French rule (20) and toppling the English (16). Reverse 73 at the base of this axis signifies that part of the life's work could only be achieved by her efforts, alone. Its 37, a king Key, represents one aspect of the Dauphin, indicating that he may not be trustworthy due to its "challenge" position. These numbers and Keys help to illustrate St Joan's inclination towards high aspirations, unswerving devotion and allegiance and being drawn to perform gargantuan, humanitarian deeds.

Inner Square: St Joan's two aces in her amazing inner square make it extremely powerful. You only get four numbers from its periphery and if you pair its diagonals by ignoring the heart number, you add a further three. The inner square's ruler is 19. When you imagine or take out its Tarot Keys, consider how well they graphically depict the "Work" of the physical plane. Note the treachery, betrayals and heartbreak in the two 57s, the 3 of Swords, as well as the martyrdom when reduced to their 12s, the Hanged Man. Now see the ability to lead and conquer in the incisive nature of the two 52s, the Queen of Swords, and in their reversals which reveal two dashing, crusading, Knights of Wands. Then contemplate the bizarre, the unknowable and secrets, plots and schemes in their root 7s or maybe you see St Joan as the Charioteer or the "Warrior" taking control of her country's destiny?

Pairing the inner square's diagonals, 55 adds the Ace of Swords to the mix, depicting good and evil in the life as well as sudden, radical change. Two obvious instances of radical change can be seen manifesting at important junctures in her life. One occurred when she changed her circumstances from a simple county girl to being a flag bearer and fighter in men's garb and the other when she was captured in battle, by the English swiftly changing from a freedom fighter on the battle fields of France to that of being a prisoner. 27, another Ace, bestows inspired ideas and actions and multi-talents. 72 contains elements of "the protector and the keeper of secrets".

In this case, less numbers from the inner square may facilitate less deviation in the Life Work, similar to Oprah's, which has even fewer. Even St Joan's Star supports this as no new numbers appear in it. However, an abundance of sword Keys appear in her SDLD with 6 accentuating them by being her heart number, LPN and goal rulers. In many ways, they came to represent the actual weapon or method used to physically free France from England. This can be seen in the imagery of The Devil of her LPN15; England can be perceived as the oppressor (the devil) with the chains on this Key representing France being bound to England. Was this the divine intent in each 6 to ultimately use the sword of "Zain" (seventh Hebrew letter) to sever France's ties to England in order to achieve her earthly assignment?

57 forms part of the inner square and the first mini-diamond. Being intensified it enlivens depth of feeling in the areas of loyalty, commitment, compassion and empathy. St Joan exhibited these qualities – her heart literally bled for her beloved country which was in foreign hands. Multiple 57s and their 12s most likely increased her sense of patriotism and martyrdom which compelled Joan to rise to "the cause" which would satisfy her innate sense that she had a "life mission" to perform which was fanned by her crusading Knight Keys. 57's Tarot image of three swords through the heart brings another notion to mind, that each sword may be seen as depicting the three betrayals she suffered: firstly, by the hand of King Charles Vll when he chose to turn his back on his female protagonist, the second as the English church finding her a heretic, and the third, when many of her beloved countrymen and women turned against her.

The way that St Joan's numbers are "Divinely contrived" to suit her earthly purpose is truly awesome; especially those that make up her magickal facets and LPNs. The 12s from her year number, and also from the reductions of 57/75 and 39/93, strongly point to a life of voluntary sacrifice and service for the Greater Good by one who is inclined to martyrdom (12s and paired 33). The two 75s from the 57s bring a new slant to their interpretation. In Joan's case, they show how she was capable of expressing virtuous principles in that she chose to accept the barest minimum for her valiant efforts choosing to give what she received as payment, such as money, gifts and rewards, to the underprivileged and in so doing demonstrating her charitable nature. Materially, she had little to show for her hard won victories yet, when you reflect on her life, she achieved the impossible and could have been very wealthy if she was selfish by nature. This notion of unselfishness is reinforced further by the ruler of her number-lines which is 74, the number of the "Saviour" or the "Good Samaritan" which bestows these traits upon its bearer. However, the flip side to 74 is when its recipient is placed in times of need. This aspect of 74 was evident when Joan was completely dependent upon others for her needs thus exhibiting the reciprocal, give-and-take nature of this number.

Other Salient Features: The emphasis in what has been addressed so far, has focussed upon life events that were signified by many numbers other than those being activated in St Joan's first life cycle. More proof that numbers, not traditionally regarded as being active, will be highlighted as her story unfolds further.

Two 53s flank both diagonal sides of the SDLD and the Star. They correspond to the Knight of Swords portraying an indelible image of St Joan astride her valiant steed charging forward, intent on meeting her enemies with the sword of St Catherine and righteousness held high in her hand – a special sword that was believed to have magical powers. Upon instructions from her "Voices", this sword was found in an old, forgotten trunk among other implements, behind an altar in a church exactly where she was told it would be located. The two 53s as the Knight of Swords indicate one-pointedness and a passionate, unswerving devotion to a cause. Its reversal, 35, sees Joan standing firm in her resolve and always en garde, ready to attack or defend, forever remaining vigilant until her work is complete. It also depicts defending an untenable position – she would become France's ultimate sacrifice!

SD LDR56 represents being repeatedly thwarted by the Dauphin's deception and delaying tactics. His deception culminated in her capture and being burned at the stake (35, a figure leaning heavily on a staff, in front of several wands in the 9 of Wands card!). Tarot Keys for 35 and 62 depict a maiden bound, weary and fenced off by staffs in one card and bound, blindfolded and almost enclosed by swords in the other – she was personally inhibited by difficult situations, often beyond her control, yet she was able to transcend them and liberate France! Link paired 58, 62 and 15 to 16, 35 and 56 and a common theme of being inhibited, tied up and imprisoned becomes apparent.

These powerful images and their combinations confirm that obstructions, delays and waiting for the right moment to act would play a prominent role in this life especially when two 56s are present in the SDLD with one being the all-powerful SDLDR. A major instance of this occurred when Joan first heard her 'Voices" (clairaudient aspect of 56) when fourteen but did not take action until seventeen when she finally took up the banner to fight for her people. Others were when the weak Dauphin continually thwarted her plans by being devious and indecisive. The positive aspects of these hindrances were shown in her as an army leader who could use setbacks for gain by using the time to contemplate and plan manoeuvres, regroup and prepare for the next move. This allowed her to exploit the potential contained in 56 and in her WNLG14.

Two paired 73s the 5 of Pentacles, depict the importance that religion and church figures played in Joan's life. 73 signifies how she ended up being shunned by the church which is graphically depicted in the exoteric image of this Tarot Key. Esoterically, however, it depicts St Joan's challenge to never lose her trust and faith in God.

LDRs20, on the other hand, gave Joan prudence, unstinting energy, perseverance and strength as well as the ability to cope with enormous tasks and stress. It also represents the harsh, contrived sentence imposed on her by the English clergy. They gave her neither the right to legal counsel nor the right of appeal. Almost all numbers dealt with so far have been purposely chosen to demonstrate that they are not contained within St Joan's "active" life cycle. To further this, her supposedly "inactive" LC2 and family of LDR2s gave her strong political leanings, as well as a strong chance of being involved in wars (see links to wars in the LD2s of the Dalai Lama, Ghandi and Bill Clinton).

SDLDR56 clearly depicts St Joan's connection to Higher Forces via clairaudience. When seventeen, she knew that it was time to come forward and make "God's Mission'" known, through her. This was an auspicious time for her. This age linked to the 17 in the first and fourth cycles, promising fame, fortune and infamy – this was a destiny moment – *her* moment to shine and literally be a "star"! But, her LCR17 in all probability depicted her future downfall. This "17 synchronicity" is fascinating. It becomes even more so when 17 is sometimes spoken of as being one of the numbers of God which may be implied as St Joan being one of God's messengers.

Yet another bizarre coincidence occurred when these events took place. 17 can have sexual identity issues! The quirky links to this were that Joan cut her hair short and was dressed as a man from the time she entered the army to protect her from molestation. This is an intriguing way of expressing this facet of a 17. She was not only dressed as a man but also took on a role customarily given to a man – a very unorthodox turn of events for those narrow-minded times! (A diminutive associate of mine also has a LCR17. Her sexual identity idiosyncrasy is expressed when she describes herself as "having the body of a man". Interestingly, she is flat-chested and she also has a deep voice for a woman!).

Intensification of Royal Keys: Another fascinating point is the extraordinary amount of royal or "people" keys that are present in the Tarot images of several of Joan's paired numbers. From a personal perspective, these cards bestow leadership and high-ranking potential by the stations in life that they represent. Her LCs almost exclusively pair and reverse to represent Kings, a Queen, Knights and a Page, which is unusual. Another Page and two more Knights can be found in the baseline and SDLGs and a Queen in the SDLGR, with another one in 38 being the reversal of WNLDR's 83. From this prevalence, was St Joan destined to be among the elite and/or become a person of high-ranking? Given her extraordinary abilities and undertakings at such a young age, coupled to the idea that LCs may well represent past life attributes, one cannot help but speculate that she may have drawn on past life ranking and capitalised on it by taking it to more advanced levels? For instance, had St Joan incarnated from a prior high-ranking and/or military background? Would this account for her extraordinary ability to sway a nation, successfully lead armies, counsel a King and be the people's hero (paired 79) at such an incredibly young age?

Number-line rulers: When you have few numbers to work with, as in this case, calculate the Wheel's number-lines in your search for more information; they might just provide you with what you are seeking. Joan's SD number line rulers are: $15 + 28 + 16 + 15 = 74/47$.

28/82 that rule the SD spiritual axis provide important additional information. They tell you that Joan was born with the innate trait of developing strong leadership abilities that entail power struggles. They also tell you that she is likely to have the courage to stand up for herself, her convictions and the rights of others (74). To substantiate the strength of these particular numbers in her character, take into account that 28/82 also rule the WN inner square and the red triangle of the WN Star. Intensification like this, especially from their positions, almost guarantees that Joan would become embroiled in power struggles of some kind at some stage in her life. From the WNLD, the spiritual number-line adds to 46/64. These numbers are not found elsewhere. 64 is very interesting from the point of view that it relates so well to betrayal, collapse and witnessing of many deaths which were all major aspects of her life.

WN Additions: WNLG14, WNLG21, WNLGR51 and WNLDR83 are the only new numbers you get from St Joan's WNLD. WNLG14 is significant because it bestows organisational ability especially in the sense that it can be used to unite her divided country by embracing a common cause. WNLG21 depicts her advancing status both mundanely and spiritually. WNLGR51 as the King of Swords bestowed her with razor sharp leadership potential and a formidable demeanour. WNLDR83 enhanced her creative, intuitive faculties in devising strategic tactics that enabled her to sense what her enemies might do, thereby giving her an "edge".

Active Mini-diamond: Having dealt with many numbers that are not contained in St Joan's currently active LG/C cycle to demonstrate that they were indeed "alive" and working, we shall now turn our attention from them to concentrate on her first cycle's active numbers.

It is of great interest to see that the numbers in Joan's active first LG/C cycle reflect those of her LCR17, LPN15 and LDR56. Do these strong connections indicate why her soul influence began so early in her life? For instance, 16 that forms the base of this cycle could represent her early "spiritual awakening" and wanting to change her country's circumstances for the better. 16 also signifies the possibility of imprisonment which she also endured during this cycle. 15, 16 and 17 point to her early rise to power, fall from Grace and early demise. Her death in this time span is reflected in the 19/10/1 that rules this mini-diamond and her inner square (the presence of a combination of 15, 16, 17, 19 and 10 often forewarns of a death or close encounter with death if the person happens to be in the "right" circumstances for that to occur).

When fourteen, St Joan first heard her "Voices" while praying in anguish for the plight of her people. Her "Voices" were that of Archangel Michael, St Catherine and St Margaret. They transmitted to her that she was the maid chosen by God to liberate France from English rule and see to it that the Dauphin, was to receive his rightful place and be crowned as Charles VII, all of which she accomplished. Her mission was to break the fetters (15) that bound her country (LG24) captive to English rule (WNLGR 51?). Did St Joan perceive England as the devil in Key 15? Was this her challenge? Did she see her country being chained to England and literally set about to cut free (15) her king (51), country and countrymen (24) with her mighty sword (heart 6)?

At its highest level, 15 (curiously, The Devil) can depict liberating oneself through unswerving discipline, focus and devotion from earthly attachments and choosing to follow a Saintly Path. St Joan certainly used her LPN15 in these ways as she literally personified non-attachment to materialistic things by releasing herself from and transcending common earthly desires, pressures and connections. This demonstrates how esoteric 15 as a number can operate at high moral, religious or spiritual levels rather than as attachment to materialism, possessions and relationships when activated exoterically.

Perhaps the same notion could be applied to St Joan's SDLDR56. Does it signify on its highest level the ability to receive clairaudient messages channelled from Higher Beings? This is apparent in her communications with and allegiance to her "Voices". (As an aside, Leonardo da Vinci has 56 ruling his number lines. It makes you wonder if his genius was a result of being a human channel for Superconsciousness?). Maybe these ideas will be more fully explored by those who share a passion to seek a greater understanding of the significance and meaning of what compound numbers symbolise. In conclusion, it is my opinion that this case study shows St Joan, to be an advanced, enlightened soul, using the active mini-diamond's numbers - 15, 16, 17 and 19, its cycle ruler, in their esoteric capacity.

(See Book 2: Chapter 11 and 13 for St Joan's year of capture and day of death)

 **HANDY TIPS**

Set up a pictorial representation of your WNLD putting Tarot cards in place of the number to gain deeper insights and understanding from it. Thoroughly absorb each image. Allow each Key's special qualities to imprint its attributes on your mind. Muse over their names, images, numbers and Hebrew letters and their symbols. Reflect on how they mirror your life. Learn as much as you can about yourself from them remembering that all is not revealed at one attempt. Begin by applying their positive aspects to your life and watch it change for the better. To assist you with this, the front cover displays my WNLD with its corresponding numbers. **NB:** WNLG82, which is my true third goal, is reduced to 10 and depicted by the Wheel of Fortune only for the purposes of the cover. Normally, a homemade Key would be placed underneath the Wheel of Fortune Key with an 82 inscribed upon it.

Cutting up pieces of card and writing a Key's name and corresponding number on them, readily substitute for repetitive Keys, those that go beyond 78 and reduced Keys. Making them in different sizes has the advantage of being able to place a reduced Key on its parent Key to expose the LD "layers". Greater, personal insights can be uncovered in this way.

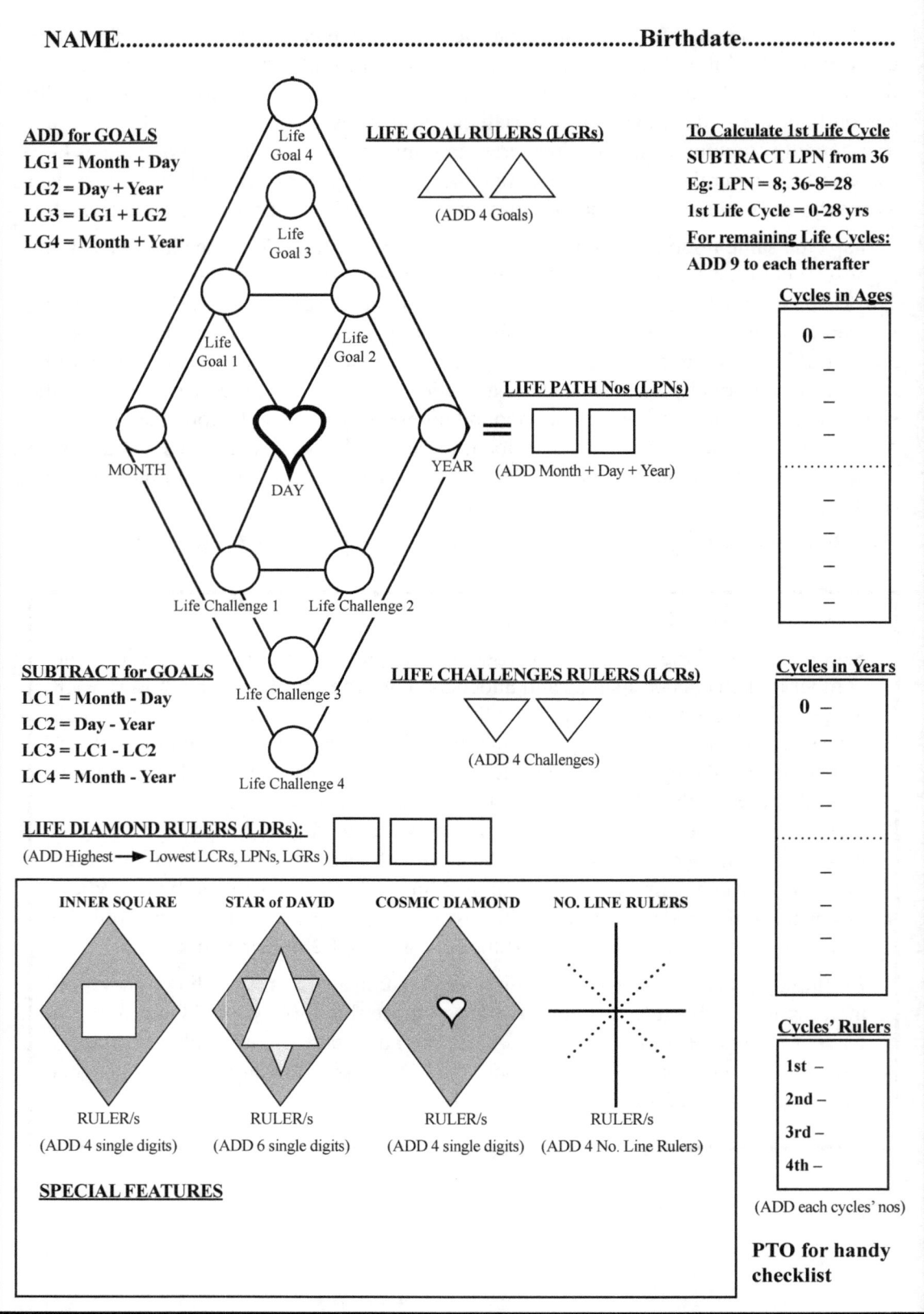

WHEN ZERO CHALLENGES "DISAPPEAR"!

Abbreviated Terms used for *Single Digit Life Diamonds* in this Chapter:

- ❖ LD = Life Diamond
- ❖ SD = Single Digit
- ❖ SDLD = Single Digit Life Diamond
- ❖ SDLG = Single Digit Life Goal
- ❖ SDLGR = Single Digit Life Goal Ruler
- ❖ SDLC = Single Digit Life Challenge
- ❖ SDLCR = Single Digit Life Challenge Ruler
- ❖ SDLDR = Single Digit Life Diamond Ruler
- ❖ LG/C = A Life Goal and its Life Challenge combination
- ❖ SDLPN = Single Digit Life Path Number

Abbreviated Terms used for *Whole Number Life Diamonds* in this Chapter:

- • WN = Whole Number
- • WNLD = Whole Number Life Diamond
- • WNLG = Whole Number Life Goal
- • WNLGR = Whole Number Life Goal Ruler
- • WNLC = Whole Number Life Challenge
- • WNLCR = Whole Number Life Challenge Ruler
- • WNLDR = Whole Number Life Diamond Ruler
- • WNLPN = Whole Number Life Path Number
- • PYN = Personal Year Number

CHAPTER 10
WHEN ZERO CHALLENGES "DISAPPEAR"!

ZERO CHALLENGES *REPLACED*

Perhaps one of the most exciting things about introducing WNLDs is that zeros, which only appear in SDLDs challenge positions, frequently *disappear*. Zeros disappear due to being replaced by real numbers in their companion WNLD – but *not* in every instance. Hence, zero replacement is one of the exceptional features that WNLD's produce. It is a great boon to numerology for, when the zero is replaced, its lack of specific directions is happily eliminated! Traditionally, the zero is commonly written up as being the number of "choice" – no wonder, when it contains limitless possibilities (refer to 0 in Appendix 1). Generally speaking, depending upon the choices made and actions taken under a zero's activation or influence, either success or failure is the outcome.

In essence, this broad generality was all that one had to go by in the past. Now that we have a number to work with, definitive guidelines can be accessed and used with confidence. This is groundbreaking and definitely worth celebrating. At last we can obtain specific directions from the number that replaces the zero having explicit details to go by instead of being forced to play guessing games in our summations. We are no longer ships without a compass when zeros appear in challenge positions – especially when quadruple zeros occur, as in Reg's case study (later in the chapter). However, there are times when some LD's zeros cannot be replaced due to their mathematical compositions or when a birth date's numbers are very low, e.g. 2-2-2000. WNLDs such as Sir Edmond Hillary's and Albert Einstein's retain the zero from their SDLDs. The other WNLDs that follow theirs make remarkable changes to their zeros providing us with precious indications from what each veils.

Chapter 10 – When Zero Challenges "Disappear"!

EXAMPLES: Sir EDMUND HILLARY and ALBERT EINSTEIN

SIR EDMUND HILLARY: 20-7-1919 = 47/11/2 - First to conquer Mount Everest

	9		SDLGR = 26/8		27		WNLGR = 161/8
	4				67		
	9	4			27	40	
7	2	2	SDLPN = 11/2	7	20	20	= WNLPN: 47/11/2
	5	[0]			13	[0]	
	5				13		
	5		SDLCR = 15/6		13		WNLCR = 39/12/3

SDLDR = 52/16/7   WNLDRs = 247/184/13/4

TRADITIONAL METHOD – (SDLD)   **WHOLE NUMBER METHOD – (WNLD)**

ALBERT EINSTEIN: 14-3-1879 = 42/6 - Famous scientist/mathematician/physicist

	1		SDLGR = 14/5		28		WNLGR = 140/5
	2				56		
	8	3			17	39	
3	5	7	= SDLPN = 15/6	3	14	25	= WNLPN: 42/6
	2	2			11	11	
	[0]				[0]		
	4		SDLCR = 8		22		WNLCR = 44/8

SDLDR = 37/19/10/1   WNLDRs = 226/19/10/1

TRADITIONAL METHOD – (SDLD)   **WHOLE NUMBER METHOD – (WNLD)**

 **HANDY TIP**

When zeros appear in SDLDs, especially if they remain or appear in a WNLD, use The Fool Key to interpret it first in its inception or initiation mode i.e., as a 0, and then in its culmination, fulfilment mode as a 22; Appendix 3. Also consult Appendix 1 for the interpretations of a 0 and a 22.

Three case studies follow containing examples of zero challenges being replaced by their true numbers in their WNLDs.

The Life Diamond

CASE STUDY: CYNTHIA : 19-5-1949 = 47/11/2

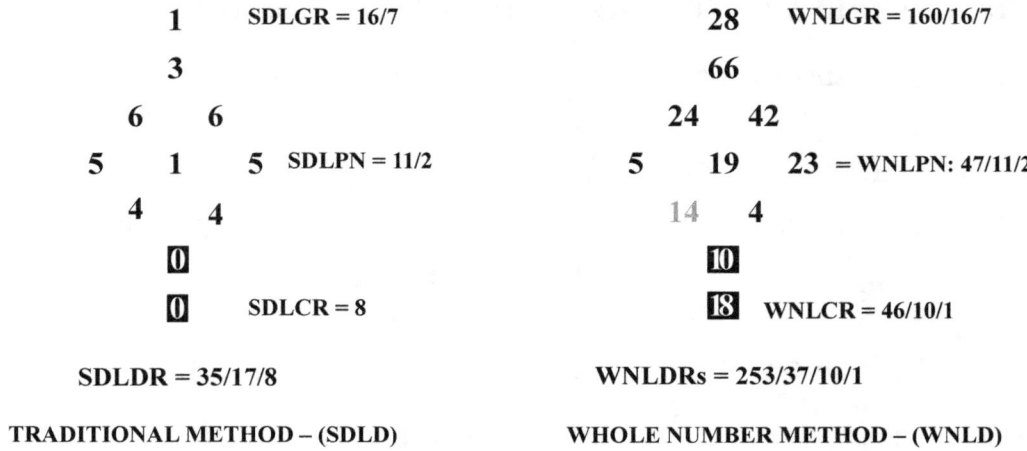

TRADITIONAL METHOD – (SDLD) WHOLE NUMBER METHOD – (WNLD)

Cynthia's WNLD presents us with new and very exciting directions when WNLC10 and WNLC18/9 suddenly make their welcome appearance where her SDLD zeros were. The emergence of these numbers reveal exactly what each of Cynthia's zeros conceal. Their "veils" have been lifted and now that we have tangible numbers as guides, definitive signposts are exposed and, as a result, the information that they bring to her WNLD and indeed to her life, can be put to excellent use. As you will come to see, Cynthia's WNLC10 and WNLC18 supply her with very specific traits, skills and directions whose singular nature and indications could not possibly be determined from her zeros when using traditional methods.

For Cynthia, we will use her true challenges, WNLC10 and 18, as a means to explore other LD features. For instance, we can weigh and consider esoteric influences; past life influences; possible karmic implications; the way a challenge and its goal work together; and how the work of a cycle can carry over into the next. This helps to get an idea of specific lessons to be learnt and the life work to be done. Carry over themes occur when either lessons are not learnt and/or the work of the cycle is unfinished or if the numbers of the next cycle indicate same or similar themes. Parallel themes occur when numbers in consecutive cycles are repetitive or have similarities that produce same but different slants to a theme. Cynthia's 10 and 18 provide us with an excellent example to use to investigate these features. By studying them along the following lines, your interpretive and analytical skills will advance because you are learning to synthesise many WNLD aspects and recognise how ongoing themes can cover a very long period of time.

Do Challenges Represent Past Life Works and Karma?: To recapitulate before moving on, LC numbers quite possibly signify gifts and talents brought over from past lives as well as representing current life obstacles (karma or lessons) and the need for continuous personal adjustments (dharma or growth). They can be positively expressed even though challenges are traditionally labelled as "negative indicators". It may pay to refer back to

Chapter 10 – When Zero Challenges "Disappear"!

Chapter 2 where several suggestions were given for past life and karmic implications and for positive and negative expression of goals and challenges.

Esoteric WNLC10: To use the LCs as reference points to what has been brought over in this lifetime is, of course, conjecture and open to question until further research either verifies or refutes this notion. However, I think it would be safe to consider that Cynthia's WNLC10 and 18's attributes signify many things from a past life – your job as the numerologist, is to select what is appropriate to her and her life and also what you consider to be likely to unfold, given what you have before you.

WNLC10 could denote that Cynthia has already reached a point of culmination in certain aspects of her past lives and, as a result, is poised, ready to begin new ones in this lifetime. Taking this line of reasoning, we will explore esoteric aspects of a 10, and its Tarot Key the Wheel of Fortune. (An exoteric approach was mainly used in delineating Bill, Hugh and Oprah's WNLC10s in the previous chapter.) Esoterically, Key 10's "Wheel of Life" basically represents *perpetual rotation and cyclicity* depicting involution and evolution and the cycles of life. It signifies constant flux and change manifesting in our everyday lives as we continually struggle to adapt and adjust to daily affairs. In this way, the Wheel plunges us into a fertile field in which personal development undoubtedly occurs as a consequence of being subjected to constant change. The Wheel's cycles are ruled by Cosmic and Karmic Laws. This tells us that our actions determine outcomes according to these laws. When under the Wheel's direct influence remember; *what you sow, you also reap* or *what goes around, comes around!* From this we are able to gather many clues as to what Cynthia's experiences may be.

To broaden esoteric parameters further in an effort to gain more from the significance and meaning of what 10, its Key and its position are representing for Cynthia, other clues can be drawn from the Hebrew letter's symbol for this Key. The letter is "Kaph" denoting a *"closed fist"* which represents *"clasping or grasping"* something. Being on the spiritual Path, this would be very good knowledge for Cynthia to have. Simplistically, it would help her to realise that she has the innate ability to grasp the meaning behind things. She also has the ability to hold fast to things which will sometimes serve her well and other times, not. Her work would be to differentiate between which of these promotes her evolution and which negates it as the Wheel manifests both pros *and* cons!

The pain of adaptation to the Wheel's (life's) ups and downs will most certainly test Cynthia's mettle. What she can definitely anticipate is that, although she has finalised some or one particular aspect or phase of herself in a past life or lives, this is the lifetime she has chosen to make changes to her existence that will take her a step higher on the "ladder of life". To develop new aspects of herself and initiate new things will be a big part of her "Work". This would be important information for anyone on the Path to have. For Cynthia, it tells her that she has a golden opportunity to emerge from this cycle with aspects of herself being more advanced to what they were prior to its activation. If successful, she will have a more enlightened grasp of her aspirations, her capabilities and her limitations and she will undoubtedly grow wiser from her experiences as she learns to expand her boundaries. (Expanding boundaries and gaining wisdom stem from the planet Jupiter which rules this

Key. It provides you with another way of perceiving growth and evolutionary themes in the 10. Knowledge of planetary or zodiac rulers and their specific attributes also adds to your skills at interpreting Keys and numbers. See their allocations in Appendix 2.)

As a number, this WNLC can be expected to bring Cynthia more onerous lessons during its cycle with the aim of facilitating growth. This possibility furnishes you with yet another clue – anticipate that this may not be a good time for Cynthia due to 10's "testing" nature. She may experience such things as being dominated by others, the use and abuse of power and attacks on her self esteem. If these conjectures are correct, we would anticipate seeing Cynthia's life experiences manifesting some of these aspects we would presume she has chosen to work on in this lifetime, in order for her to come into her own. For instance, Cynthia may have "chosen", through the 10/1 to become more self-assertive, independent, and shoulder heavier responsibilities. If these conjectures are correct, Cynthia will lift herself "up" and endure the pain and suffering that higher levels of self-awareness and capability often entail knowing that there is "no gain without pain". Also, having a WNLC10, she has more than likely brought over many inherent skills, has earned rewards for past life efforts or experienced her fair share of good and bad fortune which will help to prepare her for this life's tasks. Armed with this information, Cynthia might be excited about rather than daunted by what her WNLC10 prospects would bring. This comes from having a broader knowledge from which to capitalise on the positive and negative possibilities contained in this number. The main test for you, the numerologist, is to appropriately fit the above clues and their possibilities to Cynthia's life and decide how she can turn them into positive outcomes.

Esoteric WNLC18: Fascinatingly, WNLC18 also has strong esoteric evolution and change connotations to it which links it to those that are similar in her WNLC10. The major differences between the way that evolutionary unfoldment is accomplished is that Key18 promotes *voluntary* change whereas Key 10 *imposes* change. You can see how beneficial it is to have Key18 follow Key 10. Wisdom garnered from 10's cycle (Jupiter signifies the gaining of wisdom), can be capitalised on in 18's cycle. In 18's cycle, forced change gives way to self-imposed change where Cynthia is handed back the controls. Apart from that, WNLC18 may suggest that, in past lives, Cynthia could have accumulated occult knowledge, was clairvoyant, and had healing abilities and/or a religious background. These notions stem from probable avenues that a WNLC18 and its root 9 might take, especially as Cynthia is exhibiting these traits. This may well be conjecture but this notion of challenges as being links to past lives and containing carried over good and bad Karma have their uses as an intuitive starting point from which an understanding of where a Life Path might be heading.

How WNLC10 and WNLG66 Work in Unison: When decoding a life cycle, you must consider that a challenge and its goal are there to reveal the specific life experiences that they represent for that cycle. Also consider that they are especially designed to work in unison. The following anecdotes show you how WNLC10 and WNLG66 did this for Cynthia.

Whilst experiencing WN10/1's activation, Cynthia found herself at the brunt of power struggles that ultimately pushed her into standing up for her rights, and asserting her

Chapter 10 – When Zero Challenges "Disappear"!

independence. This forced her to give up playing the victim by enabling others to dominate her. These are negative expressions of a 10/1. For example, she was forced to fight a large, home-building company and stand up for her rights because they were threatening to dishonour their contract. (In this instance WNLG66 represented the building company). Cynthia stood her ground, winning what seemed to her to be a "David against Goliath" battle, ending up receiving more than was promised in the original contract! Cynthia's mother passed away during this period which also helped to propel her into "coming into her own". For years prior, and while these events transpired, Cynthia's overbearing sister-in-law was constantly undermining her marriage. However, WNLC10 and WNLG66 strongly support one another. Under their combined influences Cynthia was being "pushed" into dropping the mantle of the "victim" and reclaiming her power. 66 can depict standing one's ground and being more "self-ish" which is similar in some respects to 10's, 1. This 10/66 combination brought in outside influences that were beyond Cynthia's control yet taught her how to assert herself when threatened by a building company, her sister in-law and her then insensitive husband. In a negative sense, the 66/10 pair represented an overbearing, interfering sister-in-law (66) who was creating havoc in Cynthia's marriage, an unpleasant battle with a building company (66) and the passing of her mother (10). But the positive outcome of this difficult cycle saw the emergence of a much stronger, independent, more assertive and confident woman who was now taking control of *her* life and becoming more in touch with expressing *her* needs – a positive 10 and 66! It was a life-altering cycle – a turning point for her. Cynthia commented that this was the worst period in her life.

Cynthia's WNLC10 and WNLG66 combination has other features that add further insights to the above. They are rather unique in that one is a *tens* number and the other is a *master* number as well as being a *queen* Key. These three factors intensify the vibrational field of this cycle as each operates at higher frequencies thereby demanding more of Cynthia which bears out why she has painful memories of this period. The insights that can be gleaned from their attributes give clear indications as to what this period may evoke. They provide you with clues that can be used when combining 10/1 with the 66 to anticipate that Cynthia's sense of self might be challenged by *people and corporations* during their reign as 66, being a *royal* Key includes high profile women, society, people, businesses and corporations under its umbrella and 1 from 10 can signify domineering people. Because of their high powered nature, 10 and 66 indicate that this is likely to be an onerous cycle. Having advance knowledge of this would not only help to prepare Cynthia for what might eventuate but also help her to at least understand the processes involved. Knowledge such as this can be very settling in trying times because it would give Cynthia a sense of the bigger plan for her.

Cynthia's WNLC10 cycle proved to be the catalyst that drew on her many 1s. In so doing, Cynthia "came out". She demonstrated this by unshackling herself from inhibiting influences stemming from the two 15's on her SDLD's baseline and reinventing herself under the 10's energies with the help of her two 13s on her SDLD's spiritual axis – *"death of the old Cynthia"*. Using 10's traits, she learned to assert herself and express her needs; using 15's traits she let go of several incumbrances and by using 31's traits, she extricated herself from the incessant wrangling (31) that was making her life miserable. Upon entering her WNLC18 cycle, Cynthia took this newly discovered sense of self and maturation to grasp what was impeding her personal growth a step further by seeking courses and people who supported her "emergence".

How One Cycle Carries Over Into the Next: Cynthia's numbers provide us with an excellent example of how the work of the WNLC10 and WNLG66 cycle flows into the next. WNLG28 provides us with an instant clue of this continuance because it reduces to an empowering 10/1 which links it to the previous cycle's WNLC10/1; except that we now have a hidden 10/1 in a *goal* position. Therefore, themes involving confidence, independence, self-awareness and self-improvement will continue unfolding and being tested, perhaps more overtly, as a goal. The theme of Cynthia's struggle to be seen, heard and valued as an individual in her own right from the previous cycle carries on. Ongoing "power-plays" (28/82) continued. Cynthia was learning from her relationships and circumstances how to take ownership of her life (28/10/1). She moved from being dominated and overruled (negative 2, 8 and root 1 from 28) to reclaiming her power and becoming a force to be reckoned with (positive expression of these numbers if not taken to extreme). These new strengths and attitudes got rid of an interfering sister-in-law and created a role reversal in the marriage because Cynthia reclaimed her personal power.

WNLC18 carries on 10's gift of evolving one's self, albeit in different ways to the 10. If you look at 18's Key, you will see how narrow the Path of Enlightenment is and that it undulates as it rises many times towards the mountains in the distance. These rising undulations represent Cynthia's many ups and downs over the course of time as she strives to become more. This mimics the cyclic, rotational nature of the Wheel as it teaches by what is learned from its ups and downs, too. These similarities help us to deduce that the striving of the 10 cycle is definitely persisting throughout the 18 cycle.

Outcomes: After years of suppression and financial limitations, Cynthia's innate (or brought over) gifts and rewards could be seen surfacing under her WNLC10 and WNLC18. WNLC18, for instance, endowed her with *reorganisational skills*, which she applied after the emotional hurt and turmoil of the WNLC10 period to help transform herself and reinvent her life using a variety of self-help and spiritual practices. Her father passed away during this period (WNLG28 reducing to 10 – loss of a senior family member) and Cynthia became quite wealthy from her inheritance. Several factors that point to coming into money during this time span were: 28 which equates to the "rich merchant", its root 10 being the Wheel of Fortune signifying wealth, and The Moon, WNLC18, the promise of an inheritance (10 and 66 also have possibilities of becoming wealthy in them as 66 is a "wealthy" queen which reinforces the possible wealth aspect in the 10.) As the numbers and Keys suggest, these were life-changing phases in Cynthia's life.

These 10 and 18 anecdotes serve to prove that replacing zeros with numbers have provided invaluable guidelines that refine our ability to forecast life-long trends with greater precision. These trends help to verify the first impressions from WNLC10 that one of Cynthia's major tasks in this life, is to become more independent and learn not

Chapter 10 – When Zero Challenges "Disappear"!

to rely on others too much for support. This runs counter to her LPN2 – which provides us with a paradox – we have assertiveness (10/1) conflicting with compromise (2) and independence (10/1) conflicting with togetherness (2)! Now we need to look for other numbers in her LDs to support this "10/1" theory. Other powerful indicators are, of course, the heart 1, the two paired 10s from the third and fourth SDLG/Cs, crowning SDLG1, crowning WNLG28 that reduces to 1, and finally, the "1 family" of the WNLDRNs. So, the appearance of WNLC10 would be viewed as a "trigger" for Cynthia to begin to emerge as a person in her own right and WNLC18 providing back up for that. Her LPN, on the other hand suggests that Cynthia's main lesson is to learn to integrate her "1" and "2" aspects by not compromising her sense of self in relationships.

Reg's LDs, that follow, provide us with yet another example of whole numbers replacing SD zeros. As with Cynthia, we will be mainly concentrating on their replacement. He has a WNLC18 and three WNLC9s which will be treated from a different angle.

When comparing their LDs, you may notice that Cynthia and Reg share similar numbers. In so doing, they also share similar, but different life experiences, which you will come to recognise as you become more skilled at delineating. Take their WNLG24s for example. Cynthia expresses her WNLG24 as being an avid gardener. Reg expresses his WNLG24 more widely, by also being an avid gardener as well as spending extended periods living, working and travelling in country areas. In addition, he spent a few very successful years cultivating crops. Moreover, their WNLC18s have developed along similar lines. Cynthia is presently using hers along limbic healing lines and may develop into a medical intuitive, given time. Reg is using his for his earth energy and spirit clearance work. Both Cynthia and Reg are spiritual and mediumistic. These are proving to be salient trends for each. Such examples as this help to support the theory that the numbers in a LD are there to exert their influence for *life* – not just exclusively for when their cycle is activated.

CASE STUDY: REG, REG: 3-12-1929 = 36/9

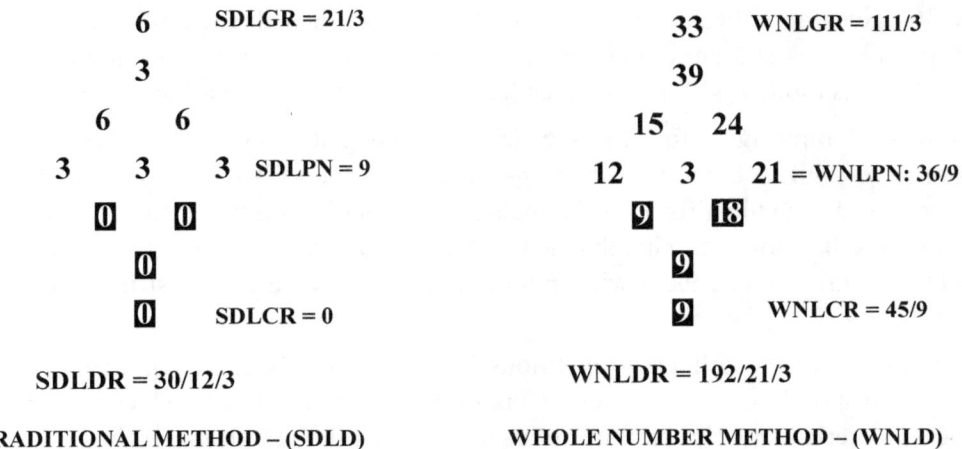

```
                6      SDLGR = 21/3                    33      WNLGR = 111/3
                3                                       39
            6       6                                15      24
        3       3       3   SDLPN = 9              12      3      21  = WNLPN: 36/9
            0       0                                   9      18
                0                                           9
                0       SDLCR = 0                           9      WNLCR = 45/9

        SDLDR = 30/12/3                              WNLDR = 192/21/3

    TRADITIONAL METHOD – (SDLD)              WHOLE NUMBER METHOD – (WNLD)
```

From Four Zeros to Four Numbers: With the focus being mainly upon the replacement of the zeros in Reg's WNLD, you are able to see a distinct contrast between it and the SDLD. Reg's WNLD now has numbers filling every challenge position including his challenge ruler position. As in Cynthia's case, Reg's "new" numbers immediately provide specific guidance that is masked by his SDLD zeros. It is a pity that his numbers are so repetitive as a variety of numbers would have supplied a better example. However, it serves to demonstrate what the whole number method can do. To see his true life goals and that each is a different number when you look back at his SDLD, is a great help when delineating his Life Path.

With so many 9s, Reg actually personifies The Hermit Key in real life. He is extremely kind, genteel and wise, always ready to help and guide anyone in need by devoting his life to their cause. An aura of reclusiveness or "absence" enshrouds him as you might expect. Naturally, multiple 9s intensify these attributes and predispositions as well as giving greater clarity to his Life Path.

When *True* Challenges Indicate Present Life Trends: On another tack, LPN9 and three WNLC9s, inspires the thought that this incarnation's focus is on tidying up loose ends from past lives. Precious indications from them give rise to considering notions that this incarnation could be one of culmination and of perfected works and at the same time, one that paves the way for a new phase to begin in the next life. Without them, such guidelines as these could not be entertained. Reg's SDLGR21 supports this idea. It signifies aspiring towards completing phases and cycles so that new, elevated cycles can begin. Add to this Reg's SDLDR30. It also supports this theme as it denotes building for the future, the successful completion of tasks and the solving of long-standing problems.

To date, Reg's life has borne out much of the above. Success, power, status, accomplishment and endings and beginnings intersperse his life. From his many talents represented by the multiple 3s, 6s and 9s, he made and lost a lot of money and pursued several successful careers. With the numbers that he has, no wonder he is so creative (39/93 rule his number lines!), has had so many flourishing professions (6s), has travelled extensively within Australia (24 and 9) and lived in so many places (repetitive 6s and 60s). The presence of many 36s gives him "broad shoulders" that provide him with the ability to take on heavy responsibilities and large undertakings. Their reverse 63s represent the powerful influences that his mother, sister and wives (past and present) have had on his life.

Reg is now a "shining light" for others. Spirituality, integrity and ethics are very much at his core (9s). WNLC18 and the strong psychic influence of The Moon intensify his highly specialised, psychic gifts. Reg channels them through his unique talent in the field of earth energies. It is not surprising that he is writing a book documenting his astonishing findings (18). With so many 9s, it will, in all likelihood, receive wide distribution when published.

To be able to accurately delineate repetitious LCs, as in Reg's case, you need to rely upon their corresponding goals as well as taking note of other influences coming from cycle rulers, esoteric symbols and their rulers as well as other major numerological data.

Chapter 10 – When Zero Challenges "Disappear"!

This will help you get clearer directions and finer details that are more likely to manifest during their active time spans.

When faced with so much repetition and little relief in a LD such as Reg's, clearer indications of the Life Path are more easily obtained due to the absence of any great deviation. Many repetitive and negative tendencies were experienced from this phenomenon during the first round of his LG/Cs when life experiences either demanded much or were quite harsh, thus moulding Reg and steering him towards uncovering his true Path. As a result, this tendency greatly diminished when Reg's orientation reversed with well-earned success, peace, harmony and contentment becoming dominant features when he "raised the bar" and found his own true Path.

The next case study is not only another good illustration that important information can be gleaned from the numbers that replace zeros but also that a specific angle of a LD can be studied in order to bear out an emerging hypothesis. This time, we have a WNLC16 and a WNLC18 zero replacement. Each of these numbers, on their own, can be regarded as rather threatening. When you have them together like this, you can be expected to be a little uneasy about the way that they might manifest. This is the proposition that is being focussed on for Amelia. We are going to study her LDs in an effort to uncover clues that point to her tragic death. (Both Cynthia and Reg have WNLC18's appearing in their WNLDs but so far have not experienced a tragic event in their lives.)

CASE STUDY: AMELIA EARHEART
AMELIA EARHART: 24-7-1897 = 56/11/2   **DIED at age 39**

```
          5    SDLGR = 21/3              32      WNLGR = 192/12/3
          8                               80
        4   4                           31    49
       7  6  7  SDLPN = 20/2          7   24   25 = WNLPN: 56/11/2
        1   1                             17    1
          [0]                             [16]
          [0]  SDLCR = 2                  [18]  WNLCR = 52/7

       SDLDR = 43/7                    WNLDRs = 300/75/12/3
```

TRADITIONAL METHOD - (SDLD)   **WHOLE NUMBER METHOD – (WNLD)**

Numbers That Signify a Potential Tragedy: The presence of 16s, 17s, an 18, 64s and an 80 plus a hidden 57 as the reverse of 75 in the WNLDR family, combine to auger the possibility of a tragedy. However, both tragedy and fame can be found in Amelia's LDs. The 17s and two paired 47s (achieving one's dreams) plus her crowning WNLG32 (victory) at the zenith of her WNLD and paired 60 (earned success) are good indicators of fame. They are further supported by her SDLD's LGR21 and the 19 found in her WNLGR192. Fame will not come easily, however. It will come as a result of great struggle and personal hardship. Paired 44, 57s, 58 and 76s, two SDLC1s and SDLPN20, WNLG31 and WNLG80 lead to this conclusion as there is a strong theme of personal struggle, adversity or hardship inherent in them. Two paired 10s from her SDLD and two 12s appearing in the WNLGR and WNLDR positions further support that supposition. However, I would lean heavily towards struggle being a major theme as WNLG31, the Tarot Key actually named "struggle", happens to be Amelia's *Achievement Number!* (Book 3: Chapter 2.)

Having determined these background possibilities, does the stress factor inherent in these numbers incline you toward considering a negative connotation for her WNLC16 and WNLC18? Amelia's story provides us with the answer.......

First and foremost, Amelia was a pioneer (inner square ruler, 10/1; spiritual axis rulers 19/10/1) in the field of aviation. She was the first woman to become a pilot (innate in her SD/WNLC1s but possibly more so in her SDLDR's reversed 43 as 34, the 8 of Wands which is often linked to air travel). At age thirty-four and ten months, she set out to cross the Atlantic single-handed, in a flimsy, unsophisticated aircraft of the time. Amelia landed in Ireland after completing the fastest crossing (34) of the Atlantic on 21st May 1932 – a great victory (WNLG32).

When aged thirty-nine years and eleven months, she took off on 2nd July 1937 on an even more courageous solo attempt to cross the South Pacific – sadly, never to be heard of again. This was a great tragedy which is what 16 and 18 can produce. Together with 34, they indicate that she had the potential to be accident-prone. If this is what you anticipate, the *timing factor* needs to be addressed in an effort to pinpoint such a possibility. This is another angle to study that is absolutely imperative in such cases.

How Do You Ascertain the *Time* for a Tragic Event?: Because Amelia is a LPN11, you need to calculate her age cycles to ascertain which one she would be activating for the event, to get further clues. She provides us with a wonderful example of helping to solve the age-old dilemma of deciding whether to use a 2 or an 11 for these calculations. Obviously, the use of either positions her at different age cycles. I prefer to use her LPN11 for reasons given in the following and in Chapter 12.

Timing her LDs by using a LPN11 in preference to her LPN2, to calculate her age cycles, places Amelia's first solo flight in the final year of her *second* cycle. Her second solo flight occurred almost at the end of her fourth personal year during the *third* cycle (she was under an auspicious PYN13/4!). This meant her "threatening' WNLG80 and its accident-prone WNLC16 were activated. They much more so depict a life-threatening experience than her WNLG49 and WNLC1 do. 16 on its own can herald an accident! Its combination with 80 helps to reinforce thinking the worst during that cycle.

You cannot work on the assumption that these two numbers will bring about Amelia's death. So, the next step for you to take is to link these numbers to other LD or major personal numbers that support your theory. For example, Amelia's SDLD's number-line ruler reverses to make another 16. This 16 and SDLDR "shadow 34" are constellation numbers that always hover in the background waiting to add their influence to the mix when the right kind of occasion presents for them to become active. 34 can auger a swift, forceful event, similar to 16. As this data builds, the possibility of a tragic accident is beginning to become more ominous. Two paired 48s and two 10s that make up the SD third cycle plus 16, 18, 34 and 80 do not bode well as an active set of numbers for the event.

To add to this, the SD third cycle ruler is 18, the number of tragedy! Now check the WN third cycle ruler and you get 194 =14/5. Break it up into its number pairs and you get 19 and reversed or shadow 49. Both 19 and 49 can trigger a death. Princess Diana had two 49s in her Yearly Diamond's goal sector when she died in her tragic car accident. 19 is also common among "death" numbers as is 14. So, both SD and WN third cycle rulers support the mounting picture. Amelia is surrounded by an extremely powerful, potentially destructive, force field. Although Amelia exercised the enormous bravery inherent in her active WNLG80 it was linked to the accident-prone Tower, WNLC16, taking the place of her SD zero! – who knows, a bolt of lightning or a storm may have brought her down like that depicted on its Key. Add 18's Key to the mix and you get The Moon, night-time and The Moon Key being ruled by Neptune which equates to the sea! Was she brought down at night, in a storm at sea? Was she the victim of an unforeseen catastrophe (16)?

Putting the Pieces of the Puzzle Together: Amelia's combined indications lead to forming the conclusion that her WNLCs do, in fact, raise alarm bells and that she may very well be in peril. These assumptions are strengthened due to being linked to several other potentially threatening numbers that were also active at that tragic time. As a consulting numerologist, the direction gleaned from her numbers would be to issue a warning that things may go awry sometime during this period and that all human attempts should be made in an effort to lessen any likelihood of things possibly going wrong, especially if contemplating or being engaged in anything hazardous.

To time a possible demise during that daring attempt, more detailed figuring needs to be carried out like calculating Yearly Diamonds, Personal Months and Personal Days (all in Book 2). Her Numeroscope would also hold essential keys to help with timing events (Book 4). For instance, Amelia's Yearly Diamond for age thirty-nine, when linked to her LDs, graphically depicts a probable demise for that daring attempt. To cite two important instances, the Yearly Diamond and current Decade's Diamond had strong links to her LPN as both of their rulers were 11; exactly matching it. Amelia's is a telling example of when the true numbers that are revealed in the WNLD, especially in the case of zero replacements, give more precise directions.

WHOLE NUMBER LIFE DIAMOND WORKSHEET

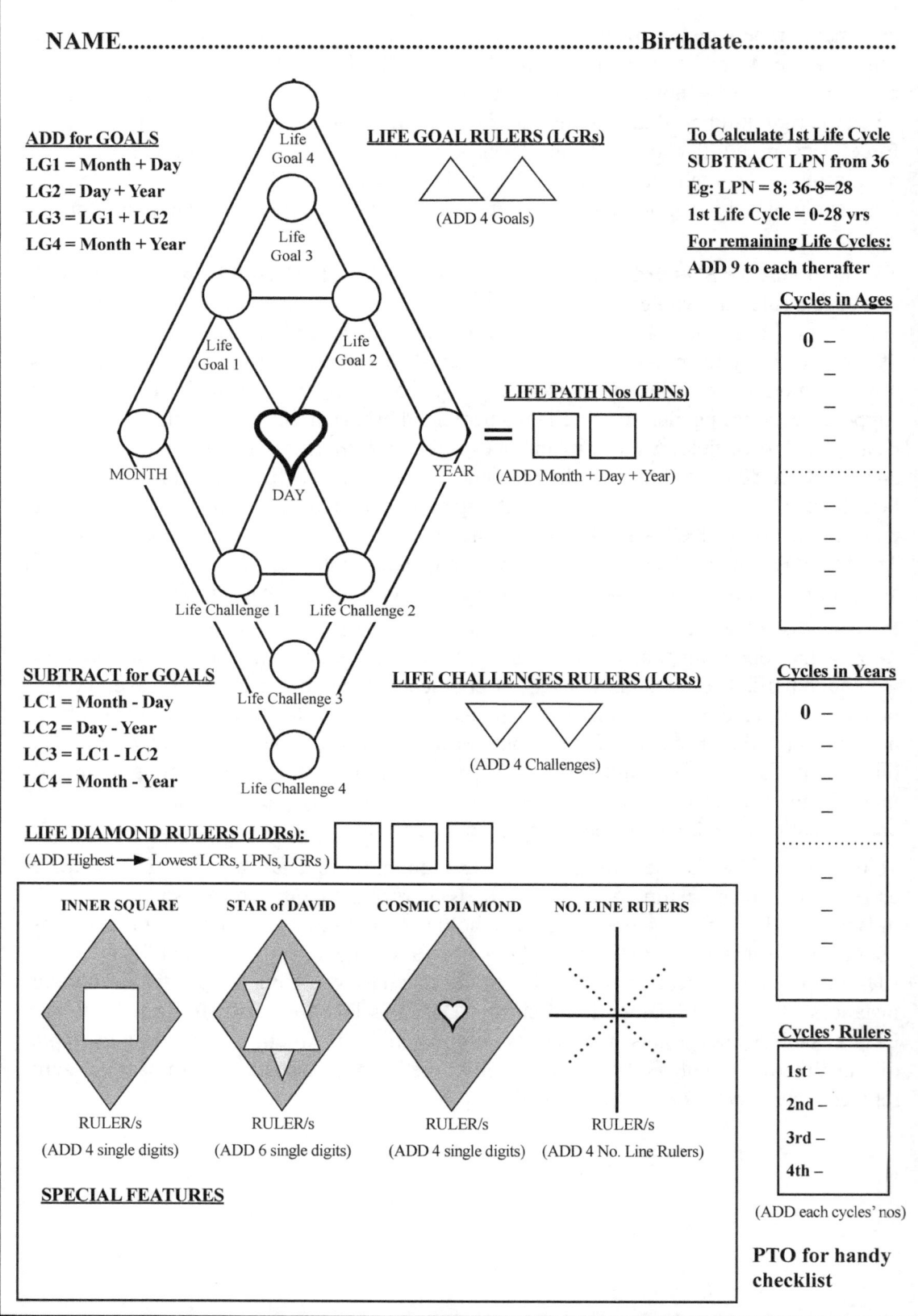

HOW TO CALCULATE AN INTERIM LD

Abbreviated Terms used for *Single Digit Life Diamonds* in this Chapter:
- ♦ LD = Life Diamond
- ♦ SD = Single Digit
- ♦ SDLD = Single Digit Life Diamond
- ♦ SDLG = Single Digit Life Goal
- ♦ SDLGR = Single Digit Life Goal Ruler
- ♦ SDLC = Single Digit Life Challenge
- ♦ SDLCR = Single Digit Life Challenge Ruler
- ♦ SDLDR = Single Digit Life Diamond Ruler
- ♦ LG/C = A Life Goal and its Life Challenge combination
- ♦ SDLPN = Single Digit Life Path Number

Abbreviated Terms used for *Whole Number Life Diamonds* in this Chapter:
- • WN = Whole Number
- • WNLD = Whole Number Life Diamond
- • WNLG = Whole Number Life Goal
- • WNLGR = Whole Number Life Goal Ruler
- • WNLC = Whole Number Life Challenge
- • WNLCR = Whole Number Life Challenge Ruler
- • WNLDR = Whole Number Life Diamond Ruler
- • WNLPN = Whole Number Life Path Number

CHAPTER 11
HOW TO CALCULATE AN INTERIM LD

HOW TO CALCULATE THREE TYPES OF *INTERIM* LDS

Knowledge is power. Education, in whatever form or field, facilitates expanding and enriching levels of knowledge. As a consequence, your powers are increased as you accumulate greater understanding and wisdom from the knowledge gained. Hence, this chapter provides you with greater knowledge of yourself by introducing three additional methods that extend LD dimensions further. These additional methods allow you to access unexplored dimensions about yourself that the SDLD and WNLD have not yet uncovered. Their inclusion provides you with the opportunity to make more informed, life-affirming decisions that help you to become all that you wish to be.

HOW TO CALCULATE THREE TYPES OF INTERIM LDs

1. Inclusion of WHOLE NUMBERS as they appear in the goal area.
2. A TENS NUMBER/S *interim LD*.
3. A MASTER NUMBER/S *interim LD*.

Just slight adjustments are all that is required to learn how to calculate your interim LDs. Their proper place is to fit *between* the SDLD and the WNLD. They are essentially an extended version of a SDLD. Once calculated, they create a natural progression from SD → *interim* → WNLDs. On occasion, you may get two personal, interim LDs. Emma provides us with such an example. She has a first type of interim LD and she has a tens interim LD.

The first type of interim LD is mandatory and the easiest to do. It is always calculated prior to any other interim version. For the first type of interim LD, you retain the SD baseline as it is but you do *not reduce any of its compound goals wherever they may occur*. This is similar to the WNLD in the way that you do not reduce its goal totals, either. When you keep the goal totals as they are in this LD, it often produces a mixture of SD and whole number goals like in Emma's, or all of its goals can be whole numbers like in Daniel's. But, in interim LDs, the challenges *never alter*.

The other two types of interim LDs are founded upon retaining any tens or master numbers that occur naturally in or can be derived from the birthdate. Emma, Mozart, Bill Gates and Annie Besant provide examples of using *tens* in their baselines. "50 Cent" supplies us with a *master number* example that appears in his baseline. Do not reduce any compound goals, challenges or LPNs that may appear anywhere in these LD's calculations. Any changes within them naturally flow on to alter some or all of their rulers. As you would expect, ruler totals increase as a direct result of retaining higher numbers in the basic calculations. If changes occur to the challenges due to using tens or master numbers in the baseline, *all* LD rulers become greater.

Each interim LD in the following case studies brings forth its own unique dimensions that the SDLD or WNLD are unable to bring to light. For this reason, they are worth calculating especially if they reveal vital information that these two LDs do not contain. Interim LDs consisting of SD baselines will be introduced first. You will find that some LDs lend themselves to this way of extending their parameters much better than others – Daniel's is an excellent example of dramatic changes occurring throughout the interim goal sector.

EXAMPLE 1: DANIEL JACOB RADCLIFFE: 23-7-1989 = 57/12/3

```
           7      SDLGR = 23/5                  16      LGR = 68/14/5
           8                                    26
      3    5                                    12   14
   7  5    9      SDLPN = 21/3             7    5    9   = LPN: 21/3
      2    4                                    2    4
           2                                         2
           2      SDLCR = 10/1                       2   LCR = 10/1
      SDLDR = 54/9                          INTERIM LDR = 99/45/9
           SDLD                                   INTERIM LD

                                    34      WNLGR = 194/14/5
                                    80
                                30      50
                            7   23      27  = WNLPN: 57/12/3
                                16      4
                                    12
                                    20      WNLCR = 52/7
                        WNLDR = 303/78/15/6
                                  WNLD
```

The Life Diamond

Best known for his acting role as **"HARRY POTTER"**, DANIEL'S interim LD provides us with a superb example of changes occurring to all four of his interim goals. This is basically brought about by having a 7 and a 9 in the baseline (pair them and you have the number of the "hero"!). Higher SD baseline numbers are more likely to produce compound numbers for their goals. Note how Daniel's LGRs and LDRs are elevated to higher numbers due to not reducing the goals' totals. By revealing the goals' interim parent numbers, you are able to immediately deduce other very relevant facets of Daniel's make up, capabilities and life experiences from their appearance which is the purpose behind constructing them. They reveal information that might prove to be vital to a person's further understanding of themselves, their life and their possibilities which can then be brought to their awareness and used to their advantage.

Emma provides us with two interim LDs. This is due to the fact that she has a "hidden" tens number in one of her birthdate's numbers. Hers happens to be a tens reduced number which is derived from her year number, 1990 = 19 = 10. The first interim LD works with a SD baseline watching for any whole numbers to appear in the goals sector from its calculations. The second interim LD uses the "hidden 10" on the baseline derived from her year number which alters several of her goals and challenges. These "new" numbers add further dimensions to her character and possibilities.

EXAMPLE 2:

EMMA CHARLOTTE DUERRE WATSON: 15 - 4 - 1990 = 39/11/2

```
                5      SDLGR = 21/3                         5      LGR = 39/12/3
                8                                          17
            1       7                                  10      7
        4       6       1   SDLPN = 11/2           4       6       1   = LPN: 11/2
            2       5                                  2       5
                3                                          3
                3      SDLCR = 13/4                         3      LCR = 13/4

        SDLDR = 45/9                              INTERIM LDR = 63/36/9

            SDLD                                        INTERIM LD
```

— 162 —

Chapter 11 – How to Calculate an Interim LD

```
              14     LGR = 66/12/3
              26
          10     16
       4     6     10   = LPN: 20/2
          2     4
              2
              6     LCR = 14/5
       TENS LDR = 100/46/10/1
       TENS INTERIM LD
```

EMMA is best known for her supporting role as **"HERMIONE GRANGER"** in the *Harry Potter* films. The major difference between Emma's first interim LD and Daniel's is to notice that only two of her goals change to compound numbers; not the complete set as in Daniel's case. Nevertheless, vital information is gleaned from her two compound goals and new LGR and LDR totals. Her tens interim LD however, brought forth compound numbers in every goal placement and altered three of her challenges, as well, which meant that new ruler totals have appeared in all major LD extensions in the tens LD. Perhaps one of the tens or master number LD's most significant feature is to reveal a hidden LPN. In Hermione's case, hers is 20. 20 exposes another layer of Hermione's character and possibilities providing further important guidelines.

It is amazing how much explicit information can be retrieved from a birthdate when utilising these specialised techniques to bring out other personalised dimensions. When you analyse Emma's LDs, you can appreciate how well her personality fits the character of "Hermione". The same can be said for Daniel in his "hero" role as "Harry".

An excellent case study for you to practice on is that of actor, CAMERON MICHELLE DIAZ. She was born on: 30AUG1972. Her birthdate produces all four LD types. (Use the baseline: 8 – 30 –10 for her *tens* LD). Cameron has what I consider to be a "star signature" in her SDLD. The numbers that I find consistently appearing in people who reach stardom in whatever field (or become famous for whatever reason) often have conspicuous 17, 18, 19, 21 and a 31 in their SDLD or among their LDs. Check out her SD cosmic diamond.

CASE STUDY: MOZART

MOZART provides a particularly good example to use to support the value of introducing interim LDs due to his SDLD containing so few numbers. Research has shown that repetitive numbers explain the reason behind extremist behaviours or uncommon interests

The Life Diamond

or talents. This was so in Mozart's case. However, restrictive LDs like Mozart's blossom and bloom due to the addition of interim LDs and WNLDs. Their inclusion reveals the hidden potential and exclusive Life Path directions that his SDLD's fail to expose on their own.

Not surprisingly, Mozart's numbers give rise to unique LDs. They provide the opportunity to explore to what extent interim LDs contribute to uncovering hidden, useful details as well as expanding on the personal directions that each can provide. His first interim LD reveals three tens in its goals making this LD more demanding in addition to lifting it to a higher frequency. A tens interim LD is created from Mozart's year number which hides a 10. It produces compound numbers in each goal position as well as replacing Mozart's two zero challenges. Note the appearance of paired 79 that takes their place. Being the number of the hero, it accounts for Mozart's popularity and notoriety. Note the dramatic differences between Mozart's SDLD to his WNLD.

MOZART: 27 - 1 - 1756 = 47/11/2   **DIED at age 35.**

	2	SDLGR = 6			2		SDLGR = 168/15/6
	2				20		
1	1			10	10		
1	9	1	SDLPN = 11/2	1	9	1	= SDLPN: 11/2
8	8			8	8		
	0				**0**		
	0	SDLCR = 16/7			**0**	SDLCR = 16/7	

SDLDR = 33/15/6   INTERIM LDR = 69/15/6
SDLD   **INTERIM LD**

	11	LGR = 69/15/6			20	WNLGR = 168/15/6	
	29				74		
	10	19			28	46	
1	9	**10**	= LPN: 20/2	1	27	19	= WNLPN: 47/11/2
	8	1			26	8	
	7				**18**		
	9	LCR = 25/7			**18**	WNLCR = 70/7	

TENS LDR = 114/60/15/6   WNLDR = 285/96/15/6
TENS INTERIM LD   **WNLD**

Chapter 11 – How to Calculate an Interim LD

Mozart's LDs provide an excellent opportunity to blend together the different features that each contains. This will challenge your ability to be able to pluck different components from each that go together to validate certain traits and themes. The following synopsis shows you how to do this as this is essentially what you are aiming to achieve.

Begin by scanning each LD. Search for what each one has to tell you and note any salient features. Each of Mozart's LDs are very distinctive. Many of his repetitive numbers and his two zeros are replaced in his extended LDs. Their replacements provide specific information which coalesces to reveal firm directions and individualistic idiosyncrasies.

While scanning Mozart's SDLD, note how number-pairing forms four master numbers, four 19s and four 18s including two 20s, two 80s, a 90 and a 29 which reduces to 11. Also note the high potential for attaining mastery stemming from the SDs and number-pairing of his SD inner square. Thank heavens for this technique which allows us to expose hidden traits and directions with so few SDs to decipher! The SD Star of David comes in handy, too. It provides two new numbers. They are 28 and 10 which relate to power struggles, others using money as power and ups and downs.

Now scan the dynamic changes occurring in Mozart's tens interim LD. Although several numbers repeat those when paired in the SDLD, like 10, 11, 18, 19 and 29, which do not add any new data, they at least reveal a layer of the "parent" numbers that spawn the SDLD's goals. This is vital information to get. So are any new numbers that appear in this LD. The new numbers paired are: 17/71, 78/87 and 79/97 *which only appear in this LD*. And, all of Mozart's interim LD rulers have increased. Take especial note of its LPN 20 which brings an additional number to his LPN family. Mozart's extended LDs provide an opportunity to combine interpreting SDs, number-pairing and whole numbers altogether. The same approach can be applied to Mozart's WNLD. Seek new numbers or outstanding features as you scan its make-up.

Having done the preliminaries, begin the interpretations. Remember that you are dealing with a male genius living an extraordinary lifestyle who acquired great wealth and fame and entertained royalty and high society. So, which numbers denote these features? A 17, 18s with several 19s and a beneficial *heart* 27 plus many tens and master numbers all suggest the potential for talent and the development of specialist skills as well as the ability to distinguish oneself, especially when most are reversed to make 71, 81 and 91. Mozart also has two interim 79s – the people's "hero". And 96 brings him before the masses. As far as royalty is concerned, look for royal keys. Mozart has a 26 (Page), 25 (Knight), 52 (Queen) and a 51 (King). The presence of 10, 17, 18 and 19 and 22, 79, 88 and 90 are a strong recipe for genius, fame and fortune but are mostly challenges which tend to detract somewhat from their beneficence. Add to this notion The Tower, plus treachery within the all-powerful tens interim third LG29, reversed 62 and intensified 18s. This combination may have been enough to bring about Mozart's downfall. Was Mozart handicapped by his genius and eccentric behaviour depicted in his 19s (unconventional behaviour), 18s (psychological disorders), 0s (wisdom or folly) and WNLCR70 (eccentricity)? Did his 1s make him too headstrong or reckless when combined with his paired 22 and double 0s (The Fool) in his SDLD?

Several reinforced 18/81s (with paired 88 and two paired 80s and 90s) indicate not only a high capacity for genius, but also the tragic and treacherous nature of Mozart's life. This is strongly supported by WNLG64 (reversed) and the powerful WNLCR7 which is really a high powered 70 at that. 7, 18, 64 and 70 imply that secrets, plots and schemes and the hidden and the unknown to be strong factors in Mozart's life. 18 is well known for its deceptive qualities. Add several 18s to interim LG29 and paired 29 in his SDs to reinforce this theme. They contain potential defamatory situations. Combine several 19s with them and you have a strong case for broken promises and contracts along with having the ability to earn a high rank in life (as 91s). So here we have a see-sawing picture (70, many 10s and 18) of fame, fortune and deception that caused eventual ruinous outcomes (64).

Money is the bane of most aspiring artists. Mozart was no exception. It is interesting to note how many "money" numbers appear in all of his LDs demonstrating how finances were integral to his life. "Money" numbers are: LPN2, LC8s, interim 10s and LGR69, WNLC26, WNLG28 and WNLCR70 and LG29. Compound 88 and two 80s with a 90 are, too. They indicate attaining *and* losing wealth. WNLC26 coupled to top 22 and bottom 00 in the SDLD, strongly hint at gambling problems or at least taking risks with finances. Mozart's heart 9 tends to magnify these traits. WNLCR70 at its worst suggests lack of control, chaos and anarchy as well as excessiveness and an unbalanced nature or life – a ruling WNLCR after all! Mozart's financial situation was never stable (70, WNLC26 and horizontal central 88), being mainly reliant on the generosity of benefactors, WNLG74.

The threat that Mozart's love of pleasure and self-destructive behaviours posed for his health and eventual collapse is evident in the 2s, 6s, 7s, 11s and, especially, WNLG64 (10 of Swords). Finally, top SD paired, 22 can presage a state funeral or a very public one. In Mozart's case, it was the reverse. He was buried in an unmarked grave.

This brief exposé shows you how to criss-cross between each LD to synthesise corresponding pieces of information that substantiate Mozart's life as he lived it. It gives you a taste of what very advanced practices can produce. This brief interpretation is based upon integrating a full set of LDs and their various facets to blend them together to produce common themes. I believe this to be the next area of numerology to develop – finding *sets* of numbers that describe similar probabilities, themes and states of affairs.

As we near the conclusion of this chapter, BILL GATES' LDs are reintroduced. This is because his birth date not only provides us with a zero replacement but also because it lends itself to producing an extraordinary tens interim LD as a result of his month number being a 10, his birthday number being a 28/10 and his year number being a 20. The baseline for this interim LD will have the numbers 10 - 10 - 20 as its foundation. They produce an interim LD that shows a very rare example of an unprecedented array of numbers. Their outstanding potential, in some ways, outstrips Mozart's!

In Bill's interim LD to follow, note how every single one of its numbers are exactly ten times higher than those in its companion SDLD (except for the zero) which gives you some idea of the enormity of the potential and the power that Bill's interim LD numbers represent. They have been discussed at length in previous case studies; therefore,

Chapter 11 – How to Calculate an Interim LD

although phenomenal, they need no further mention except to say that they verify Bill's unprecedented array of gifts and talents and truly remarkable life. The intensification factor in his interim LD due to multiple numbers and repetitious Tarot Keys spirals well beyond the norm. The Wheel of Fortune (five 10s), the 4 of Wands (two G30s and CR30) and the 10 of Cups (one 50), in particular, may indicate his unprecedented success in the business field and amassing of incredulous wealth (*five* interim Wheels of Fortune and *four* paired Wheels of Fortune!).

EXAMPLE 3: BILL GATES: 28 - 10 - 1955 = 58/13/4

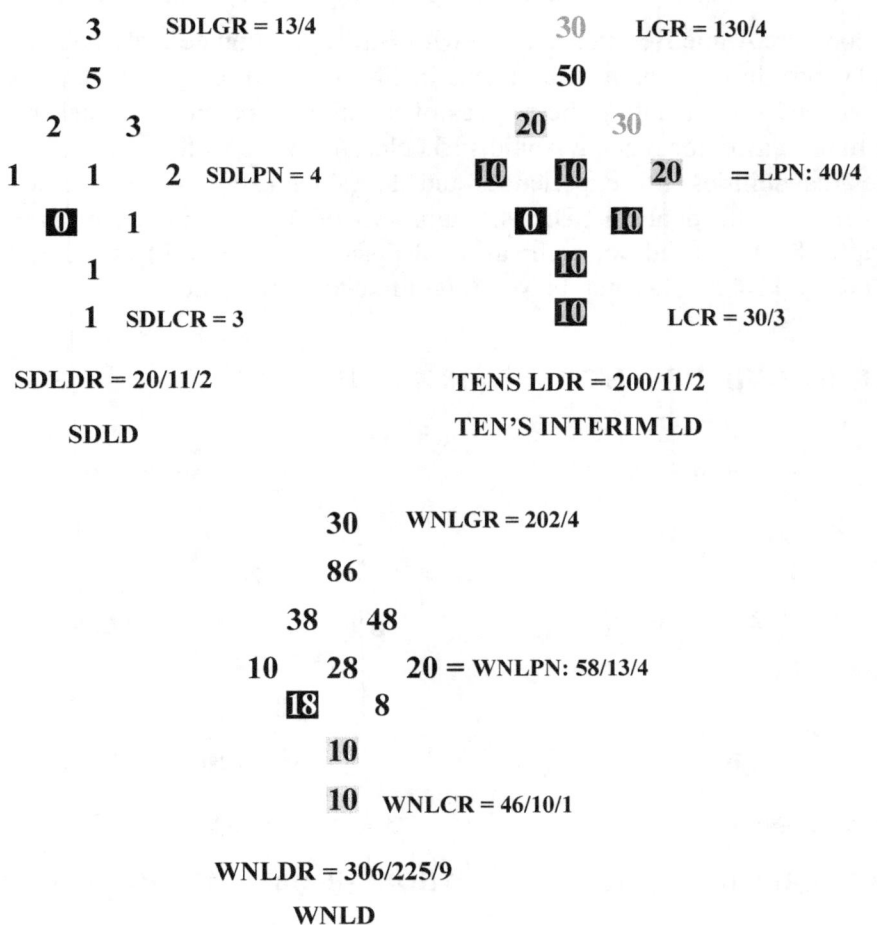

ANNIE BESANT'S LDs also deserve a place here because her SDLD replicates Bill's. This provides us with an opportunity to study the unique differences that two people with identical SDLDs such as theirs possess. When you are confronted with identical SDLDs, setting up the interim and WNLDs enables you to quickly and easily determine individual differences. That is what makes their inclusion so important otherwise, the contrasting

The Life Diamond

or like natures of the subjects would not become obvious if these extra steps were not taken. Rare examples such as these are especially interesting from a numerologist's point of view.

Annie's SDLD contains a zero which is replaced by a WNLC9 in her WNLD. Unlike Bill's numbers, Annie's do not lend themselves to creating an interim LD as it turns out to be her WNLD which is a unique feature in itself! Yet the differences that occur between the two LDs, when you construct them for Annie and Bill *personalise* them for each, making their individual differences shine forth. It is that that makes the inclusion of this added approach so unique. Bill's interim LD is such a classic. It is so rare and such a fine example of its type. Annie's is a fine example from the standpoint that it endorses the place of the WNLD and zero replacement in numerological computations.

When you compare Annie Besant's WNLD with Bill's, you immediately become aware of the similar but different paths they chose in life. One can only speculate that they are both advanced souls availing themselves of the highest potential in their numbers. This is the main reason for placing Annie's LD close to Bill's so that the differences in personalities, capabilities, life experiences and directions can be compared with each other when faced with identical SDLDs. Highlights of Annie's life were given at the end of Chapter 8. If you did not compare Paul Foster Case (3OCT1884) and Aleister Crowley's (12OCT1875) LDs, maybe you might like to do them now?

EXAMPLE 4: ANNIE BESANT: 1 - 10 - 1847 = 31/4

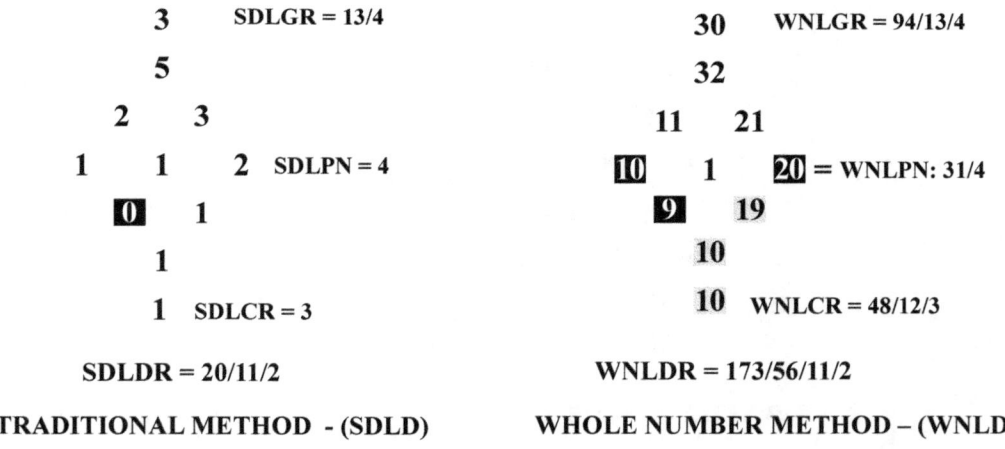

TRADITIONAL METHOD - (SDLD)　　WHOLE NUMBER METHOD – (WNLD)

As with Emma, above, two interim LDs come next. One is an ordinary interim LD while the other uses the 22 from the year number to create a *master number*, interim LD. The personality chosen for study is the opposite of Annie's and Bill's.

Chapter 11 – How to Calculate an Interim LD

EXAMPLE 5: CURTIS JAMES JACKSON III ("50 CENT"): 6 - 7 - 1975 = 35/8.
Curtis is a famous rapper who has turned his life around from that of a ghetto mentality to becoming rich, famous and gaining prestige. The film, *Get Rich or Die Tryin,* in which he stars, tells his sordid life story. In real life, he was actually shot nine times by a rival gang member. 50 Cent's array of LDs provide us with a master number interim LD which is also his WNLD because his day and month numbers are only single digits. However, this man has made an effort to become lawfully rather than unlawfully successful and for those who know his story, his numbers are very interesting when you take his personal history into account. Note the triple 41s in the SDLD (two in his inner square) and one more in the potent position of third goal in the WNLD. (41 bestows the potential to become rich but not everyone does due to individual differences.) As you now know, fame and shame often come with a prominent 17 and 16 combination which remain in all three LD's challenge areas. I wonder if Curtis will use his 11s in the future to educate others from his life experiences (wayshower aspect of SDLDR9 and interim LDR9). Do his LGR12s (Hanged Man) hint at struggle (SDLC31s), for personality transformation and ascension in this lifetime due to multiple 12/21 pairings in his SDLCs and two of his squares?

```
              2       SDLGR = 12/3                    11       LGR = 57/12/3
              5                                       23
          4       1                                 13    10
        7     6     4   SDLPN = 17/8              7    6    4     = LPN: 17/8
          1       2                                 1    2
              1                                        1
              3       SDLCR = 7                       3       LCR = 7
     SDLDR = 36/18/9                       INTERIM LDR = 81/36/18/9
          SDLD                                    INTERIM LD
```

```
                  29       LGR = 111/3
                  41
              13     28
            7     6     22   = LPN: 35/8
              1       16
                  15
                  15       LCR = 47/11/2
         MASTER LDR = 193/157/13/4
         MASTER INTERIM LD also WNLD
```

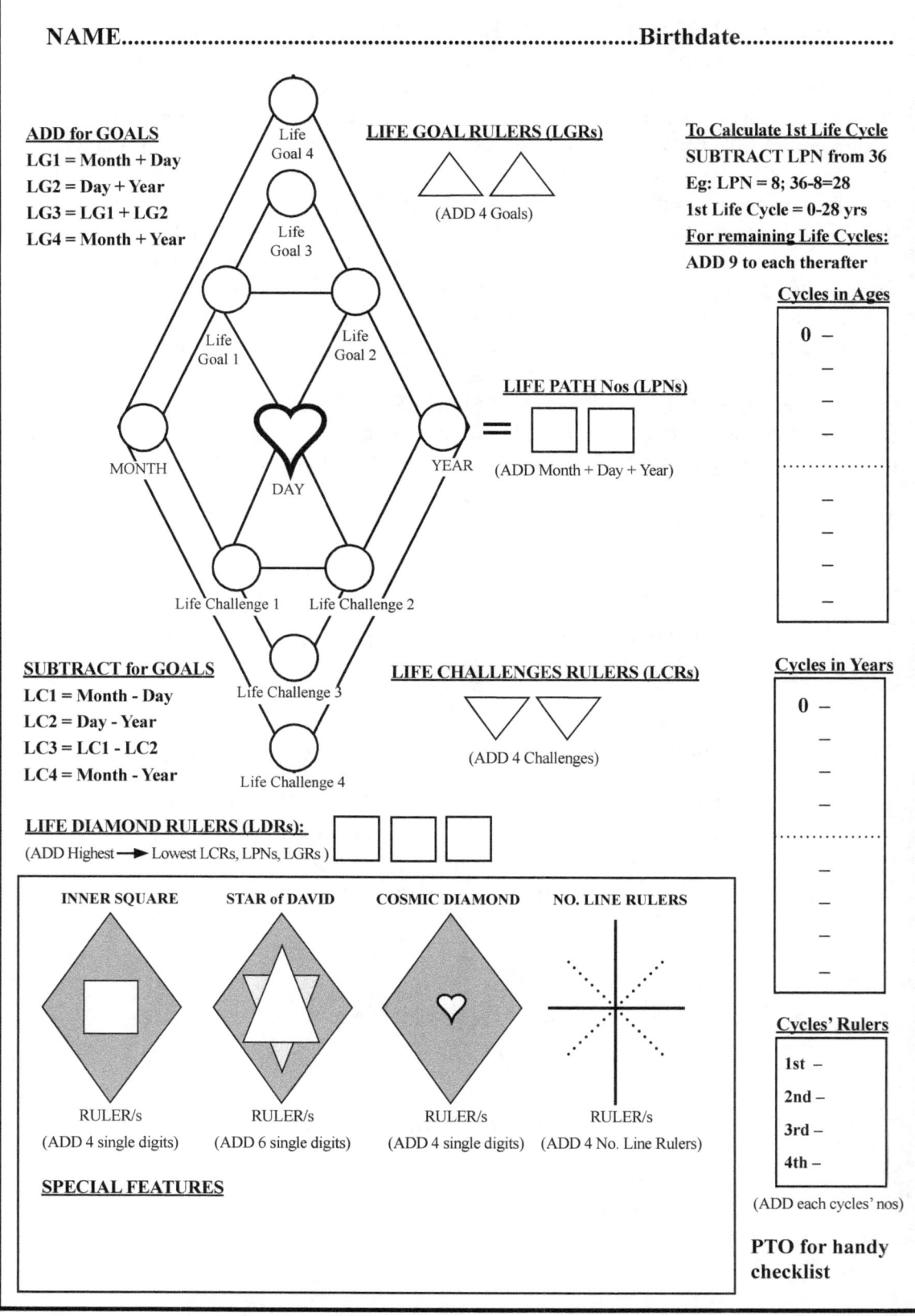

THERE IS LIFE BEYOND THE FOURTH LIFE GOAL

Abbreviated Terms used for *Single Digit Life Diamonds* in this Chapter:

- LD = Life Diamond
- SD = Single Digit
- SDLD = Single Digit Life Diamond
- SDLG = Single Digit Life Goal
- SDLGR = Single Digit Life Goal Ruler
- SDLC = Single Digit Life Challenge
- SDLCR = Single Digit Life Challenge Ruler
- SDLPN = Single Digit Life Path Number
- SDLDR = Single Digit Life Diamond Ruler
- LG/C = A Life Goal and its Life Challenge combination

Abbreviated Terms used for *Whole Number Life Diamonds* in this Chapter:

- WN = Whole Number
- WNLD = Whole Number Life Diamond
- WNLG = Whole Number Life Goal
- WNLGR = Whole Number Life Goal Ruler
- WNLC = Whole Number Life Challenge
- WNLCR = Whole Number Life Challenge Ruler
- WNLPN = Whole Number Life Path Number
- WNLDR = Whole Number Life Diamond Ruler

CHAPTER 12
THERE *IS* LIFE BEYOND the FOURTH LIFE CYCLE

THE FOURTH LIFE CYCLE AND BEYOND – *A Second Chance at LIFE!*

To remain under the fourth life cycle's influence for the rest of the life suited Pythagoras' time when people generally died in their fifties and sixties. But many live beyond 100 years, today. This is almost twice as long as people lived in his day. Therefore, this outdated approach needs to be amended to suit the present day reality that life continues for much longer. It is accomplished by limiting the time span of the fourth life cycle to *nine years only*. When the end of the fourth cycle is reached, it completes a *round* of life. Then the life cycles are recommenced starting at the first life cycle and allotting nine years to each cycle thereafter; it could not be simpler. (Refer to Chapter 5 for calculations that divide life cycles into rounds.)

Research was begun into those who have lived long enough to reactivate old life cycles in order to validate amending this system. From this research, findings showed that *same, but different experiences* were repeated during a matching, reactivated cycle. This phenomenon was commonplace. It corroborated the updated system. Not only that, forecasts for reactivated life cycles could be based upon past experiences as parallel experiences from the past repeatedly re-emerged in them. This provided a sound premise upon which to anticipate that future events and circumstances, whether the same or masquerading in a different guise, were likely to surface at some point during the reactivation of a "twin" cycle. As you will find in two examples that follow, they can even occur very close to exactly the same time in the reactivated cycle.

The best thing about these new methods is that, by renewing life cycles, past mistakes can be corrected as the likelihood of them repeating under each cycle's reactivation is almost guaranteed. You get *a second chance at life!* Not only that, you bring a *new reality and new perspectives* to each reactivated cycle. This is due to accumulating maturity and wisdom from the vicissitudes of life.

If you are at an age when you are reactivating life cycles, reflect on the high points that occurred in the past, during the same cycle being renewed. For example, if it happens to be the first mini-diamond, reflect on the major events, aspirations, thoughts, feelings and actions that manifested during its former activation. Think back to when you were a child, teenager and young adult. Bring back memories about the influential people and friends who helped to shape your life. Then think about where you lived, went to school, began your first job, married or found a partner, bought your first home and possibly started a family. If you happen to be single when you reactivate this cycle for the second time, there is a good chance that you could remarry, start a new career, purchase property or become a grandparent during its renewal; these are its parallel experiences.

When reactivating a cycle, gather as much information about its numbers with a view to forecasting the future partly *based upon earlier experiences*. Apply all of the tools you know. Use SDs, number-pairing and WNs. Do not forget its rulers. To know something of what occurred during a twin cycle's previous activation would be most helpful as this information provides guidelines for what is likely to resurface or redevelop as parallel experiences when it is reactivated.

Perceive the reactivated cycle's numbers as combining to describe the specific arena in which a mixture of new and old takes place. Projections should facilitate extension, consolidation and resolution of past experiences, coupled with embracing new possibilities that ensure ongoing growth, new karma and works. Success depends upon facing and handling the specific opportunities and lessons inherent in each cycle. Avoid enabling past mistakes and outworn attitudes and behaviours to determine the future. Find ways to resolve them and move on and up.

What Reactivated 9-year Cycles Involve
- Calculations that extend the 9-year life cycles *beyond* the fourth life cycle
- Continued SD, WN and Tarot Key analysis
- Recall of experiences during initial cycle activation
- Anticipation of repeat tendencies during each reactivated cycle

An important thing to bring to mind when the first and the second mini-diamonds' cycles are reactivated, is to remember that they are derived directly from the earth or horizontal axis which forms the LD's baseline. Their focus is mainly upon materialism and everyday affairs when they are activated for the first time. However, when mature years are reached, a shift in focus to a deeper appreciation of life becomes more evident. Spiritual influences often enjoy higher prominence during their reactivation with forecasts reflecting a combination of mundane and spiritual projections.

The following case studies break with tradition and present examples of the continuation of life *beyond* the fourth life cycle. Sadly, good case studies are difficult to come by as this can prove to be difficult information to find, yet it is vital to confirming this hypothesis. This is due to most seniors being either unable to pinpoint earlier experiences or live

The Life Diamond

very ordinary lives once retired or do not wish to make their life story public. Reg's life experiences that follow enable us to compare the initial activation of his life cycles with their reactivation.

CASE STUDY: REG – 3DEC1929 = 36/9

REG: 3-12-1929 = 36/9   A = 77   CURRENT LIFE CYCLE: 73 ⇒ 81 YEARS

	6	SDLGR = 21/3		33	WNLGR = 113/3		0 - 27
	3			39			28 - 36
6	6			15	24		37 - 45
							<u>46 - 54</u>
3	3	3 SDLPN = 9	12	3	21 = WNLPN: 36/9		55 - 63
0	0			9	18		64 - 72
	0				9		⇒ 73 - 81
	0	SDLCR = 0			9 WNLCR = 45/9		82 - 90

SDLDR = 30/12/3   WNLDR = 192/21/3

TRADITIONAL APPROACH   WHOLE NUMBER APPROACH CYCLES   9 YEAR CYCLES

Summary of Parallels between First and Fifth Life Cycles

A heavy reliance is placed on letting each data box below speak for itself. Life experiences that demonstrate repetitive themes and mature development are highlighted in each. Note a mixture of extending, paralleling and new experiences occurring during the second activation of Reg's first mini-diamond when compared with its initial activation; this is what you can expect to find.

<u>1st LIFE CYCLE: 0 - 27 YEARS</u> `3+3+6+0=12`	<u>5th LIFE CYCLE: 55 - 63 YEARS</u> `12+3+15+9=39`
• Difficult early life • Overbearing, domineering mother • Left school → entered art college • Art awards and exhibitions • Moved interstate to be in art community • Unsuccessful art career - no money in it • Took over father's building business and became very successful • Local and interstate travel for career	♦ Very unhappy married life (wife controlling and self-serving like mother) ♦ Abundant money-making period ♦ New direction → restaurant trade ♦ Divorce ♦ Overbearing relative bought into business ♦ Sold above ♦ Sold share in large, opulent country home ♦ Psychic abilities germinating

Chapter 12 – There *is* Life Beyond the Fourth Life Cycle

Summary of Parallels between Second and Sixth Life Cycles

Noticeable differences occurred between these twin periods. They provide a wonderful illustration of parallel experiences taking place – variations of living and working in the country during both cycles (24). Two important events occurred that prove the theory that we can re-encounter like experiences during reactivated life cycles; Reg's mother passed away two years into his second cycle's first activation and his overbearing, female relative sold her share in their successful business when exactly two years into its twin, sixth cycle!

2nd LIFE CYCLE: 28 - 36 YEARS	6th LIFE CYCLE: 64 - 72 YEARS
3+3+6+0=12	3+21+24+18=66
▪ At 30, mother passed away	❖ New directions
▪ Continued successful building career	❖ Created country/seaside tourist resort
▪ Much country travel due to building career	❖ A huge financial success
▪ Country life brought entertainment, concerts and dances	❖ Sold gourmet restaurant - relative leaves
▪ Fleeting romances	❖ At 66 remarries - very happy
▪ Several interstate holidays	❖ Sold up everything and moved interstate
▪ Mundane affairs ruling Reg at this point	❖ Psychic abilities and spiritual outlook intensifying

Summary of Parallels between Third and Seventh Life Cycles

Reg's third life cycle equates to The Devil Key, depicting materialistic leanings during its activation – its exoteric connotation. This is plain to see in the third cycle but spiritual interests are burgeoning during the seventh life cycle. With new interests and more mature perspectives, Reg transcends the need to fulfil materialistic desires by replacing them with firmly entrenched, spiritual aspirations and unconditional service – 15 and 33 shifting to esoteric mode.

3rd LIFE CYCLE: 37 - 45 YEARS	7th LIFE CYCLE: 73 - 81 YEARS
6+6+3+0+0+0=15	15+24+39+9+18+9=114
✧ Father passed away	✹ Grandchildren born
✧ At 36 married	✹ New homes
✧ Son born	✹ Spiritual directions and earth energy work
✧ Marital, rural home	✹ Travel: urban, country and interstate due to earth energy work - networking
✧ Dinner parties, social events, friendships	✹ Channel for 'Spiritual Guides, Star Entities'
✧ Career change from building to restaurateur	✹ Documentation of earth energy findings continues
✧ Ruled by materialism, money and status	

The Life Diamond

Although very reluctant to include myself as a case study, I felt forced to do so because, as already mentioned, it is difficult to find people who are willing to share their life story publicly and, at the same time, have experienced clear-cut lifestyle changes between twin cycles to prove their reactivation. I am also a good example of a LPN10 and the decision that must be made whether to choose the 10 or the 1 to subtract from 36 to ascertain the length of the first life cycle. Using this updated system is one way of substantiating both theories in one.

Another way is to use a significant life event to confirm using the higher of the two LPNs and check it against both LPNs especially *when a second round of life cycles has not begun*. Bill Clinton and Alan Bond's life experiences follow mine to substantiate using their higher LPN11 in preference to their LPN2 (same as for Amelia Earhart's LPN11/2: Chapter 10).

LOUISE: 27-6-1939 = 55/10/1   CA = 68   CURRENT LIFE CYCLE: 63 ⇒ 71 YEARS

	1	SDLGR = 12/3		28	WNLGR = 113/3		0 - 26
	1			82			27 - 35
6	4			33 49			36 - 44
							45 - 53
6	9	4 SDLPN = 19/10/1		6 27 22	= WNLPN: 36/9		54 - 62
3	5			21 5		⇒	63 - 71
	2			16			72 - 80
	2	SDLCR = 12/3		16	WNLCR = 45/9		81 - 89
	SDLDR = 43/34/7			WNLDR = 305/35/8			
TRADITIONAL METHOD			**WHOLE NUMBER METHOD**				**9 YEAR CYCLES**

Summary of Parallels between First and Fifth Life Cycles

These two cycles show clear indications of a mixture of experiences that were extensions of the old cycle coupled with paralleling and new experiences emerging in its renewal. The most obvious parallel experiences were the death of my father and the death of my partner which happened *exactly four years into each cycle*. The timing of their deaths, although separated by many years, was exactly one month apart! This revelation was truly inspiring in the light of verifying this updated system. (Note that Reg had similar events two years into each of his second and sixth cycles when two high profile women "left" his life.)

Another major parallel experience can be drawn from marrying in the first and taking a new partner in the fifth cycle. These are exciting details that confirm reactivation of cycles. Other parallels to be noted in the two cycles are: similar but different teaching, surgery, property and inheritances. A major shift towards astrology, Theosophy, metaphysical, and spiritual aspirations occupies the main focus in the reactivated cycle which were quite the opposite of the materialistic leanings that dominated the first (and second) cycle. Lecturing to adults, not children, was another same but different trend resulting from a changing reality that produced new directions.

FIRST LIFE CYCLE: 0 - 26 YEARS 6+9+6+3=24	**FIFTH LIFE CYCLE: 54 - 62 YEARS** 6+27+33+21=87
▪ Born into a large family - controlling mother ▪ Father seriously ill ▪ Father died when I was four ▪ Inheritance passed into mother's care ▪ Surgery ▪ Teaching career - young children ▪ Married a controlling husband ▪ Built home ▪ Extremely ambitious teaching career ▪ Study and promotion ▪ Main focus: career, materialism and status	♦ Travel as lecturer - astrology and metaphysics ♦ New partner - died 4 years into cycle! ♦ Close sister passed away ♦ Inheritance – "divorced" myself from siblings due to malice over sister's estate ♦ Health breakdown and severe depression ♦ Bought and sold property ♦ Surgery ♦ Occult studies, numerology research and writing ♦ Main focus: spiritual aspirations and service

Summary of Parallels between Second and Sixth Life Cycles

Now into my sixth year of my sixth life cycle, several parallel experiences have already occurred during its revival when compared with its twin cycle. The most outstanding example of this would be to use the illustration of the death of my baby boy that occurred under the 9-4-4 of my second mini-diamond. 9-4 can typify the death or loss of a male as well as bringing in a new male or the birth of a son. What I consider to be the paralleling experience of this event when I renewed this mini-diamond was when my treasured son abandoned me soon after entering it (the years did not coalesce this time). It was just like experiencing another death – the loss of another son! Other good examples of same but different life events are easily seen in each cycle's comparisons. Opposites, bringing new, yet similar, experiences, are mostly found in the shift of focus from the mundane to the spiritual.

The Life Diamond

SECOND LIFE CYCLE: 27 - 35 YEARS	**SIXTH LIFE CYCLE: 63 - 71 YEARS**
9+4+4+5=22/4	27+22+49+5=103/4
• Surgery	◆ Dedication to numerology research
• Children born	◆ Books written on numerology findings
• Dedication to teaching career continues	◆ Two grand daughters born
• Death of a son due to a fatal car accident	◆ Advanced breast cancer diagnosed
• Promotion - increased salary	◆ Son 'divorces' mother - severe depression
• Difficult relationships with subordinates	◆ Serious health issues - re-invention of self
• Struggle with workload and health	◆ Meditation and advanced occult studies
• Another promotion - attendant responsibilities	◆ Spiritual directions, service
• Main focus: family, career, material security and status	◆ Main focus: occult studies and research. Completion of books. Goodwill.

Bill Clinton's LD is being reused again, for three purposes; firstly, to further substantiate the theory that we can and indeed do, go beyond the fourth life cycle; secondly, to use his LPN11 instead of his LPN2 to calculate his age cycles; and thirdly to demonstrate how to forecast when someone has just moved into a new cycle. Bill's LPN11 will accelerate him through his cycles placing him in his fifth life cycle during the time of his infamous trial. The numbers in its mini-diamond clearly portrayed this life episode much more so than if we were confined to working with his fourth life cycle using a LPN2.

CASE STUDY: BILL CLINTON

BILL CLINTON: 19-8-1946 = 47/11/2   **CURRENT LIFE CYCLE: 53 ⇒ 61 YEARS**

		1	SDLGR = 16/7		28	WNLGR = 160/7		0 - 25
		3			66			26 - 34
	9	3		27	39			35 - 43
								44 - 52
8	1	2	SDLPN = 11/2	8	19	20 = WNLPN: 47/11/2	⇒	53 - 61
	7	1		11	1			62 - 70
		6			10			71 - 79
		6	SDLCR = 20/2		12	WNLCR = 34/7		80 - 88
	SDLDR = 47/11/2			WNLDR = 241/205/16/7				

TRADITIONAL APPROACH   **WHOLE NUMBER APPROACH**   **9 YEAR CYCLES**

Chapter 12 – There *is* Life Beyond the Fourth Life Cycle

Bill's trial was held on the cusp of his now fifth mini-diamond. Being on the cusp of a cycle signifies the *transition period* when one moves from one cycle to the next. It is good to be able to bring to your attention a case study depicting the *cuspal* period that occurs during a transition between cycles. The cuspal period is the "shadow period" that refers to when the influences of the old cycle have not fully dissipated and are still having subtle effects on the new cycle which is slowly gaining strength. The same can be said of the new cycle – that it subtly influences the end of the old cycle as it is losing power – one waxing as the other wanes. When interpreting this period, both cycles need to be worked together during the first and final years.

Although just into reactivating his first/fifth life cycle, Bill was still under the waning influences of his fourth life cycle. This meant that elements of Bill's fourth cycle were still influencing this cycle during his trial. For example, power struggles, WNLG28, which are easy to picture in a courtroom scene, were still carrying over from the fourth cycle. It, and its WNLC12, The Hanged Man, turned his whole world upside down when his "Judgement Day" arrived (WNLCR11). His newly activated Justice Key brings us to the fifth cycle and its numbers.

Several other fifth cycle numbers combine with 11 to confirm that Bill was reactivating them. For instance, under the growing influence of his now fifth, life cycle, Bill fought (8) his court case (9) to protect his reputation (paired 81 and 91). Bill's SDLG9 depicts the law, legal personnel and lawsuits. Link it to the WNLD's WNLC11 and you get a definite warning of possible litigation proceedings which helps to substantiate the fact that this cycle was being renewed as his life experiences were dominated by the judicial system (11), ethics (9) and broken promises (19) at that time. Also, consider his paired 79 and 17 that perfectly describe the "people's hero's" (paired 79) lawsuit (9) which was globally publicised (97), making him The Star (17) in his own scandalous story (17). Then SDLC7 hints at something hidden – that incriminating dress!

Despite contrary indications, Bill was found not guilty of the charges brought against him and continued to enjoy unprecedented approval ratings in his job as President (19, The Sun). After all, he does have the Sun, Moon and Star, as well as the 10 of Pentacles (78) in this mini-diamond! I guess that we could have expected this outcome as he is indeed blessed with those beautiful numbers! 78 can bring a sudden end to a way of life which occurred soon afterwards when Bill's term of office drew to its natural conclusion and he left the Presidency. 78, as the 10 of Pentacles, often signifies moving house, a redundancy package and/or a comfortable, happy retirement.

Without delving further, all of these numbers gave clear indications of Bill's time in court, retirement and moving house. They verified that his first cycle was being reactivated. We can also say that LPN11 worked extremely well as the number to use to calculate his age cycles.

Next, Alan Bond's case study is being used to exemplify choosing his LPN11 over its LPN2. A major life event is chosen as the catalyst for choosing between them.

The Life Diamond

CASE STUDY: ALAN BOND

ALAN BOND: 22-4-1938 = 47/11/2

```
              7      SDLGR = 28/10/1              7    LGR = 37/10/1
              6                                  15
           8     7                             8     7
         4    4    3  SDLPN = 11/2           4    4    3  = LPN: 11/2
            0    1                              0    1
              1                                  1
              1    SDLCR = 3                     1   LCR = 3
         SDLDR = 42/24/6                   INTERIM LDR = 51/24/6
              SDLD                             INTERIM LD
```

```
              25     LGR = 163/10/1
              69
            26    43
          4    22    21  = LPN: 47/11/2
            18    1
              17
              17   LCR = 53/8
         WNLDR = 263/74/11/2
         WHOLE NUMBER LD
```

ALAN BOND'S winning of the prestigious America's Cup on 26SEP1983, provides an excellent example of choosing his LPN11 over his LPN2 because the numbers of his fourth life cycle best reflect that auspicious event when he was 45. For this momentous occasion, if a LPN2 is used, it places him in the second year of his third LD cycle. On the other hand, if a LPN11 is used, it places him in the second year of his fourth LD cycle. To validate this choice, Alan's life events must match either cycle's numbers. The best way to find which cycle was activated is to pluck each from his LDs and analyse them separately against his life experiences at that time. Their cycle rulers must also be calculated to help with your findings. To methodically analyse each cycle, is the only way to decide which LPN to use when confronted with a LPN11 (or a LPN10).

Chapter 12 – There *is* Life Beyond the Fourth Life Cycle

Prevailing circumstances surrounding an event provide the clues. Your role is to find the numbers that describe it. Cast your eyes over each cycle's numbers to see which best suits the events of the time. Then use the numbers from that cycle to analyse the situation and verify your findings. Both of Alan's third and fourth LD cycles are laid out below for study.

THIRD CYCLES:

	14/5 **LG6** 13/4			95/14/5 **WLG69v** 112/4	
LG8		**LG7** = 15/6	**WLG26**		**WLG43** = 69
LC0		**LC1** = 1	**WLC18**		**WLC1** = 19
	1 **LC1** 2			35/8 **WLC17** 18	
	7 (LG6 + LC1)			86/14/5 (WLG69+WLC17)	

THIRD CYCLE SD RULER = 23/5   **THIRD CYCLE WN RULER = 174/12/3**

FOURTH CYCLES:

	11/2 **LG7** 10/1			29/11/2 **LG25** 46/10/1	
MONTH **4**		**3** YEAR = 7	MONTH **4**		**21** YEAR = 25/7
	5 **LC1** 4			21/3 **LC17** 38/11/2	
	8 (LG7+LC1)			42/6 (LG25+LC17)	

FOURTH CYCLE SD RULER = 15/6   **FOURTH CYCLE WN RULER = 67/13/4**

From the above, Alan's fourth SDLD cycle is favoured as it depicts his life events for that time extremely well. One only has to think back to this momentous occasion and remember the blaze of publicity that surrounded him in his moment of glory. Paired 37 (SDLD) and hidden WN38 (from 21 year + LC17) beautifully reflect this as they are linked to the media. When you are endeavouring to prove or disprove a theory, ideally, neither of these numbers should appear anywhere in his third SDLD or WNLD cycle otherwise that would confuse your findings.

This cycle's hidden 10s as opposed to 1s in the third cycle provide a very good indication that something momentous is likely to occur due to 10 signifying culmination, climax and finalisation. You also get year 21 and hidden 21 appearing in the fourth cycle but not in the third. They signify much the same as 10 and 21 reinforce a final achievement here.

The fourth cycle in the WNLD contains the Knight of Wands (25) and two Queens of Swords (52). They intensified Alan's unwavering focus (Knight) and shrewdness (Queen) on winning the America's Cup. The SD cycle ruler 15 reverses to 51, the ambitious King of Swords. Having kings and queens with 17, The Star, in these cycles all combine to point to rising to the top or gaining recognition in some way which go well together to fit this grand occasion. All of Australia saw Alan as the knight in the Knight of Wands, WNLG25: an inspirational, active, crusading knight, which was very much fanned by media acclaim and coverage (paired 37 and hidden 38) that he received. His top SDLG7, The Chariot, enabled him to exploit his talents to the full and be in charge of his current life circumstances. The enormous popularity and encouragement that he received from the Australian people was also reflected in this 7. To make this even more exciting, this WN cycle's ruler is 67, the Knight of Pentacles. This Knight signifies the proud realisation of one's labours! Further to this, this is an auspicious cycle for Alan because it contains his LPNs and interim LD ruling numbers, with 47 in particular, signifying the potential to manifest a Life Path dream.

If Alan's LPN11 and not 2 was chosen to work with, his LPN11 reveals that he won the prestigious America's Cup during the second year of his fourth life cycle, not his third. The numbers and Keys of the fourth cycle describe this famous event better.

By contrast, if his LPN2 was used, Alan would have been activating his third life cycle's numbers at that time. This cycle better describes when he was busy building his commercial enterprise under his SDLG/C 6/1 pair and WNLG/C 69/17 pair. 69 in particular signifies a burgeoning money-making period. This was the period when Alan was using his 69's Ace of Pentacles for his shrewd real estate deals, loans and investments. These are traits that this Ace specifically depicts. His LPN11 would put him at the third cycle for that period of his life.

When Alan reactivated his first cycle, he totally ruined his reputation ending up in jail (cycle ruler 16) for massive embezzlement (paired SD 44, 48, 40s and 80s). Note this cycle's emphasis on money numbers and the Fool's folly in the SDLC0! Also note WNLG26, the number of greed. SD cycle ruler 16, activated his "fall from Grace" or "Humpty Dumpty" syndrome. Linking 16 to his WNLC17s, the fallen "star" and active WNLC18, the number of tragedy and the reckless Fool (0) made an awesome group of numbers that together brought about his toppling from power *if* his empire (16) was built upon shaky foundations.

(To confirm the above findings, Alan's Yearly Diamonds should be calculated. You will find them in Book 2, Chapter 12)

Some Final Points to Ponder

Once the first life cycle is over, astrological associations can be made to the lengths of time it takes to live through the long periods that separate the beginning and end of each cycle's reactivation. Eg, 27 years elapse from the end of a 9-year cycle to the beginning of its next activation. If a full round of four, 9-year cycles from beginning to end is calculated, 36 years have elapsed.

Lunar and Saturn return astrological associations can be approximated to each 27 year period. Three Jupiter returns equate to the 36 year period which standardise a round. More fascinating however, is that Jupiter rules the Wheel of Fortune Key which in turn governs the laws of cyclicity and change and the mechanisms of involution and evolution.

THE NATURE OF NUMBERS AND TAROT KEYS

CHAPTER 13
THE NATURE OF NUMBERS AND TAROT KEYS

Numerology and Tarot address the infinite range of possibilities that each of us has the potential to attain *according to the nature and position of our numbers, our level of evolution and personal preferences.* What this means is that we can choose to become a saint or a sinner or develop somewhere in between.

LDs have similar properties and can also be expressed at different levels in the above ways but there is another factor to consider. LDs are self-help tools that are based upon sequential stages of chronological growth containing varying dimensions and layers within their cycles that are governed by the element of time. Where you are now is not where you will be in the next moment, day, year or decade; you bring a renewed reality to each interpretation of a LD which allows for penetration of its deeper layers. This implies that all that LDs signify, cannot be revealed from a single interpretation as their layers cannot be fully realised or accessed until the element of time has taken its course. Liken a LD to the proverbial "onion" and its layers. As more wisdom and more experience, knowledge and understanding are gained over time, layers within the LD can be peeled away to uncover its next "hidden" layer.

WAYS THAT NUMBERS AND TAROT KEYS ARE INFLUENCED

The following list provides some examples of how the expression of a number or Tarot Key is coloured by a plethora of existing determinants; it is by no means exhausted.

- Current level of evolution
- Racial heritage, religion and family conditioning
- Sex, age and status
- Current spiritual, mental, emotional and physical focus/states
- Predilections (ethics, beliefs, politics, work, likes, dislikes, specialties, habits)
- Current environmental conditions and security status
- Current goals and dreams
- Ability to discriminate and make right choices
- Personal accountability for thoughts, words and actions

THE NATURE OF NUMBERS AND TAROT KEYS

Background information plays a major role in extracting appropriate guidelines from a LD's extensive range of possibilities. Therefore all LD indications must be carefully weighed and measured against the above points. This needs to be done in an effort to ascertain how to apply the correct level of interpretation to its numbers and Keys. Always be mindful that every LD and Key embodies infinite levels of possibilities in order to accommodate the vast ranges of human potential, capabilities and levels of attainment. Another important point to bear in mind when interpreting a LD is to address the fact that its numbers and Tarot Keys either depict you or represent others. When it relates to others, their personal idiosyncrasies, perceptions, prevailing moods and circumstances – whatever is affecting *them* – will impact on *you* thereby affecting and colouring your responses. Therefore, it is essential that you learn to distinguish between when numbers are describing someone or something other than you.

To put this another way, when numbers and Keys are active, they need to be seen in the light of either being *the initiator* when *you* are the instigator, agitator, aggressor, inciter or mover – or the *recipient* when you are the object, target or victim of another's' actions or external forces – or *inert* when you and/or others choose to be indifferent, complacent, submissive or passively resistant. Numbers and their Keys are also expressed in a constructive, consolidating, modifying or destructive mode. There are times when they represent corporate bodies and institutions and their personnel. At other times, the element of the unknown or unforeseen can be dominant factors. To be ever mindful that their fields of experience can be activated in these ways is essential to accurate forecasting.

The above points are fundamental determinants that need reinforcing at this time because they directly impinge upon how numbers and their Keys are likely to manifest. Knowing that they have the capacity to materialise in a variety of levels, ways and varying degrees of intensity, helps us to learn how to apply them to our lives and make the most of their attributes and guidance. Ignorance on the other hand places us at the mercy of their energies and forces which often culminate as undesirable outcomes.

When we exercise our knowledge and understanding of how numbers and Keys operate, we are utilising our free will and our ability to learn to use and control their energies, forces and specific attributes. We do this when we consciously and discriminately exercise their powers while concurrently taking into account prevailing conditions and circumstances that happen to be active at the time or might be activated in the foreseeable future. However, there are times when karma and the unknown and unforeseen become overriding factors acting as catalysts that introduce, reinforce, consolidate or finalise certain details or phases in our lifelong journey. This is when we feel that we are at the mercy of things beyond our control until the luxury of hindsight makes what we have experienced, and why we have experienced, it clear.

At times, taking control of your destiny can be confrontational *only if you let it*. This results from uncovering single or groups of numbers or Keys that have inherent negative connotations. There can be nothing more unnerving to those who succumb to fear and trepidation when these occasions arise. Unfortunately these people are easily put off by their fears which is a pity because the solution to their problems often lies in their numbers and Keys.

When faced with what appears to be a negative influence stemming from certain numbers, the antidote is often found by initiating counteractive strategies that mitigate it. The way to do this is to look for or imagine situations in which their opposites can be employed and formulate strategies that cultivate desired outcomes. As simple as it might sound, this is one way to magickally manipulate negative potential with the intent of initiating desired outcomes that are in agreement with beliefs and spiritual aspirations. Consequently, the inherent tests, trials and tribulations that appear in the negatives can be turned into triumphs. Sometimes, all that is needed to promote positive outcomes is a change in attitude that thwarts the continuance of entrenched, disadvantaging behaviours. (Book 2's Chapter *How to Work with Numbers and the Tarot* depicts 31 to exemplify this.)

The trick is to see a "testing" number's gifts in a positive light when pitted against the background of life knowing that negative experiences, as unpleasant as they may be, are paradoxically our best teachers. They undoubtedly promote greater understanding and the attaining of wisdom by presenting specific lessons that guarantee personal growth. Especial gifts are always contained in them that open doors to new horizons. In reality, they are doorways to growth. The way to gain access to them is invariably through the conscious application of self-correctional behaviours via the pain of adjustment.

THE ROLE OF TAROT

Combining Tarot with numerology adds an abundance of tried and true information to it that has accumulated over the ages. Utilising Tarot expands numerology's traditional, number range from 0 to 9 to 0 to 78. Because Tarot also embraces positive *and* negative likelihoods, 156 delineations become instantly accessible as it has 78 positive interpretations and 78 negative interpretations. Access to this extensive range of Tarot delineations immensely increases the scope of predicting reliable outcomes when you consider the limited range of numbers that have been employed until now.

This Tarot/number-range can be increased further. Some compound numbers in the range from 79 to 99 can be reversed allowing additional access to the Tarot. These numbers are 81, 82, 83, 84, 85, 86, 87 and 91, 92, 93, 94, 95 and 96. For example 81 can be interpreted as 18 and 82 as 28 and so on. If a number like 97 exceeds the Tarot range, it can be reversed to create 79 and reduced to 16. 16 can then be reversed to create 61 and then reduced to 7. Finally, 7 is reversed to bring forth 70. This procedure opens up 97's full set of numbers to access its other dimensions.

SINGLE DIGITS HAVE A COMPOUND NUMBER REVERSAL

Because a hidden zero holds a place before all single digits, a number pair can be formed from them such as 80 from 8. Several of these pair's delineations and images are dissimilar but 3 and 30 are unusual as both suggest prosperity. 1 and 10 are another such pair as each depicts life and death in albeit different ways. Ponder these Tarot Key pairs to gain further insights.

THE ROLES OF THE TEN AND ITS UNIT DIGIT WITHIN COMPOUND NUMBERS

The ten and its unit digit within a compound number have their own individual yet unified role to play when esoterically expressed. Imagine them performing as a duet. Each plays a different role within the harmony. The tens number takes the lead acting as a vehicle for its unit digit's qualities and characteristics to be expressed through itself. Consequently, the unit is coloured and modified by its ten and vice versa. For example, the *strength* of the 1's qualities and characteristics will be evident by its *position* in the compound number. It will either be "up front" in its expression if a ten or, seeking expression *through* the ten by adding further dimensions to it if a unit. Therefore, although the ten digit is dominant, it is also infused with the qualities and characteristics of its unit – the two synchronise to become one.

To cite an example, this synchronicity can be found in the subtle differences at work in 12 and 21. In 12, the dominant, self-sufficient 1 actually veils a soft heart at its core (2) when its sharp veneer is penetrated. One of my dearest sisters was born on the 12th of the 12th. My pet name for her was "The General" (she actually worked at a military hospital as a very senior nurse and earned the rank of Major in the army reserves – no small feat in those days!). Her external self was officious, stern and stiff – the 1. But, become injured or upset, her sympathetic, caring 2 shone through her austere 1, for she was in actual fact the sweetest, kindest person you could know (2). In her senior years, although quite ill, she strove to better the conditions of the elderly through political channels – her 2. Despite her somewhat stoical demeanour (1), she was much loved by all and many attended her funeral.

I have experienced just the opposite in the 2 in 21, which masks a strong, self-serving will (1) behind a soft guise (2). To coin a phrase, 21s can be like the proverbial "iron fist in a velvet glove". I have a friend born on the 21st who has a very sweet demeanour. But, she is a typical pessimistic 2-type. She is critical of others, whinges and whines about everything and into the "why me" sort of thing. She smiles as she offers her friendship and support but dig behind the 2 and you will find that it is all on *her* terms – her 1 coming through her 2! So, when you least expect it, a rather dominant 1 can suddenly pop out, seeking dominance rather than cooperation. Another trait is seen when promises of assistance under the projected sympathetic, caring guise of the 2 are reneged on. Can you see the differences between how the numbers in a 12 and a 21 can be modified by the positions that they hold in each number?

To put things in a different way, the ten is the instrument through which its unit works. Together they are complete like a tap cannot run without water or the boat will not sail without wind or a book is blank without its words. The tap, boat and book are the instruments in each case representing a ten that provides the medium through which its unit can be expressed.

TENS NUMBERS

By their nature, tens numbers are extremely powerful. They always require special consideration. This is mainly due to the ten's zero and the fact that it raises the frequency levels of its root digit by one or several octaves thereby intensifying its effects. Extra potency emanates from the zero as it is pregnant with budding potential. Therefore, things are bound to happen in more productive, prolific, profitable or obstructive, destructive ways.

Always give tens numbers special treatment bearing in mind that they are ten times more powerful than their root digit. Tens numbers behave similarly to master numbers. They operate at higher vibrational levels which consistently demand more by intensifying experiences and outcomes. Greater levels of joy, success and good fortune, responsibility or stress are commonly experienced whilst under their influence. Old ideas suggest that protection is inherent in a ten's zero. This view appears to enjoy some credibility. 20 for example, sometimes manifests a miracle of some kind. On the other hand, 10, 20 and 40 are tens numbers that often present a crisis of some description or portend a death. There are so many variables to weigh and consider that it is imperative that caution and flexibility are used when interpreting powerful numbers.

The basic quality of a ten is that it always signals the *culmination* of something while simultaneously signalling some form of *new beginning or emergence*. Take any ten's age for example. It not only completes a decade but also heralds the beginning of a new decade as a *new reality* is birthed at its beginning and developed until the next ten's age is reached beginning the process over again.

A ten's attributes must be carefully measured against a person's abilities, circumstances and level of evolution in an effort to ascertain its correct application. Always take into account that every number embodies infinite levels of possibilities in order to accommodate vast ranges within human ability and development. This must be done when considering the innate potential of any number in relation to its subject – especially when dealing with a high tens number like 90 or any very high number, for that matter.

Tens "Gifts" *promote personal growth via extension of the self* as a result of the many trials and tribulations that need to be overcome while under their influence. Often hidden talents, greater strength of character and unknown capabilities are exposed during tens' "testing" times regardless of whether these periods are experienced as positive or negative.

MASTER NUMBERS

Master numbers are treated in the same way as tens numbers because greater demands and higher expectations apply to them, also. Therefore, experiences are usually intensified making many demands which challenge their recipient to operate at higher levels. *Multi-tasking* is a keyword that comes to mind. When a master number appears, know that you have the ability to juggle more balls in the air or imagine that you are being promoted and, as a result, have more responsibilities and expectations placed upon you because you have demonstrated that you are capable of handling them.

However, there is a subtle difference between a ten and a master number. It is that the *completion and emergence* factors in a ten do not apply to the master number as *mastering something* does not apply to a ten. Nevertheless, in their specific ways each describes evolution and the potential to take things to the next level.

WHERE TO LAY EMPHASIS – THE AUTHENTIC OR THE REVERSED NUMBER?

Another important detail requires attention. This is when you find yourself confronted with a compound number and its reversal and you need to decide which of the two is the stronger. Is it the authentic compound number or its reversal that is dominant? My developing view on this is that it is the reversed or hidden compound number because the actual number seems to be more automatically expressed as it is less restrained by not being obscured. Take 35 and 53 for example. If 35 is the present number, its traits would be more readily apparent whereas 53 would appear as part of the psyche that is struggling to emerge.

35 and 53, as a pair, happen to be two very different numbers. If you take out their Tarot Keys you will find this to be graphically so. 35's image is that of a standing figure that appears to be wearied by life's accomplishments (they are signified by the Wands in the background) while 53, on the other hand, depicts an energetic knight on horseback with sword held aloft charging in or out of life's circumstances whichever the case may be. Each Key clearly shows two starkly different ways to materialise. The visible number may be more automatically or comfortably expressed whilst its reversal may indicate symptoms of a yearning or a striving to manifest what it indicates. In 35/53's case, a way of interpreting each is to see 35 as being stuck in a rut or an unpleasant situation and 53 as yearning to be free of its encumbrance. In an effort to establish which of the pair is dominant, judge which characteristics are more overtly expressed and those that are "latent". Then ascertain which number or Key is being more overtly expressed for *that time* as they can quickly switch roles.

This is an example of another illustration of how to use the Tarot Keys' images to distinguish between obvious and subtle effects. If 73 is the authentic number, anticipate seeing circumstances already unfolding in the life that encourage the development of self-reliance stemming from the effects of experiencing loss and/or hardship. If these factors are dominant, then 37, being 73's reversal, may be expressed as a yearning to be wealthy, to be highly regarded, to achieve status or be noticed or to have things come more easily and not have to strive so hard or suffer being alone in the world. 37's yearnings for success or life to be compassionate and/or caring or indulgent are not to be viewed as "bad" things. They may well represent the driving force behind the seemingly oppressed 73 to learn ways to make life better or to learn the paradox of *richness in less* or the *richness of developing Inner Light, Trust and Faith.* Herein lie important clues that show the way out of 73's seemingly oppressed conditions.

Being able to work with compound numbers in this manner might open up a clever way to discern where the emphasis lays in this life by using the actual and its hidden number to uncover obvious and obscured life directions that are latent within each. Maybe the overt number could be perceived as old work being brushed up on whilst the covert number could be perceived as new work for this lifetime? If these notions were found to be so, then the covert number would reveal hidden, present life possibilities.

When dealing with paired core numbers in a LD, I tend to regard the heart number as the tens number in each case. If the heart number happens to be a 6, then "sixty whatever" is the "present" or authentic number while its reversal, "something 6", is the number struggling to emerge. When pairing numbers from the cosmic diamond, I use the month and the year numbers as the tens number as they are "given" numbers because their goal and challenge are contrived from them. When pairing the numbers from the spiritual axis, I read them as going upwards for the top pair and going downwards for the bottom pair regarding the third LG/C as being the tens number in each case.

NUMBERS AND TAROT KEYS AS INDIVIDUAL OPERATORS

There is yet another idiosyncrasy about numbers and their corresponding Tarot Keys that needs to be addressed. It is when you become aware that a number acts as a separate entity in its own right with the same being said for a Tarot Key. These are the occasions when either the number or the Tarot Key appears to be completely "divorced" from the other and cannot be merged. Either the number or the Key clearly signifies which is the major tool to employ in the divination. However, it pays to check both out before reaching that conclusion, just to be certain. 40 and its Page of Cups Key come to mind. They present a good example of when the number and its Key operate more or less independently from each other. For example, 40 as a number in its own right is often found to be experienced as a testing time when things tend to unfold in onerous ways. The Page of Cups Key on the other hand, does not give this indication as it often presages a birth or something joyous in the making. (The final chapter in Book 2 covers this phenomenon in detail.)

OPPOSITE DEPICTIONS IN SOME TAROT KEY PAIRS

To make a further distinction, some Tarot Key pairs by themselves, depict clearly opposite scenarios. A good example of this is when you compare the images and meanings of the Tower with its pair the 7 of Swords. Look at each and you will see that the Tower depicts being unceremoniously evicted by forces beyond your control while its reverse, the 7 of Swords depicts a *planned* escape. To cite another example, 7 as The Chariot shows being in control of a situation whereas 70 depicts procrastination and juggling opposing situations in an effort to harmonise constantly changing conditions. They are enlightening when viewed as each other's reckoners. 7 has a tendency to become too one-pointed, rigid and/or controlling. 70 disturbs the status quo via changing circumstances and conditions that teach adaptability. When combined, the ability to remain calmly in control amid periods or situations dogged by flux and change is the desired point of attainment. Looked at in this light, 7 and 70 are the perfect antidote for each other when either goes to extremes.

37 and 73, 35 and 53, 26 and 62 and 46 and 64, are other excellent examples that show stark differences between how Tarot Key pairs can represent opposing aspects. Copy 7 and 70's example above to see how one Key can give the answer or remedy to the other if it is negatively inclined. For example, Key 45's answer to its despondency lies in Key 54. Here we see the Page "clearing the air" and ridding himself of life's obstructions. Being a sword key, it suggests that one needs to be pro-active and a tad ruthless to do this.

NUMBER, TAROT KEY OR TAROT SUIT INTENSIFICATION

Repetitious numbers or Tarot Keys or Tarot Suits signal an *intensification* of a particular field of expression. They help to establish where to place *emphases* and how to *time* anticipated eventualities.

FINALLY

In conclusion, the propositions expounded in this book are in their infancy. An open mind is required to test and accept or reject what is being put forward. I hope that fellow seekers will become involved in this process and bring to it something of their own, thereby helping to make a unique contribution to this science. I strongly urge that research is carried out in your life and the lives of famous, infamous and familiar people to validate these propositions for yourself. My advice to you is to think outside the square, give *your* ideas a try and find what works best for *you*.

Further insights into the nature of numbers and their Tarot Keys are expanded upon in Books 2, 3 and 4. They provide different observations and aspects to ponder; in particular, refer to Book 2 and Book 3's final chapters.

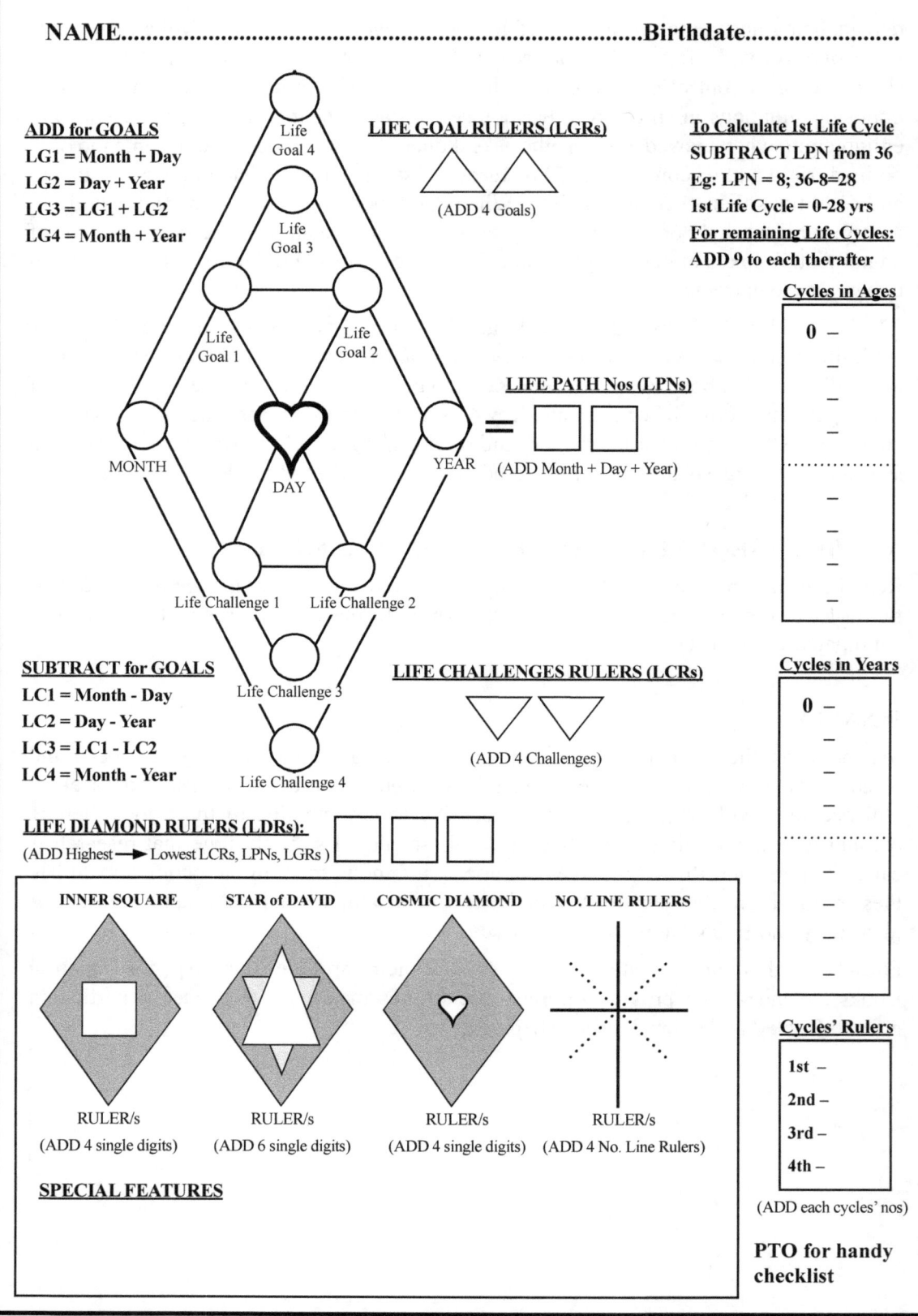

APPENDICES

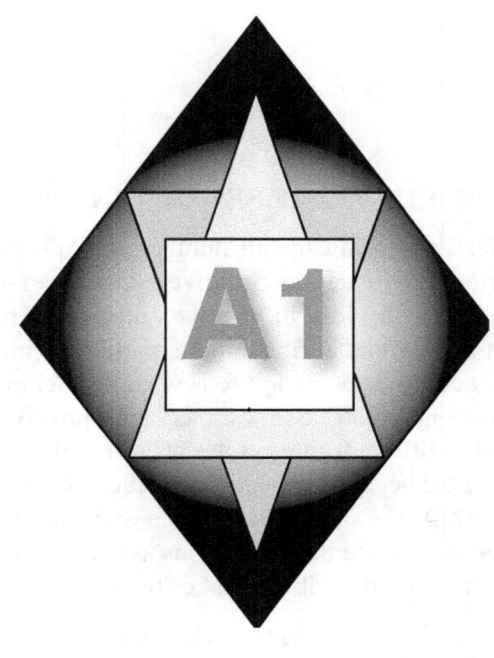

PREAMBLE TO APPENDIX 1

HOW NUMBERS FROM 0 TO 99 ARE SET OUT IN APPENDIX 1

The heading "opportunities" appearing for all numbers in Appendix 1 embraces both the positive and negative attributes of each, as negative experiences invariably veil important lessons that, without fail, eventually lead to positive outcomes. The term "gifts" represents what I perceive to be the most special attribute that a particular number possesses. The idea of being able to ultimately achieve success in life is what lies behind the use of both of these terms. In this way, all experiences can be viewed as being positive. To perceive a negative as an intrinsic "gift" sheds a different light on the way in which we have worked with the significance and meaning of the negative aspects of numbers, heralding a welcome change in viewpoint and perception. Apply the same notion to the word "Karma". It engenders the idea of retribution but, when seeing it in the light of actions as continuing adjustment according to our life works, as Paul Foster Case describes it, takes the punitive sting out of it.

Bear in mind that this branch of extended numerical representation is in its infancy; hence the interpretations that follow are by no means exhaustive nor are they set in concrete. Please view them as a springboard to greater things. Add and delete, as you become more accustomed to each number's unique qualities, nature and attributes. The delineations for each number are based upon actual life events drawn from observations and research data.

Each Number in Appendix 1 is treated in the following ways:

1. Because the LD's numbers and cycles are either lifelong or long-term, interpret them as having enduring, developmental qualities.
2. Each number is linked to its Tarot Key for quick conversion to the Tarot.
3. Opportunities describe probable positive and negative outcomes.
4. Gifts refer to the most rewarding features found in each number.
5. Tens and Master Numbers accompany their related root digit, as there are subtle links from one to the other. Consequently, you will find 1, 10 and 11 up to 9, 90 and 99 grouped together. This group precedes all compound numbers which begin at 12.
6. Interpretations for each compound number's reversal from 12 onwards appear as a pigeon pair, eg 12 is followed by 21; 49 is followed by 94.

APPENDIX 1

NUMBERS 0 ⇒ 99 and their MEANINGS

0

Tarot Equivalent: The Fool or Universal Source - Ain Soph.

Opportunities: Firstly, 0 signifies two things in one. It signals a state of preparedness and readiness for a new cycle/phase/project to commence when it is a 0 or, it can signal the *full completion* of a cycle/phase/project when it is a 22. As a 0, it is **action poised and ready to go!** 0 signifies a stage of readiness to begin a *higher phase* of spiritual development or to take a skill, project or business to *higher levels* of attainment, production, expansion and so on. It contains all of the necessary ingredients to accomplish this in a most individualistic way, which is coloured by its ruling tens digit if it has one. When 0 appears with a tens' number it *raises* its vibrational rate, thereby *intensifying* experiences according to the tens' numbers' qualities and attributes. They are raised to *new vibrational heights* performing like master numbers. 0 contains unlimited potential and free choice that can have severe ramifications if wrong choices are made under its influence. Unlimited potential and possibilities are present in the "pregnant, awaiting state" of the 0. 0 can be likened to the "womb of matter" - the breeding ground of each and every possibility where literally everything that is created has its inception. Other 0 attributes are: Utopian ideals. Carefree nature. Freedom of expression. Open to risk-taking. Lacks self-discipline. Ruled by Uranus.

Gifts: *Evolution!* Upward, spiralling growth. Raising the bar. Initiatory stages. Protection.

1

Tarot Equivalent: The Magician

Opportunities: All 1s signify efforts to concentrate energies and forces in order to manifest one's own identity, creative powers, and special skills. Issues pertaining to self-esteem, self-worth and self-realisation. Struggle to develop independence and self-awareness because often dominated by others until pro-active independence is achieved. Rebelliousness and resentment towards authority figures and organisations develops due to self-expression being inhibited. Learns best from direct experience. Does not like to be told what to do or how to do it - sometimes to own detriment. New beginnings. Originality. Initiator. Inventor. Pioneer. Leadership ability. Talented. Skilled. Resourceful. Writer. Literature. Medicine. Dominance issues. Assertiveness rather than aggressiveness. Selfishness. Life and death sometimes, especially with 4, 10, 13, 15, 16, 17, 18, 19, 20, 21, 22, 27, 40, 46, 55 or 64. Ruled by Mercury.

Gifts: Development of self-awareness. Learning self-sufficiency. Focussing powers.

Tarot Equivalent: The Wheel of Fortune

Opportunities: 10 is 1 at a higher level of expression. Divine protection but not to be abused or taken for granted. Creative and innovative drive of the 1 intensified. Aspirations. Increased power. Goal-setting. Reputation. Publicity. Rotation, cyclicity. Ups and downs. Temporary states of existence. Remaking of the self. Opposites, such as: success/failure, give/take, gains/losses, good/bad luck, and good vs. evil. Issues to do with sexuality. Taking things to their conclusion. Beginning over again but at a more advanced level. Generosity. Plastic surgery. Culmination may mean new beginnings, death or greater expression of independence. Promotion or increased powers. Inheritance. End of life. Dissolution of outmoded forms. Man-made and natural laws. Death sometimes, especially with 1, 4, 13, 15, 16, 17, 18, 19, 20, 21, 22, 40, 41, 46, 64 or 55. Rules the hips, buttocks and blood circulation. Ruled by Jupiter.

Gifts: Completion. Originality taken to advanced levels. Regeneration, renewal and growth.

Tarot Equivalent: Justice

Opportunities: 11 is a Master Number. It intensifies 1 and 10 attributes. 11 highlights the relationship factor between you and life. Developed sense of comparison. Sees differences through related connections. Spirituality. Metaphysics. Insightful. Foresight. Visionary. Idealism. Perfectionism. Acutely perceptive. Accuracy. Hypersensitivity. Allergies. Equality. Impartiality. Self-righteous. Prudish. Duality. Procrastination. Dependence/independence issues. Victim/saviour complex. Self matters. Self-focus. Independence/control issues. Identity issues. False modesty. Nervousness. Guilt. Fear. Jumping to conclusions. Love of beauty and culture. Humanitarian. Teacher. Education. Judgement. Stocks and shares. Politics/politician. Innate business sense. Partnerships, marriage/divorce, contracts. Surgery. Karma. Governs kidneys, loins and lumbar region of spine. Ruled by Libra.

Gifts: Ability to correctly weigh and measure the outcome of actions as a result of the development of discrimination and right reasoning. Mediation and resolution. Reaching mutually agreeable outcomes. Increased psychic sensitivity. Meditation.

Appendix 1

2

Tarot Equivalent: The High Priestess

Opportunities: All 2s basically represent opposites, conciliation, compromise, relativity, duality of forces and balance via disturbance. Relationships, partnerships and unions of all kinds - also separations. Diplomats and diplomacy. Mutually acceptable negotiations. Peaceful revolution; seeking peace via non-violent means. Mood swings; moody. Finances, trade, banks, real estate, transport and travel. Surgeons and surgery. War or warring factions. Ambiguity. Things slow to develop. Martyr. Great sensitivity to others. A commonality with others. Crass manipulator for own ends. Co-dependence issues. Taking second place. Putting others needs before your own. "Doormat" syndrome. Mealy-mouthed. Brooding. Reflection and duplication; things happening twice. Reflection of opposites eg. life/death; war/peace; truth/deception; active/passive; cause/effect. Cannot say no. "People-pleaser"; pleases everyone ending up pleasing no-one. Self-negating. Manipulator. Procrastinator. Confusion. Stupidity. Self-pity. Avoidance behaviours. Ruled by the Moon.

Gifts: Diversity. Arbitration. Wisdom.

20

Tarot Equivalent: Judgement

Opportunities: 20 expresses 2 at higher levels. Divine protection from the 0 but not to be abused or taken for granted. The masses. Extreme conditions, increased responsibilities, demands and workload. Enormous fortitude. Abundant energy reserves. Potential for great achievements from stretching, striving and straining of the self. Ability to persist against great odds. Ability to withstand heavier burdens and increased stress, tension or pressure. Great gains and/or hidden talents surface from hardship. Stressful situations. Important decisions. Determining matters. Putting off the inevitable only to have to face greater obstacles later on. Bringing something of long standing to a close. Executives and administrators. Illness; major surgery. Removal of a body part. Cancer related issues. Life-changing experience. Renewal. Miracles. Miracle cure. Life threatening experience or death sometimes, especially with 1, 4, 13, 15, 16, 17, 18, 19, 10, 21, 22, 40, 46, 64 or 55. Ruled by Pluto.

Gifts: Transformation. Renewal of something. The 'Phoenix' syndrome.

22

Tarot Equivalent: The Fool

Opportunities: Also refer to 0. 22 is a Master Number. It intensifies 2 and 20 attributes. Significant time in your life. Rise to power and glory. Genius. Far-reaching abilities. Risk-taking, either courageous

The Life Diamond

or reckless. Impulsive, knee-jerk actions. Scientific work/interests. Mathematics. Numerology. Architecture. Carpentry. CEO's. Large corporations. Stocks and shares. Public servant or employee within large corporations. Large negotiations. The public. Public recognition. Seeking those of like mind. Unions. Joining groups. Humanitarian. Utopian ideals. Increased pressure and demands. Severity. Crisis. Psychic curse. Unplanned turn of events. Life-changing or threatening event. State of health thwarts attainment of goals. Surgery. Loss, grief, bereavement. Death sometimes, especially with 1, 4, 13, 15, 16, 17, 18, 19, 10, 20, 21, 40, 46, 64 or 55. Sometimes high-profile funeral. Shin, ankle problems. Ruled by Uranus.

Gifts: Ability to handle large enterprises or undertakings. Great work.

3

Tarot Equivalent: The Empress

Opportunities: All 3s basically represent growth and expansion, birth, children, relatives, friends, social events, creativity, artistic and literary expression, languages and scholarliness. Also, communication, celebration, entertainment, excitement and short distance travel. Social activities. Fertility/sterility, pregnancy, miscarriage or abortion. Self-indulgence. Superficiality. Love affairs. Tendency to overwork, scatter, have 'too many irons in the fire' and flighty. Easily distracted from goals, directions or projects - always something else that appears more alluring. Something in the making. Limitations to creativity. Deprivation. Wears heart on sleeve. "Foot in mouth" disease. Interfering. Gossip-mongering. Pretence. Tells lies. At its highest, 3 represents wisdom and worth, harmony and action, perfect love, tenderness and soul force. At its lowest it signifies the damned, the infernal judges and the infernal furies - the wrath of God. Ruled by Venus.

Gifts: Manifestation of ideas/talents. Understanding. Abundance. Happiness and joy. Pro-creativity. Strong maternal tendencies.

30

Tarot Equivalent: The Four of Wands

Opportunities: In 30, all 3 attributes are capable of manifesting at higher levels. Divine protection but not to be abused or taken for granted. Contentment. Fulfilment. Achieving goals. Conclusion of a project. Giftedness. Pride in efforts. Successful, combined efforts. Dreams of creating an ideal home and family. Building strong family foundations and relations. Family oriented. Move to a larger or more prestigious home. Establishing a family enterprise. Family celebrations and struggles. Great creative talent. A recognised artist, writer, actor, speaker, etc. Extreme limitations to creative expression. Extreme privation. Self-undoing. Chip on shoulder. Bigot. Family disintegration. Crumbling foundations. Astronomy and astrology.

Gifts: Rewards commensurate with effort.

Appendix 1

Tarot Equivalent: The Seven of Wands

Opportunities: 33 is a Master Number. It intensifies 3 and 30 attributes. Loyalty. Generosity. Supremacy. Seeking a personal best. Rising to the occasion. Coming out on top. Fighting for your rights. Struggling to stay on top. Turning obstacles into stepping-stones. Bravely facing challenges. Defiance. Feisty when roused. One-upmanship. Chip on the shoulder. Language barriers. Unconditional service. Generosity. Wanting for nothing. Things handed on a platter. Miserliness. No sooner is something attended to than another takes its place. Loneliness at the top. Hobbies. Pride. A braggart. Big-noting oneself. Sees oneself as a hero. Talks or gossips endlessly. Wears heart on sleeve. A bore. Parenting issues. Pregnancy; birth. Sometimes twins with a 9 or a teacher of young children. Mother fiercely devoted to family, children and relatives. Foster or adoptive parents. Works with children. A protector of children. Children at the forefront. Naivety. Dereliction of duty.

Gifts: Selfless-service. Abundance. Fertility. Beneficence. Creativity. Oration. Literacy. Valour.

Tarot Equivalent: The Emperor

Opportunities: All 4s represent basic insights that give rise to logic, reason and reality. Development of finely tuned or detailed technical skills. Also, details in life that concern personal security, boundaries, restrictions, disciplines, finances and family protocol. Medicine, astronomy, mathematics, accountancy, draughtsmanship, surveying, economy, real estate and trade skills. Numerology. 4 is patient and plodding but can be overbearing. A positive 4 personifies rational observation, reality checks, practical, methodical application of reasoning powers and skills, strength of character, magnanimity, applied understanding, order and control of personal affairs and material success. Those who express 4 in this way can be held in high regard and seen as mentors. Paternity. The father or father figures. Familial ties. Leaders. Authorities. Bureaucratic organisations. Need to break family ties to grow. Strong need for security and firm foundations. Death sometimes, especially with 1, 13, 15, 16, 17, 18, 19, 10, 20, 21, 22, 40, 46, 64 or 55. Ruled by Aries.

Gifts: Development of order, organisation, stability, logic and reason. Strong paternal qualities.

Tarot Equivalent: The Page of Cups

Opportunities: 40 expresses 4 at higher levels. Divine protection but not to be abused or taken for granted. Incredible insight. 40 often appears to be a very difficult, testing number. It epitomises earnest endeavours and the struggle endured to reach the pinnacle of success. It also strongly points to karmic implications and experiencing rewards and punishments that are commensurate with intent and ethics that lie behind work, choices and actions. Sometimes extreme hardship. "Forty days and nights in the desert" or "the Dark night of the Soul" syndrome. Very bad luck. Bankruptcy, or threat of. Loss, mourning, grief. Tests, trials and triumphs. Severance. End of a phase. Inheritance, death and taxes. Death sometimes, especially with 1, 4, 13, 15, 16, 17, 18, 19, 10, 20, 21, 22, 40, 46, 64 or 55.

Gifts: Alleviating karmic debts. Strengthening of character. Endurance. Self-discipline. Completion.

Tarot Equivalent: The Four of Cups

Opportunities: 44 is a Master Number. It intensifies 4 and 40 attributes. Achieving mastery or acclaim in a chosen field. Inventive. Increased status, capabilities, common sense and logic. Broadening of horizons. Entrepreneurial activities. Offers. Proposals. Capitalising on money-making opportunities. Ability to seize upon opportunities. Future financial planning. Retirement and insurance schemes. Investments. Borrowing. Inheritance. Time out for re-evaluation purposes. Bankruptcy, or threat of. Harsh conditions. Delays. Extreme hardship. Heavy restrictions. Intense re-evaluation of life. Searching for answers. Inner conflict and discontent. Danger of giving up under pressure. Complacency. Disinterest. Avoidance behaviour. Laziness. Missing the best opportunities. Moody to the point of neurosis.

Gifts: Amazing opportunities. Reconnection to your spiritual self. Mastery of a skill or aspect of personality.

Tarot Equivalent: The Hierophant

Opportunities: All 5s basically represent change that evokes uncertainty and the need for adaptation and adjustment. They also signify freedom of expression, the five senses, sensory experimentation and experience, inquisitiveness, inconstancy, instability, restlessness, change and adversity. Also, creative self-expression that involves exploration, discovery and courage. Divorce, separation, infidelity, sexual desires, activity and preferences. Travel, holidays, recreation, hobbies, studies, gambling and substance abuse. Ruthlessness, intolerance, insensitivity. Religion. Welfare services. Social welfare institutions. Rehabilitation facilities. Marriage. Love and love affairs. Children's issues, such as education. Ruled by Taurus.

Gifts: Development of intuition. Change due to unfolding circumstances, growth and maturation.

Appendix 1

Tarot Equivalent: The Ten of Cups

Opportunities: 50 expresses 5 at higher levels therefore, elation or the pain of adjustment may be intensified. Divine protection from the zero but not to be abused or taken for granted. Achievement of hopes and dreams not necessarily in material terms. Abundance. Perfect home and family. Family celebrations. Marriage. Blended family through remarriage or new partnering or fostering. Merging families. Family crisis. Shattered domestic bliss. Broken home. Separation of family members. Family discord. Lack of family support. Low domestic standards. Devastation. Messy household. Falling into disrepute. Ruthlessness, cunning and domination.

Gifts: Crowning glory. Happiness and contentment.

Tarot Equivalent: The Ace of Swords

Opportunities: 55 is a Master Number. It intensifies 5 and 50 attributes. Social activist. Welfare institutions/services. Sincerity of purpose. Integrity. One-pointedness. Ability to cut to the heart of a matter. Radical life-changing events. Crisis. Complete change to circumstances eg rags to riches or vice versa. Life threatening experience. A chip on the shoulder. Sees life too intensely - severely. Living a life of regrets. Guilt ridden. Often lives by the code of "do as I say, not what I do". Vengeance. A back-stabber. Extremely judgemental. Callous. Black thoughts. Severe judge. Lawyer. Doctor. Fearful. Eccentricity. Sexual deviance. Good or evil tendencies. Death or loss sometimes, especially with 1, 4, 13, 15, 16, 17, 18, 19, 10, 20, 21, 22, 27, 40, 46 or 64.

Gifts: Works for the greater Good.

Tarot Equivalent: The Lovers

Opportunities: 6 is generally about all things related to love, marriage, separation, work, colleagues, daily routines and affairs and personal habits, health, hygiene and diet. 6 also depicts parents, family, homes and domestic issues, real estate and travel agencies. Development of the finer senses. Appreciation of art, singing and beauty. Beauty products. Good food and wine. Also innate appreciation of beauty, peace and harmony, routine, order, work. Loyalty and devotion. Purposeful, reserved, discreet, conservative, shy and conformist. Single-minded. Can be a workaholic. Nit-picking and critical, fastidious and extremely productive or indolent, disorderly and shabby. Commerce, trade and banking. Employees and subordinates. Carers. Takes calculated risks. A collector or accumulator - a connoisseur. A musician. 6 is also the number of adjustment, which means that success is born from discrimination followed by right choices and actions. Ruled by Gemini.

Gifts: Discrimination. Industry, versatility, resourcefulness and flexibility.

The Life Diamond

60

Tarot Equivalent: The Six of Swords

Opportunities: 60 expresses 6 at higher levels of expression. Divine protection but not to be abused or taken for granted. Increased sense of personal power and capabilities. High attainment. Earned success and its rewards. Reverence. Adulation. Honour. True giftedness. A great work. Architecture. Persistence and perseverance. Profession that offers potential for brilliant future. Unswerving faithfulness. Nurturer. Carer. States of equilibrium, peace, harmony and balance being tested. Facing security issues. Very hard work. Harsh work or living conditions. Troubled life. Moving away from disturbing conditions. Distressing family problems, family cleavages or upheavals. Severe or chronic health issues. Travel may be for spiritual reasons or to better your position in life or for health reasons or to escape. Legal issues related to family or work issues. Big decisions accompanied by big adjustments like leaving home and country. Family loss, wills, inheritance or alimony.

Gifts: Learning to *be* and *do*. Enlightened self-direction. Fine-tuning.

66

Tarot Equivalent: The Queen of Pentacles

All Queens represent women whom you respect, have a position of authority and wield their power (albeit positively or negatively). Because a Queen holds a commanding position, this can be transferred to 66, giving its owner an innate capacity to rise to the top or be very influential when it is active. In female charts, Queens represent actual personality traits, whether consciously or unconsciously expressed. In both female and male charts, a Queen represents the women whom they attract, e.g. mothers, sisters, influential relatives, teachers, wives, girlfriends, business partners, colleagues, authority figures or specialists in their particular fields, and so on. Apply these guidelines to 24, 38 and 52 which are also 'queen' numbers.

Opportunities: 66 is a Master Number. It intensifies 6 and 60 attributes. Integrity, self-discipline, health and diets, work and ethics are challenged under this master vibration. Therapeutic professions. Advanced, discriminative powers. A time for inner searching and analysis. Higher aspirations. Idealistic tendencies must be couched within realistic parameters. Extremely resourceful and tenacious. Promotion. A fighter for rights but can become the victim of others' deception. A champion of the underdog. Sly. Issues to do with unfaithfulness, lies, deceit and hypocrisy. Danger of becoming obsessive and extremist. Good intentions can be thwarted. Get behind the friendly, helpful demeanour and you'll find the following traits; a force to be reckoned with; a martyr, who hurts oneself to hurt others; one who secretly likes to make others suffer. Master manipulator for own gain. Shrewd. Money hungry. Vengeful. Punitive. Into payback. Fickle. Jumps to conclusions. A know all. Powers of persuasion. A survivor at others' expense. Jealous of friends. Controlling, wants own way. Dishonest, untrustworthy. Plays by own rules. Severe or chronic health issues. Family loss, wills, inheritance, disputes over estate matters. Extremely industrious or apathetic and into avoidance behaviour. Doing the barest minimum. Passive resistance. Stubborn to own detriment. Unfaithfulness. Difficulty in getting in touch with your female or male side. Damaged sense of femininity or masculinity. Sexual concerns often stem from this.

Gifts: Great humanitarian. Sympathy, compassion and empathy. Inner wisdom. Healing powers. Being able to walk in another's shoes.

7

Tarot Equivalent: The Chariot

Opportunities: Seven virtues, seven vices and seven deadly sins make a highly complex number. Rules the seven chakras and metaphysics. Cyclic completions. Phases ending. Number of the people. Learning the power of words. Persuasive speaker. Perfection, eccentricity, probing and penetrating, research, analyst. Deliberate self-limitation or confinement. Religious or spiritual bent or outright sceptic. Well-mannered, knowledgeable and thoughtful or ill-mannered and ignorant. Openness or rigid and fixed in thoughts and ways. Metaphysical and occult interests. Happy in own company especially with a 1. Self-imposed limitations. Need for privacy. Need for rest and recuperation. Health concerns. Travel for health reasons or over water. Losing things or forgetfulness. Hidden matters surface. Secrets. The unknown and the unforeseen. Bizarre experiences/occurrences. "Foot-in-mouth disease". Ruled by Cancer.

Gifts: Right speech. Quiet achiever.

70

Tarot Equivalent: The Two of Pentacles

Opportunities: 70 expresses 7 at higher levels. Divine protection but not to be abused or taken for granted. Charismatic. Magnetic. High aspirations. Heightened research abilities. Clever, resourceful, inventive, genius. Specialisation in one or more fields. Limitless commercial possibilities. Negotiations. Wheeling and dealing. Creation of something that has public appeal. One's fate or destiny weighed in the balance by authority figures. Weighing many variables in order to reach the best solutions. Ability to do several things at the one time. Knowing when to "switch on" and "switch off". Dealing with sudden chops and changes. Restlessness. Dalliance. Temporary state of limbo. Distractions or trying to deal with too many things at once loses focus and sight of direction or goals. Considering too many possibilities with dubious potential therefore, difficulty in making right choices. Confusion. See-sawing. Instability. Nothing definite. Volatility. Getting off track. Self-imposed seclusion. A recluse. Union of all polarities such as reflection and duplication.

Gifts: Multifaceted capabilities. Concentration. Perseverance.

The Life Diamond

77

Tarot Equivalent: The 9 of Pentacles

Opportunities: 77 is a Master Number. It intensifies 7 and 70 attributes. Perfectionist. Achieving goals. Researcher. Environmental scientist and/or interests. Environmental scientists, activists or politicians. Conscientious objectors. Probing, penetrating mind. Detectives, sleuths, solving mysteries. Searches for the answers to what appears to be unknowable. Metaphysics. The unseen and the unknown. Karmic work. Keeper of secrets. Overly accentuated control. Eccentric, quirky, perverse. Sceptic, cynic. Chaotic. Need for moderation in all things. Lying by omission. Vital information withheld. A recluse.

Gifts: In-depth research and acute analytical abilities. Strong scientific and or occult leanings.

8

Tarot Equivalent: Strength

Opportunities: Charisma. 8s give an aura of confidence and mastery of skills. Specialist fields such as: medical practitioners, bankers, economists, accountants and creative arts. Dramatics. Entertainers. Athletes. Seekers of the limelight or fame and fortune. Assets, investments, future security, loans, debts, insurance and inheritances. Death and taxes. Harsh times. Oppressive conditions that engender misery. Dominance. Cruelty. Self-demeaning tendencies. Police contact or intervention. Criminals, sexual deviants, rapists. Symbiotic relationships. Sexual expression. Weaknesses. Flattery and pride. Inflated ego. Heart and spine complaints. Ruled by Leo.

Gifts: Self-strengthening. Energy. Mastery of a profession or skill. Sublimation and control of base behaviours.

80

Tarot Equivalent: Substitute: Strength

Opportunities: 80 expresses 8 at higher levels. Divine protection but not to be abused or taken for granted. Highly skilled individuals. Great inner strength and fortitude. Self-assertion in all matters. Great achievements possible in business, sports and metaphysical fields. Big business deals and operations. Substantial financial successes. Health and vitality or the reverse. Voluntary removal of the old, outworn, outdated or inappropriate or forcible removal of that which should have been given up or let go of freely. Remaining in uncomfortable or painful circumstances longer than necessary. Being stuck in the past. Not knowing when to move on. Painful regrets. Tyranny. Abject cruelty. Domination and exploitation of the weak and infirm. Criminals.

Gifts: Mastery. Renewal.

Appendix 1

88

Tarot Equivalent: Substitute: The Tower and The Chariot

Opportunities: 88 is a Master Number- a number of extremes, severity. It intensifies 8 and 80 attributes. Strong magnetism. Temperance. Wise use of money and personal power. Accumulation of wealth. Earning good wages, sudden wealth, a windfall or scholarship. Salary increase. Good returns on investments. Large inheritance or none. Death and taxes. Monies earned and saved provide means to achieve goals. Focus is on future financial security. Insurance, assets and term deposits. Loans. Compulsive-obsessive tendencies. Too much too soon robs incentive to become greater. Oppressive conditions. Need to consult specialists. Serious illness. Life-threatening experiences. Heavy losses. Bankruptcy. Treachery. Theft. Schizophrenic behaviour. Abject cruelty. Complete domination. Annihilator. Despot. Violent, turbulent times. Threat to life. Police action. The occult. White magic. Black magic. Karmic learning.

Gifts: Regeneration. Balance of opposing forces. Personality control.

9

Tarot Equivalent: The Hermit

Opportunities: Generally all 9s are the number of the chameleon. Because it contains all of the numbers before it, this is what gives it such versatility and such a wide range of application. Whether on its own or accompanying another number it contains the potential for extremist tendencies to develop. Therefore, when delineating a 9, either singly or in a compound number, you must allow for *extremes* to occur, or at the very least allow for a wide and diversified spectrum of potential expression to be demonstrated. This slant on 9 traits will be developed more fully for the numbers 19/91, 29/92, 39/93, 49/94, etc. The simple rule to remember is that 9 *magnifies* whatever is being expressed, whether it be thoughts, feelings, emotions, desires, events or reactions, hence the tendency for the "drama Queen syndrome" and dramatic life events being played out under strong 9 influences. As a result of this intensification effect on accompanying numbers, the cause and effects can be anticipated to be more exaggerated. Dramatic, sensitive, humanitarian, way-shower, religious, legal matters, higher education, endings, loss. Double standards. Hypocrisy. Global effects. Ashram. Ruled by Virgo.

Gifts: Gaining wisdom from experience. Advisor

90

Tarot Equivalent: Substitute: The Hermit

Opportunities: 90 expresses 9 at higher levels. Divine protection but not to be abused or taken for granted. 90 can be implosive or benevolent. Modest. Compassionate. Considerate. Philanthropic. Positions of power or high status. Global or widespread recognition. Associating with those in high positions. High Court proceedings. High honours or scholastic awards. Global concerns. Publicity. Publications. High-level forums. Strong religious bent. Forced endings and beginnings. Seemingly boundless potential. Inheritance from distant relatives or grandparents. Sudden, unexpected luck. Gain with loss tendencies. Self-righteous. Superior. Haughty, insensitive and miserly. Global or long-distance travel. Tragedy. Megalomaniac.

Gifts: Way-shower. Humility. Advisor

99

Tarot Equivalent: Substitute: The Moon and The Hermit

Opportunities: 99 is a Master Number. It intensifies 9 and 90 attributes. Generally takes things to extremes; very intense. Idealist. Religious. Earnest. Humanitarian. Fame. Highly-prized honours or awards. Scholarships. Luck. High status. Global recognition. Entrepreneur. Philanthropic. Lottery win. Gregarious. Global or long-distance travel. Eccentric. Extremely passionate. Hermit-like. Happy in own company. Aloneness. Unrealistic expectations. Compulsive-obsessive tendencies. Frustrated. Quick tempered. Very defensive. Tends to blame others for own faults. Alternately positive and negative. Extremely moody. Can never be wrong. Controlling. Extremely focused or scattered. Life full of drama. The Law. Inheritance. Gain with loss. Tragedy of large dimensions accompanied by ongoing repercussions. Headaches. Karmic lessons. Confidence tricksters.

Gifts: Protagonist. Revered leader. Guru. Advisor.

12

Tarot Equivalent: The Hanged Man

Opportunities: Evolving perceptions from upsets or topsy-turvy experiences. Upsets that turn one's world upside down when one least expects it. These times of crisis tend to force viewing things with new eyes and seeing things from a fresh angle, thereby forcing new perceptions and attitudes to develop. Can be radical change for better or worse. Reversals. Role reversals. Life like being on a treadmill. A kind of a paralytic state or limbo. Suspension. Willing to make short-term sacrifices for long-term gains. Urge to get to the bottom of things. Development of metaphysical interests. Dealing with personal hang-ups. Eccentricity. Subservience. Self-sacrifice. Self-sabotage. Self-negation. Persecution complex. Martyrdom. The victim/saviour syndrome. What you give out comes back in like manner - boomerang effect. Avoidance behaviour. Suspension of activities. Ruled by Neptune.

Gifts: Versatility. Ability to see another point of view. Tolerance of differences. Sacrifice of the lesser for the greater. A complete cycle of manifestation. Submission of the lesser self to the Higher Self – 'Not my will but Thine be done'.

Appendix 1

21

Tarot Equivalent: The World

Opportunities: Reaching an important point of awareness that brings greater understanding and wisdom. Great promise. Greater accomplishment, improvement. Moving forward and upward. Elevated status. Self-awareness. Learning to temper selfish traits. Learning to forgive. Developing spiritual or unconditional love or true love. Euphoric experiences. Elation, exhilaration. Change. Cycle's close. End of a phase marks the beginning of something greater. Clashes of personalities. Self-serving behind the guise of friendship, care or support. Self-defeat. Going in circles. Loss of direction. Scattered. Stagnation. 'Iron fist in a velvet glove'. Promising the world and failing to deliver. Empty or broken promises. Death sometimes, especially with 1, 4, 13, 15, 16, 17, 18, 19, 10, 20, 21, 22, 40, 46, 64 or 55. Ruled by Saturn.

Gifts: Ascension. Becoming more. Stepping up. Liberation.

13

Tarot Equivalent: Death

Opportunities: Creative intelligence. Elimination. Endings. Circumstances force transformation and change. A complete change of perceptions, attitudes and habits. A turning point. Remaking, remodelling and rebuilding after clearing. Rejuvenation. Spring-cleaning. Purging. Destructing before reconstructing. Release of the old to make room for the new. Cutting ties that constrain and oppress. Transition. Modification. Variation. Emergence. Mixture of joy with sobriety. Fear of impermanence. Fear of letting go. Fear of the unknown. Fear of death or ruin. Loss. Life changes due to the birth of a child. Degeneration of the bones or physical strength. Skeletal problems. Resisting change. Rigidity. Scepticism. Lack of trust and faith. Clinging to the obsolete. 13 further reduces to a practical, efficient, hard working, detail-oriented, scientific, 4. Death sometimes, especially when with 1, 4, 13, 15, 16, 17, 18, 19, 10, 20, 21, 22, 40, 46, 64 or 55.

Gifts: Destruction that achieves growth/renewal. Transition. Transformation. Rebirth. Immortality.

31

Tarot Equivalent: The Five of Wands

Opportunities: Inner struggle. Genius. Over-active imagination. Brain-storming. Creative worker. Innovations. Struggle to manifest creative ideas. Struggle to be cared for, wanted and heard. Struggle to maintain focus. Struggle to complete tasks. Struggle to be steadfast. Struggle to be true to yourself. Struggle with the personality. Competitive environment. Self-preservation or protection. Eventual success. Few true friends. Others having too much influence on your life. Others taking the kudos for your ideas. Being overwhelmed by constant wrangling and/or persistent tests and trials or others' needs. Battle of wills. Leadership struggles.

The Life Diamond

Mind games. Intimidation. Submission. Giving up the struggle. Imagining wrongs that do not exist. A "stirrer", troublemaker. Pettiness. Gossip-monger. Meddling in others' affairs. Petulance. Loss of foundations/way. Hyperactive. Scatter-brained. Mental blocks. Harsh/restrictive beginnings in life. Abusive childhood. Ordeal. Not being heard.

Gifts: A fighter. A 'never give in' attitude. Cooperation. Harmony via conflict. Eventual peace. Graciousness.

Tarot Equivalent: Temperance

Opportunities: Moderation. Right observation perceives how ostensibly incongruent components can be unified to ultimately be reshaped to produce new, unified ideas and forms. Reconciler of opposites. Adaptive, creative reasoning. Change of tactics. New line of work. Changes at work. Adjusting to changing circumstances. New endeavours that embrace creative skills. Industriousness. Highly-developed artistic, technical or scientific skills. Intelligent activity. Goal-setting. Publishing. Academic awards. Legal issues. Global influences. Coming before the public. Chemistry. Medicine. Miracle worker. Health restored. Effects of consciousness on the physical form guarantees evolution. Inability to focus and draw intelligent conclusions. Fruitless efforts. Mood swings. Excesses. Chaotic conditions. Polarisation. Rigidity. Lack of cohesion. Hypocrisy. Delusion. Superficiality. Lingering or seething anger; wrath. Need for welfare services. Can be a number of death - see 41. Ruled by Sagittarius.

Gifts: Alchemy. Ability to harmonise or blend opposing forces/elements. Synthesis. Moderation.

Tarot Equivalent: The Ace of Cups

Opportunities: Joy. Win a million, lose a million. Being born into, marrying, inheriting or attaining wealth. Also loss of this status. Serving the public. Entertainer. All embracing. Harmonisation. Blending. Co-creative relationships. Unions. Marriage. Extended family issues. Innovative technician, researcher, analyst, teacher, ideas, work. Proven results from creative ideas. Manifesting goals. Modification. Completion. Everlasting. Religiosity. Burgeoning spirituality. Psychic and/or spiritual experiences. The call of the soul. Seeker of the Truth. The Path of Return. Tests of worthiness and dedication to spiritual practices. Seeking a Guru. Undivided clarity of vision. One-pointedness. Legal issues. Global concerns/travel. Life-threatening illness. Death sometimes, especially with 1, 4, 13, 15, 16, 17, 18, 19, 10, 20, 21, 22, 40, 46, 64 or 55.

Gifts: Endurance.

15

Tarot Equivalent: The Devil

Opportunities: Discrimination. Commitment. Prioritising. Marriage. Chaining yourself to that which is counter to your Highest Good. Clinging to life. Clinging to family or people or things that do not serve your best interests. Clinging to circumstances, delusions, habits and inclinations. Staying in awkward, uncomfortable or harsh situations longer than necessary. Inability to let go and let God. Sexual abuse/misconduct. Substance abuse. Addictive behaviours. Debauchery. Ruled by desires. Sometimes separation due to a death, especially with 1, 4, 13, 16, 17, 18, 19, 10, 20, 21, 22, 40, 46, 64 or 55. Ruled by Capricorn.

Gifts: High aspirations. Facing reality. Self-liberation. Non-attachment. Non-materialism.

51

Tarot Equivalent: The King of Swords

Opportunities: This is one of the four "'King" Tarot Keys. The other three "King" Keys are 23, 37 and 65. Females can display their traits, as well as attracting these types of males to them. When numbers, they bestow similar characteristics such as maturity, strength, leadership, being at the top of a chosen field, authoritarian and have an air of power and purpose about them. 51 can be extremely idealistic and in love with own ideas. Can be a ceaseless worker for a worthy cause or the underdog. This person is incisive, clever, has no time for fools and foolish things, can be autocratic and into power and control. Dynamic, energetic. Extremist tendencies. Prone to "burn-out". Cuts to the chase. Forcible. Abrupt, harsh, snarly. Crude. Derides women. Drug and alcohol abuse. Welfare institutions. Bullying tactics. Insensitivity.

Gifts: Ability to cut through the dross and reveal the Truth. Cutting ties that bind. An achiever.

16

Tarot Equivalent: The Tower

Opportunities: Spiritual awakening. Sudden insights and realisations. Life-changing events. Transformation. Sudden surprises, upsets and disruptive influences turn out to be catalysts for change. Expect the unexpected. Crisis. Change for the better. Finding your true vocation. Long-term employment. Community/humanitarian work. Sudden infatuation. Sudden decisions, action. Chaos. Something hidden causes shock when revealed, e.g. love affair or threatening disease. Dismantling. Destruction. Ruin. New property or car. Property or car problems. 16 reveals insights that expose destructive forces at work. Accident prone. Being catapulted into different circumstances. Physical collapse or collapse of life as you know it. Being at war with yourself or others. Actual warfare. Imprisonment, or the threat of. Self-confinement. Fire damage to property. Death by fire or by lightning strike. Death sometimes, especially with 1, 4, 13, 15, 17, 18, 19, 10, 20, 21, 22, 40, 46, 64 or 55. Ruled by Mars.

Gifts: A wake-up call. A cosmic kick in the behind. Adaptability.

Tarot Equivalent: The Seven of Swords

Opportunities: Strong religious aspirations. Eccentricity. To be in a position where you feel pressured into a "cut and run" situation. Hasty retreat. Eviction orders. Moonlight flit. Leaving intolerable circumstances with the bare essentials, with the intent to return to claim what is rightfully yours at a later time. Awakening to urgent needs. Running away from home. Salvaging what you can from a precarious or threatening situation. Taking back what is yours. Culling and sorting. Possession of unusual skills/knowledge. Forced to withhold information or skills. Discriminate or indiscriminate action. Taking advantage of a situation. Doing own thing. Premeditated actions. Isolating self. Lies. Stealing. Furtiveness. Stealth. Escaping from prison or prison-like circumstances. Guerrilla warfare. Gangsters. Deals behind closed doors. Severance.

Gifts: Unswerving inner beliefs. To know when to leave and what to take with you when you do.

Tarot Equivalent: The Star

Opportunities: To "star" in some way or attract the limelight by distinguishing oneself either positively or negatively. Fame, stardom. Brilliant ideas, mind and/or creativity. Recognition for special talents. Excellence in a specific or chosen field. Honours. Public honour. Success. An auspicious period. Attracting attention from others. Unexpected help and support. Being in the spotlight or winning position. Hopes and wishes. Humanitarian interests. Counselling. Metaphysical interests. Healer/healing. Health issues. A natural inclination for occult practices/study. Slander. Disgrace. Shame. Infamy. Sexual identity issues. Sexual misconduct. Failure. Litigation. Dashed hopes and plans. Death sometimes, especially with 1, 4, 13, 15, 16, 18, 19, 10, 20, 21, 22, 40, 46, 64 or 55. Ruled by Aquarius.

Gifts: Distinction. Recognition from peers or those in authority. Renewed hope. Unstinting faith. Healing.

Tarot Equivalent: The Three of Pentacles

Opportunities: Exuberance. Exhibitionism. Showmanship. Artisanship. Demonstration of skills. Holding exhibitions. A skilled professional. Sustained effort to reach higher and higher standards. Degrees of attainment - traineeship to master craftsman. Attaining professional excellence. Mastery of a skill. Diligence. Earnest efforts reap rewards. Accolades and rewards for work well done which may have taken many painstaking years to reach. Learning a new skill or trade. Seeking acknowledgment for one's talents. Outer show instead of inner glow. Rebuilding, reshaping one's life. Self-analysis. Purposeful. Renovating. Real estate or deceased estate matters. Support from those wiser or more financial than yourself. Being observed or under surveillance.

Gifts: Recognition from superiors or peers. A position of trust and distinction.

Tarot Equivalent: The Moon

Opportunities: Dealing with fluctuation and change. Solutions to problems may be found through dreams or alternate or unorthodox methods. A love of human nature. Psychology and counsellors. Psychism. Healing. Family matters. Women. Emotional upheaval. Vulnerability. Withdrawal. Deception. Forced change. Transformation. Symbiosis. Domination. Weakness. Disappointment. Mood swings. Volatility. Depression, unhappiness. Tragedy. Death sometimes, especially with 1, 4, 13, 15, 16, 17, 19, 10, 20, 21, 22, 40, 46, 64 or 55. Ruled by Pisces.

Gifts: Compassion. Psychic gifts. Self-discovery. Voluntary change as opposed to forced change.

Tarot Equivalent: Substitute: The Moon and the Hermit

Opportunities: Saintliness. Self-sacrifice. Rise to power. Earning a reputation. Great attainment. Achieving very high goals, high standard or distinguished position. Promotion, recognition or rewards for work well done. Capitalising on potential. Mastering a skill. Increased knowledge and understanding. Large corporations. Global contacts. Fight for your life or reputation. Hardship and privation. Holding grudges. Tormented. Martyr.

Gifts: Great aspirations. Empathy.

Tarot Equivalent: The Sun

Opportunities: 9 strengthens its 1. Personal power. Creative self-expression. Multi-talented. Recreation. Happiness and joy. Educational pursuits. Educational or heroic awards. Marriage. Divorce. Parenting. Fertility/sterility. Children's affairs. Children's education. Concerns about children or their education. Learning difficulties. Childishness. Legal issues. Broken promises. Broken contracts, unions or connections. Cancellations. Troubled relationships. Power struggles in relationships. End to an existing way of life. Death or loss of a family member. Death sometimes, especially with 1, 4, 13, 15, 16, 17, 18, 10, 20, 21, 22, 40, 46, 64 or 55.

Gifts: Self-awareness. Turning-point. New directions.

The Life Diamond

⟨91⟩ Tarot Equivalent: Substitute: The Wheel of Fortune and The Magician

Opportunities: Charismatic leader. Statesman. Position of great power over the masses. In a great leader we would see 91 as indicating mass appeal, or as having achieved monumental accomplishments and sometimes religious or socio-political prominence but in ordinary cases, 91 manifests similarly, yet on a much smaller scale in private life. The biggest challenge in the 91 is the ego - humility is the key. Protecting your reputation. Under public scrutiny. Winning public favour. Religious leader. Born teacher. A world teacher. Self-aggrandisement. Sudden end to a way of life. Unfaithfulness. Separation. Death or loss of a loved one.

Gifts: A Path Finder. Recognition and tribute.

⟨23⟩ Tarot Equivalent: The King of Wands

Opportunities: This is one of the four 'King' Tarot Keys (see 51 for more information). When a number, 23 bestows characteristics such as maturity, strength, leadership, being at the top of a chosen field, being an authority and having an air of power and purpose about one. Combination of creativity and idealism tinged with wisdom. An inspirational entrepreneur. Grandiose ideas. Tends to be outspoken and tactless. Makes enemies through stinging remarks and hurtful, demeaning tongue-lashings that are designed to cower in order to remain supreme. A cruel and harsh leader. Does not suffer fools gladly.

Gifts: An ideas person. Mental and physical vitality capable of sustaining prolonged, arduous labour.

⟨32⟩ Tarot Equivalent: The Six of Wands

Opportunities: Success. Psychic talents. Charisma. Magnetism. Enchanter. Many friends and admirers. Pomp and glory. Public adoration. Praise. A star or hero/heroine with adoring fans. Heroic feats. Acclaim. Praise. Elevation of status. A false hero. Falling from grace.

Gifts: Charismatic leader. Adulation.

⟨24⟩ Tarot Equivalent: The Queen of Wands

24, 38, 52 and 66 are all Queens' numbers in the Tarot. Each of these numbers represents women whom you respect and have a position of power and authority, which they wield positively and/or negatively. Because a Queen holds a commanding position, there is an innate capacity to rise to the top or be very influential when this number is present. In female charts, Queens represent actual personality traits, whether consciously or unconsciously expressed. In both female and male charts, Queens can also represent various typologies according to their elements' characteristics that are evident in the women whom they inherit or attract in their lives, e.g. mothers, sisters, influential relatives, teachers, girlfriends, wives, business partners, colleagues, and so on.

Opportunities: 24's nurture the "sacredness" of the family unit. Homely, nurturing, gardening, countryside and country related affairs. Farmers, farming. Country travel, visiting or holidaying on a farm. Overseas or long distance travel. Moving to another country. Temporary home. Florists. Authority. Taking charge. Charitable. Supportive. Intuiting others needs. Attending to affairs. Refusing charity/support. Loyalty. Traitor. Turning against another out of spite. Marriage/separation. Autocratic and abusive. Exile. Inconstancy of purpose. Degrees of dysfunction in parental pair damages children. Damaging effects of dominance from either the mother or the father. Unhealthy conditioning by parents. Immaturity.

Gifts: Getting things done. Patriotism.

Tarot Equivalent: The Two of Cups

Opportunities: Yearning for ideal relationship or marriage. Marriage. Forming a union. Commitment. Loyalty. Pleasant company/meetings. New work created from intuited ideas. Health and work issues involving another. Caring for another. Possessiveness. Undermining of a relationship. Deception, treachery, betrayal, infidelity. One infatuation after another. Separation. Moving house. House improvements. Cancelled plans, arrangements.

Gifts: Cooperation. Synchronisation.

Tarot Equivalent: The Knight of Wands

Opportunities: An idealist. Inspired fighter. A crusader. Loves to be involved in a cause. Feels it is one's duty to 'rescue' everyone. Heroic. Saviour/victim syndrome. Chases a much sought after goal. On a mission. Enterprising. Very focussed or one-pointed. Self-drivenness. Workaholic tendencies. Work involves travel. Energy, dynamism, enthusiasm. Audacious. Adventurer. Travel to a new country. Acts out of self-interests, therefore often insensitive to others needs. Impulsive. Brash. Loyal or unfaithful.

Gifts: Focus on a goal. Determination. Loyal.

Tarot Equivalent: The Queen of Swords

Opportunities: This is a Queen number (see 24). 52, being a Sword, is dual in expression, therefore expect to see opposites in character being expressed from time to time. One side of 52 can be two-faced and live by double standards or a creed of do as I say rather than by example. Its bearer is often blind to this side of their nature and can be a wolf in sheep's clothing. The other side of 52 can be a pillar of virtue, strong, faithful and powerful and extremely just and loyal. 52 speaks with authority, is incisive, can be punitive, nasty, ruthless, cunning, shrewd, bitter, vengeful and bend the rules to suit the self. Talks over you when excited. Pretender. Masks true thoughts and feelings. Hides the truth. Laughing on the outside while crying on the inside. A harsh taskmistress behind the smile. Cutting remarks. Diplomat. Other 52 attributes are; engaging in intellectual pursuits; academic advancement or awards; successful test results. Oratory and literacy achievements. 52 can bring unhappiness in marriage or dredge up unhappy memories about reasons for divorce. Separation or divorce may be viewed as a necessity to gain personal happiness. Issues surrounding abandonment. A loner. A Truth seeker. Biding one's time. Instability, upheavals, no ground under the feet. Being fleet of foot or agile.

Gifts: Incisiveness.

26

Tarot Equivalent: The Page of Wands

Opportunities: Germination of enterprising plans and ideas. Gains commensurate with integrity. Something auspicious to announce or in the making. Relaying exciting news or producing something of note. Scrutiny. Sale of assets. Small gains on investments or less than expected. Ill-advised risks or investments. Motivated by greed. Salesperson. Advertising one's ideas or wares. Confidence trickster. Scams. Risk-taking and gambling tendencies. Loss of money. Loss of integrity. Separation from a lover or relative. Feeling judged or at the brunt of compromising circumstances.

Gifts: The number of God (God: 7+15+4=26). Enterprising nature. Receiving good news.

62

Tarot Equivalent: The Eight of Swords

Opportunities: Intellectual property. Very serious or responsible outlook in relationships. Shouldering more than your fair share in relationships/work. Finds it difficult to delegate. Loyal, trusted and caring. Wears heart on sleeve. Confining marriage or commitment to someone or something. Someone or something you have an investment in keeps you confined. Falling on hard times due to run of bad luck or possible accident, death or hardship. Disappointments that have to be faced rather than avoided. Being in denial. Being surrounded by bad memories, grief, and sadness or impending loss. Anxiety. Being caught up in circumstances that are presently beyond your control. Cries for help fall on deaf ears. Unable to express the way you feel. Feeling helpless? – find appropriate help. Gloomy or harrowing phase that will pass. Malingerer. Reaping negative consequences of actions.

Gifts: Breaking free from inhibiting bonds. Finding the way out of a situation that is causing grief.

Appendix 1

27

Tarot Equivalent: The Ace of Wands

Opportunities: Inspired, innovative, pioneering, inventive, analytical and investigative. Religious leanings whether orthodox or unorthodox. Service-oriented organiser. Ability to uplift others. Self-directing qualities. Self-help; self-analysis. Ability to teach oneself. Can turn one's hand to any task when pressed to do so. A 'handy person'. Builds own house. Husbandry. Breeder. Selects mate with an eye to capitalising on best points. Savvy. Softly spoken. Temper tantrums. Lack of vitality forces aborted ideas/plans. Death sometimes, especially with 1, 4, 13, 15, 16, 17, 18, 19, 10, 20, 21, 22, 40, 46, 64 or 55.

Gifts: Inspired teacher, speaker, writer, artist, and musician.

72

Tarot Equivalent: The Four of Pentacles

Opportunities: Intuition, psychic awareness. Ability to earn and save. Investing rather than spending. Acute sensitivity to security needs. Threat, whether real or imagined, to basic security needs. Self-preservation. Protectiveness. Securing one's financial future. A need for tightening of the money belt and keeping a close watch on financial affairs. Curbing spending. Stingy, mean. Covertness. Covetousness. Hoarding. Possessive attitudes. What's mine as opposed to what's yours mentality. True mate or deceitful mate. Sees partner as a "possession". Possessiveness. Materialistic. Health crisis. Constipation. Blocked or closed chakras. Fear. Stays in unpleasant situations longer than necessary. Abandonment issues. Problems arising from deprivation issues whether real or imagined.

Gifts: Self-preservation. Conservation.

28

Tarot Equivalent: The Two of Wands

Opportunities: An entrepreneur in the making. A gift for merchandising. Good at commerce and trade. Good at handling money. Unafraid of hard work. Constant fluctuating circumstances. Financial uncertainty. Financial risk-taking. Penny wise and pound foolish. Financially dependent on others. Using money as power. Power struggles within relationships. Antagonism between partners. Competitiveness. Showdown at some point in relationships can lead to reversal of power. Trouble maker. War monger. Need for surgery and medical specialists at some stage.

Gifts: Cooperation. Seeing others as equals.

The Life Diamond

82

Tarot Equivalent: Substitute: The Wheel of Fortune and The Magician

Opportunities: Powerful leadership potential. Shrewdness in financial and business transactions. Accumulation of wealth. Building reputation and status. Establishing a business. Corporate affiliations. Property deals. Rental properties. Shrewd business sense and investment ability. Tact and diplomacy in business. Giving up your personal power. At ease with others. Good understanding of others. A doormat. Self-abnegation. Dissolution of partnership due to financial concerns and/or control factors. Cancellation of contracts. Metaphysical interests. Loss of a loved one. Bereavement. Crisis. Tension. Intolerance of others and their differences.

Gifts: Right use of power and money.

29

Tarot Equivalent: The Three of Wands

Opportunities: 9 intensifies the 2. Equality and justice. War, disruption and chaos may oppose peace, equanimity and balance. Ambassadors. Counsellors. Seekers of justice, harmony and equality. Politician. Businesslike. Learning the tricks of the trade. May not be able to delegate. Relationship problems due to imposing unrealistic ideals upon them. Searching for the "ideal" marriage, business partner or friendship. Dishonourable acts. Dishonourable contracts. Broken trust; promises. Separation. Intrigue. Secrets, lies, deception, fraud. Financial losses. Legal matters. Divorce settlements. Alimony issues. Trickery. Insincerity. Disloyalty. Hypocrites. Double standards.

Gifts: A willingness to serve others. Diplomacy. Honesty.

92

Tarot Equivalent: Substitute: Justice and The High Priestess

Opportunities: High values, ethics and morals. Great empathy. A visionary. A humanitarian. Loyalty. Devotion. Dependability. Trustworthiness. Serving a cause. Charity institutions/work. Large enterprises or enterprising ideas. Money gained through friends. Just and fair dealings. Arbitrator. Ability to right the scales, equilibrium. Warring factions. Contact with high officials, diplomats, politicians. Educators. Legal profession/matters. Legal contracts. Embittered legal wrangles. Highly emotional. Need for balance and equilibrium. Naive perceptions of others. Putting others on pedestals. Too open and trustworthy. Wears heart on sleeve. Wealthy people who see themselves as being poor. The dishevelled millionaire. Confrontational issues.

Gifts: Idealism. Eternal hope.

Appendix 1

34

Tarot Equivalent: The Eight of Wands

Opportunities: Travel. Dissemination of knowledge. Manifestation of ideas, projects. Brainstorming. Bombardment of enterprising ideas. Things speed up or unfold quickly. Spontaneity. Snap decisions that turn out to be correct or that you later regret. Jumping to conclusions. Things happening out of the blue. Surprising results. Déjà vu experiences. Things suddenly falling into place. "Falling on your feet". Actual falls. Accident-proneness, especially with 16. Increased social activity. Making new friends. Sudden offers of support from friends, relatives or business associates. Relatives. Restlessness. Suddenly applying the brakes. Sudden corrections to things that have gone off track. Superficiality. Quick to become bored; needs constant stimulus. Need to be alert to all that is going on around you. Rushing things. Premature forcing produces unwanted results. Falls. Mistiming or miscuing. Home improvements.

Gifts: Divine discontent. Knowing when to work and when to play. Learning correct application of forcefulness. Appreciation of time.

43

Tarot Equivalent: The Three of Cups

Opportunities: Creative work. Illness or circumstances limit ability to work. Ability to be productive and attend to matters. Workmates. Friendly neighbours. Family concerns. Relatives. Visiting relatives and/or friends may involve travel over water or long distances. Foster parents. Extended families. Family reunions. Family friend. Mixing in like company. Mixing business with pleasure. Secrets. Twosome becomes a threesome. Trysts. Remaining friends with past lovers. Problems due to a third party. Union or divorce due to another. Separation from lover or friends. Separation from children. Severing of ties with loved ones. Thoughtless gossip. Handicapped by illness or circumstances. Unusual or unwanted developments. Feeling untroubled by pressing problems. Allowing things to work out by themselves. Allowing destiny to take its course.

Gifts: Loyalty among friends. Celebrations.

35

Tarot Equivalent: The Nine of Wands

Opportunities: Marketing others' products. Many accomplishments, yet more to achieve. Endless work. Always one more hurdle to overcome. Battle tired and weary yet victorious through sustained courage and endurance. Resilience, defiance, resistance, stubbornness, tenacity, doggedness are all good qualities but can work against you if adhered to when a change of attitude or tactic are required. Struggle to stay in front of things. Needing support. Period of recovery. Uses illness as a crutch. Depleted health or energy due to many pressures. Exploiting energy reserves. Patience required. On the defensive. Territorial; defending one's territory. Many things pressing on the mind. Anxiety.

Gifts: Ultimate success.

The Life Diamond

53

Tarot Equivalent: The Knight of Swords

Opportunities: Travel a big part of life and work. Always on the move. Rises to a challenge. Impatient. Brave, skilful, adroit. Resourceful. Quick on the uptake. Clever. Does not suffer fools gladly. Defender of rights. An agitator. Chaotic times. Things moving in and out at a fast pace. Saint or sinner. Can be ruthless and cruel when pursuing own ends.

Gifts: Focus. Sincerity of purpose.

36

Tarot Equivalent: The Ten of Wands

Opportunities: Tackling big projects. Enterprise and discovery. Determination, grit, fortitude. High achiever. Extremely hard worker. Extremely conscientious. Weighed down with work and domestic responsibilities. Doing more than your share. Hunched shoulders/back due to carrying the world on them, hence the "Atlas Syndrome". Mental and physical breakdown due to overwork or too many pressures. Must learn to delegate and trust that others are capable of doing a good job. Local business/trade. Teaching. The perennial student. Lavish tastes. Move to a new neighbourhood. Realisation of the need to take ownership of one's life. Making responsible, even life-changing decisions. Duties, obligations and responsibilities rule this period. Compulsive/obsessive disorders. Chronic fatigue or burn-out. Double standards.

Gifts: Persistence. Oratory. Fame and glory with humility. High ethics.

63

Tarot Equivalent: The Nine of Swords

Opportunities: Self-analysis. Inner strength. Poise. Self-assurance. Composure. A patron of the arts. A deep appreciation of beauty may lead to becoming a collector. Multi-talented. Giftedness. At the mercy of controlling women. Interfering, meddling women. Malicious attacks from women. Sense of womanhood damaged from insensitive words/treatment. Women's business. Betrayal. Emotional suffering. Isolation. Illness. Depression. Guilt. Regret. Torment. Persecution. Poor sleep patterns. Sleep apnoea. Sleeplessness. Nightmares. A very distressing event. Maudlin reactions and behaviours. Self-pity. Unhealthy self-absorption. Living in the past. Mental instability. Irresponsibility. Neuroses. Anxiety attacks. Imposed or self-imposed bed confinement. Hospitalisation. Indolence. Avarice. Desire to possess without earning. Wanting to be rewarded for doing nothing eg. living off welfare. Medical intervention. Sickness benefits. Suicidal tendencies. Suicide sometimes.

Gifts: A born artist, musician, singer, teacher, speaker, writer.

Appendix 1

37

Tarot Equivalent: The King of Cups

Opportunities: This is one of the four 'King' Tarot Keys (see 51 for more information). When a number, 37 bestows characteristics such as maturity, strength, leadership, being at the top of a chosen field, being authoritarian and having an air of power and purpose about it. Loves the best of everything. Office, home and appearance reflect a love of luxury and beautiful things. Literary, artistic and scientific flair. Entertainer, performing arts, radio. Meticulous painting style. Wit and humour. Analytical. Serious. Explains things in great detail. Extremely kind, warm-hearted, loving, considerate, tolerant and thoughtful. Incurable romantic. A dreamer. Constant flux and change. Endings and beginnings. Contrasts in behaviour and circumstances. Perversity.

Gifts: Originality.

73

Tarot Equivalent: The Five of Pentacles

Opportunities: Finding institutions or others unreliable or falling short of their promises. Expecting too much of others with subsequent disappointment, resentment. Shattered trust in those who should be trustworthy. Not getting the help and support you expected. Feeling let down by others. Left to your own resources. Abandonment issues. Being forced to live in a more frugal manner. Lessons through loss or lack. Change for the worse. Being forced by circumstances to take charge of your own life. Everything will turn out successfully if you take responsibility for your own stuff. Shuns societal mores. A rebel.

Gifts: Self-reliance, resourcefulness and versatility. Self-empowerment. Hidden talents spawned from duress and endurance. Rising to the occasion.

38

Tarot Equivalent: The Queen of Cups

Opportunities: This is a 'Queen' number (see 24). New or renewed spiritual relationships. Heightened spiritual awareness and/or psychic talents. Seeking a guru or spiritual teacher. Formal or unorthodox religious, spiritual or pagan tuition. Lucrative creative talents. Love of beauty, comfort and entertainment. Highly skilled. Enforced financial controls due to impulsive spending. Structured education. Creative works reaching completion. TV entertainer. Beauty industry. Jeweller. Alternate health practitioner. Metaphysical writer/lecturer. Publishers, publishing and advertising. Forgetfulness as a result of poor attention and scattering of thought processes and energies or from having 'too many irons in the fire'. Losing focus.

Gifts: Enlightenment from greater knowledge. Focus. Birth of a creative enterprise.

The Life Diamond

83

Tarot Equivalent: Substitute: Justice and The High Priestess

Opportunities: Spiritual awareness. Spiritual growth. Potential for mastery of and profit from an art or media form. Media magnate. Business interests in the media and entertainment fields. A taskmaster. Active sports person. Making money from sporting abilities. Fond of sport entertainment. Major issues to do with finances could stem from risk-taking or impulsive, self-indulgent spending. Savings required for greater financial expenditure for improvements, replacements or maintenance purposes. Money going out faster than it comes in. Spendthrift tendencies as urges for self-indulgence or impulse spending intensify. Delusions of grandeur. Betrayal by a friend or lover. Separation. Loss of a relative.

Gifts: Right speech.

39

Tarot Equivalent: The Knight of Cups

Opportunities: 9 magnifies its 3. Visionary. Love of beauty, luxury, glamour, creature comforts, money, love and romance, sex, social activity and entertainment and holidays. These things may be highly desirable, motivating factors to its bearer. Giftedness, genius, artistic and literary talents. An abundance of creative expression that can be applied to anything. Restoration, redecoration and refurbishing. Conscientious objector. Self-indulgence. Impulse spending on luxury items. Broken romance. Heightened sexuality. Sexual misdemeanours, sexual deviance or questionable sexual ethics. Paedophilia. Voyeurism. Substance abuse. Unfaithfulness, love affairs. Betrayal, lies and deception. Escapism. Avoidance behaviour. Naivety. Lack of conscience. Gossip. Scandal. Libel.

Gifts: Artistic talent. Genius. Active humanitarian. Charisma. Magnetism.

93

Tarot Equivalent: Substitute: The Hanged Man and The Empress

Opportunities: Abundance. Artistic/literary activities. Entrepreneurial activities. Global communications (Internet). Media. Publishing. Public speaking. Teaching. Dissemination of knowledge or skills. Children. Students. Long-distance travel to visit a child. Holidaying with children. Experiencing special moments with a child or children. Sometimes birth of twins when 3 doubles or triples around a 9. Judge, courts and legal matters. Matters to do with children's' court. Custody issues. Fostering or adopting a child/children. Financially supporting a child. Wastefulness. Extravagance. Squandering. Recklessness. Spreads rumours. Infidelity. Superficial. Eccentricity.

Gifts: Broad-mindedness. Benefactor.

Appendix 1

45

Tarot Equivalent: The Five of Cups

Opportunities: Awareness of justice at work in your life. A deep awareness of the suffering of others. Time to re-evaluate present circumstances and move on. Rebuilding and adapting after change. Break with the past. New from old. Turning your back on whom or what is causing you grief. Anxiety. Disappointment Emotional hurts. Loss, grief, bereavement. Spending one's life wishing for the things never had. Focusing on regrets and a "what might have been" or "oh woe is me" and "if only" outlook. Pessimistic viewpoint. Lack of love in the life. Failure to focus on the fact that the glass is half full rather than half empty. Things are not as bad as they seem. Regrets. Scepticism. Self-pity. Worry. Inability to break with the past and/or to let the past go. Depression. Malcontent. Dissenter. Anarchist. Change of work.

Gifts: Penetration of the veils of illusion. Seeing the Light of Truth. Full appreciation of what you actually possess.

54

Tarot Equivalent: The Page of Swords

Opportunities: Pressure to adapt to the reality of a situation. Ability to sweep away the old and begin anew. Cutting away the dross. Cutting ties from those who cause pain and suffering. Endings that require new developments or strategies that more appropriately support these changes. Dogged determination to fathom things out. Researcher. Sleuth. Vigilance. A period of inner change and growth as new perspectives develop. An idea or something that has great promise. Careful development of something that has potential for widespread appeal. Introduction of a promising philosophy, science or procedures. Maligning others. Untrustworthy. Under suspicion. Playing politics. Spy. Stalker.

Gifts: Prophecy. Incisive visionary. Ability to open up your visions by not limiting your reality.

46

Tarot Equivalent: The Six of Cups

Opportunities: 46 is what I call a reciprocal number in that one receives kindnesses, gifts and pleasantries and/or gives them. It hints of family, work and health difficulties or a crisis that may be due to karmic, genetic or family conditioning. It can also signify healthy or dysfunctional family ties. Breaking free from inhibiting ties. Freeing one self from damaging family patterning. Family business. Trading in domestic goods. A tendency to wallow in the past. Revisiting old familiar places. Sudden reappearance of a childhood or old friend from the past. Return of happy and sad memories. A tendency to remain in unhealthy situations longer than necessary. Altercations with the boss. Leadership struggles. Loss. Inheritances. Death sometimes, especially with 1, 4, 13, 15, 16, 17, 18, 19, 10, 20, 21, 22, 27, 40, 64 or 55.

Gifts: Keen discriminative, reasoning powers. Learning to adjust to inevitable cyclic and developmental phases.

The Life Diamond

64

Tarot Equivalent: The Ten of Swords

Opportunities: Family, work or health crisis reaches a climax. Financial gain/loss. Family business. Work in a domestic or health industry. Adjustments at work. Modifying and restructuring daily routines. Severe crises that can be overcome. Embarrassment when with others. Self-protection. Survival tactics. Having to remain forever vigilant and keep your wits about you. Unsupported by others. Others try to bring you down. Betrayals, secret plots and schemes. Being put down by a superior. Backstabbing. Betrayed by a trusted relative or colleague. Personal suffering. Dysfunctional family. Estrangement from family. Family members turn on one another. Self-destructive tendencies. A health breakdown from overwork. Life-threatening illness or occurrence. Desolation. Annihilation. Ruin. Large financial loss. Self abuse. Going against tradition. Phase of being unproductive. Death sometimes, especially with 1, 4, 13, 15, 16, 17, 18, 19, 10, 20, 21, 22, 27, 40, 46 or 55.

Gifts: Surrender. Transcendence. Getting in touch with your mortality. Occult aptitude and interests.

47

Tarot Equivalent: The Seven of Cups

Opportunities: Major decisions. Too many options confuse decision-making. Focus. Analysis. Synthesis. Penetrating the fog. Notable achievements. Inventiveness. Practical decision-making. Sound business sense. Making money. Handling others' money and/or affairs. Fund-raising. Those who have something to offer others in the way of time, energy, money and/or goods. Seeing life with blinkers on. Self-delusion. Secrets or withholding about money and finances. Lies about money and financial affairs. Self-mutilation.

Gifts: Manifestation of talents, goals and/or dreams when focussed.

74

Tarot Equivalent: The Six of Pentacles

Opportunities: Success. Gifts and rewards. Reciprocity. Profits from creativity. A windfall. Benefactor. Generosity. Sharing worldly goods, even home. Time and energy given to others. Putting others before oneself. Helping those truly in need. Treating others as your equal. A balanced approach to all affairs. Painstaking research. Sudden change to circumstances. Overbearing. Opinionated. Insensitive. Withholding. Financial scarcity. Disappointment that wastefulness brings. Money doesn't fix money problems. Separation due to travel. Discrimination. Fear of loss.

Gifts: Ability to make a difference. Compassion and empathy for others. Humanitarianism (Jesus = 74). Self-lessness.

Appendix 1

Tarot Equivalent: The Eight of Cups

Opportunities: Monumental works. Sacrificing the mundane for the spiritual. A turning point. Reversals. Reaching a point when you are capable of sacrifice to aspire to something better and more fulfilling. Turning towards a new beginning that holds greater promise. Urge to move on and up. Always striving to better oneself. A goal-setter. Achieving a personal best. Leaving everything behind to make a fresh start. Can leave family, children or friends at the drop of a hat! A wanderer. Gypsy-like. Taking a different heading. Sudden change of religion or country. Termination of studies. Major financial decisions. Inheritance. A gnawing dissatisfaction with life or something specific, such as a crisis that may be the trigger for major changes and decisions that involve giving something up, or end something, or leave something, which is often tinged with emotions. Reckless abandonment. Circumstances force radical life-changing decisions. Being sorry for taking wrong direction. Deep regret for not having the courage to move forward and upward when the opportunity arose. Transition from life to death.

Gifts: Divine discontent. One-pointedness. Higher calling. Courage.

Tarot Equivalent: Substitute: The World, The Hanged Man, The Empress and 4 of Wands

Opportunities: Money-maker. Big business. Sound business sense. Consulting specialists in their fields. Insurance. Pensions. Annuities. Investments. Loans. Loan applications. Child seeks loan (3 from 84) without resources or any intention of paying it back. A fool and its money are easily parted. A loan for travelling purposes with a specific aim eg for health, spiritual or humanitarian reasons. Drawing on inner strength to overcome passive resistance/inertia. Reversals in friendships. Embezzlement. Fraud. Bankruptcy due to another. Reversals in income. Financial ruin. Sale of assets. Family investments. Family inheritance. Issues surrounding the foundations of what means security to you. Difficult times. Struggle. Inertia. Police matters. Death of a leader or authority figure. Abject cruelty.

Gifts: Advanced reasoning abilities. Acuity.

Tarot Equivalent: The Nine of Cups

Opportunities: 9 accents its 4. The emphasis is on unselfishness, understanding and empathy for those less fortunate. Worker for humanitarian rights or the improvement of conditions for those less fortunate. Philanthropy. Practical leader or minister. Politician, doctor, scientist, mathematician. Potential to make/lose a lot of money. Changing professions. Sabbatical. End of work. Loss of earnings. No financial backup. Greed. Faulty thinking that the world owes you instead of the reverse. Self-destructive tendencies. Bulimia, yoyo dieting. Health disorders due to poor diet. Life threatening or altering situations. An overbearing male. New male in life. Life changed due to a male's influence. Death or loss of a male. Birth of a son. Accidents.

Gifts: Sensitivity to others needs. Empathy.

The Life Diamond

94

Tarot Equivalent: Substitute: Death, 5 of Wands and The Emperor

Opportunities: 9 magnifies 4. Exercising will, logic and reason. Working out formulas or plans. Common sense. Wisdom. Tendency to go to excesses, e.g. gregarious or totally withdrawn. Yoyo dieting. Workaholic to layabout, therefore disciplinary measures needed to find the happy medium. It is important for your world to operate smoothly. Financial problems. Establishing a new line of work. Ending tutoring services. Loss of employment. Redundancy package. Retirement. Marriage proposal. Business proposal. Separation from or death of a male. Accident prone. Accidental death. Family dramas. Fetishes. Promiscuous male. Difficulties with males. Death.

Gifts: Practising harmlessness. Finding the self-discipline to control self-indulgence problems.

56

Tarot Equivalent: The Two of Swords

Opportunities: Mediumistic. Diplomacy. Being caught up in something that you are powerless to change or decide not to change for the time being. Pretending that things are better than they really are. Naivety. Refusing to see others' faults. Allowing others to interfere with your plans in the hope that they will eventually come around to your way of thinking or doing. Meditating on solving life's riddles or personal problems. Patience. Tolerance. Strategising. Manipulating. Self-searching. Being inhibited or intimidated by others. Putting things on hold. Consider, contemplate, move when the time feels right – it is all about timing! Delaying the inevitable until ready. Avoidance behaviour. Thwarted attempts at attaining goals. Voluntary time-out. Self-reproach. Grim memories of the past.

Gifts: Saintliness. Clairaudience. Intuitive insights that pierce illusion laying bare reality.

65

Tarot Equivalent: The King of Pentacles

Opportunities: This is one of the four 'King' Tarot Keys (see 51 for more information). When a number, 65 bestows characteristics such as maturity, strength, leadership, being at the top of a chosen field, being authoritarian and having an air of power and purpose about it. Money-oriented. Avaricious tendencies. Business opportunities. Learning to be versatile. Learning the importance of change. Judging the right time to make changes. Breaking with tradition and establishing a new order. Breaking family mores. Domestic changes. Career changes. Change to relationship status. Health changes. A hidden medical condition. Up against someone/something you cannot change. Rigid, dull and boring. Into passive resistance. Will not be pushed or coerced. Holding one's ground. Need to prove one's maleness or oneself. Waiting for test results or medical outcomes.

Gifts: Innate ability to judge right timing to act upon decisions that improve one's lot.

57

Tarot Equivalent: The Three of Swords

Opportunities: Intense emotional nature. Passionate. Compulsion to act. Learning compassion, sympathy and understanding from pain and suffering. Problems of the heart. Heartbreak, heartache and emotional pain. Heart disease. Heart surgery. Orthopaedic surgery. General surgery. Life threatening illness or accident. Emotional trauma. Overwhelming unhappiness. Several betrayals by loved ones. Love affairs. Dramatics. Tragedy. Depression. Attitudes/thinking distorted by harsh experiences. Ability to self-analyse and gain enlightening insights when emotional pain subsides. Feeling unacceptable/unlovable. Inability to let bad memories go. Returning to places that evoke bad memories. Doom and gloom. Bitterness. Deriving pleasure from hurting others. Revenge. Sexual deviance. Perversion.

Gifts: Empathy. Ability to walk in another's shoes. Forgiveness. The "Wounded Healer".

75

Tarot Equivalent: The Seven of Pentacles

Opportunities: Higher expression is found when the true reward is in the personal satisfaction gained from the work or the journey and not in the monetary gains - after all, the number of sacrifice (12) is contained in 75! Either bountiful or meagre rewards for hard labour. Disappointment in achievements. Less than hoped for results. Failed business enterprise. Redundancy. Abandonment. Results less than anticipated. Being forced to be satisfied with less or to reassess work practices or capabilities. Insecurity. Loss of faith. Aborted schemes. Unanticipated outcomes. Frustration. Talents unappreciated or overlooked. Test of skills. Idleness. Complacency.

Gifts: Inner rewards. Inner satisfaction. Doing the work for the work's sake rather than the reward. It's about the journey, rather than the destination. Patience.

58

Tarot Equivalent: The Four of Swords

Opportunities: High achiever despite restrictive conditions. Achieving ultimate success after struggle, striving and overcoming what seem to be insurmountable odds. Ability to achieve great works under duress or adverse conditions. Great courage and determination. Great fortitude. Great staying power/resistance. A quiet achiever. A specific kind of impediment, illness or restriction that needs to be overcome before success or improved conditions can be achieved. Self-isolation until projects reach fruition. Self-limitation. Self-confinement. Forced time-out. Forced into limbo. Rest and recuperation. Sabbatical. Relaxation. Holiday for health reasons. Ignoring a health problem. Hypochondria. Chronic fatigue. A weak constitution. Forced or self-imposed bed rest. Retirement from life. Interruption to business activities. Travel for business or health. Forced to adapt due to mistakes or severe circumstances. Imprisonment. Funerals.

Gifts: Dedication. Freedom. Recovery. Ability to overcome huge odds. After prolonged endeavour, exploitation of unique talents. Awareness of personal limitations.

The Life Diamond

85

Tarot Equivalent: Substitute: 5 of Wands, Death and The Emperor

Opportunities: Ability to overcome shortcomings and master strengths to achieve greatness. Seeks accolades for achievements. Changes in lifestyle due to changes in financial situation. Investing in a pioneering venture. Changes to business practices. Business expansion. Trade/commercial practices. Inheritance. Impulse spending. Cent wise, dollar foolish. Holidays for health reasons. Improved or improving conditions. Insurance, legal, neighbour, tenant concerns. Wrangles over joint financial issues. Wrangles over quotations. Petty squabbling. Difficulties with children. Police involvement. Struggle. Great effort for small gains. Having the rug pulled out from under your feet.

Gifts: Prioritising. Seeking just and fair dealings.

59

Tarot Equivalent: The Five of Swords

Opportunities: 9 strengthens 5. Change of religion. Stern teacher or counsellor. Importance of order paramount. Meticulous attention paid to personal details and organisation. Immaculate or messy housekeeper. Conqueror. The victor and the vanquished. Focus on winning to the exclusion of all else. Ruthless. Malicious. Nasty, bad-tempered. Altercations. The "Medusa syndrome" – the perpetrator can be so menacing as to "immobilise" others like "turning them to stone"! Annihilation. Preying on another's weakness or unfortunate circumstances. A bully or subjected to bullying tactics. At the mercy of another abusing their position or authority. Feeling demeaned and broken. Being the victim of uninhibited wrath. Merciless treatment. Cruelty. Law unto oneself. Perverted sense of justice. Control freak. Sinister. Vitriolic. Vicious attacks (verbal, written or physical) on well-meaning, unsuspecting or weak victims. A well-armed adversary in legal matters.

Gifts: Making most of the moment. Knowing how to win by losing or when to fight and when not to.

95

Tarot Equivalent: Substitute: Ace of Cups, Temperance and The Hierophant

Opportunities: Wealth, success, charisma, leader, an initiator. Planning well-considered strategies. An organiser. Judicial affairs and institutions. Welfare officials and agencies. Meticulous or messy housekeeping. Extremely critical of others. A whinger and whiner. Wears others down. Blind to own faults. Chip on shoulder. A force to be reckoned with. Complacency, ingratitude, disappointments. Assessing the pros and cons of engaging in disputes. Deciding the best time to fight or whether to fight at all. Winning by losing. The deal breaker.

Gifts: The peace-maker.

Appendix 1

67

Tarot Equivalent: The Knight of Pentacles

Opportunities: A practical, solid, dependable, ethical, trustworthy individual. Giving time, advice or financial support to others. Slow but sure success. Clever at implementing practical ideas and plans that ensure material rewards. Consolidation of tasks. Problems require systematic analysis to assess their importance and to evolve corrective courses of action. Unexpected delays or cancellations. Blockages to potential. Analytical approach. Type of paralysis and inability to move until things change or practical solutions found. Things grinding to a halt.

Gifts: A never give up attitude. Realisation of hard won goals.

76

Tarot Equivalent: The Eight of Pentacles

Opportunities: Diligence. Craftsmanship. Meticulous attention to detail. Striving to perfect a skill. Mastery. Distracted from real work. Lack of motivation. Illness makes hard work of easy tasks. Forced retirement. Redundancy. Unusual or rare health disorder. Mistakes in diagnosis due to something hidden - seek second opinions. Travel hampered by illness or unforeseen circumstances. A trustworthy and loyal employee.

Gifts: Dedication to perfecting skills and work ethics.

68

Tarot Equivalent: The Page of Pentacles

Opportunities: Agriculture. Sailing. Developing a moneymaking project. Injecting a different slant or approach into one's affairs. Ability to painstakingly manifest material things. Travel for study purposes. Residing with a billeting family for study purposes. Study under a scholarship. Domestic and/or executive tyrant. Stubbornness. Having a chip on one's shoulder. Overwhelmed by unpleasantness and feeling stuck. Placed in difficult circumstances. Wasteful and prodigal tendencies. Narrow, negative focus blocks way to liberation. Discontented with one's lot.

Gifts: Developing mastery in a particular field of expertise.

86

Tarot Equivalent: Substitute: Ace of Cups, Temperance and The Hierophant

Opportunities: A just and fair mentor. A highly motivated business executive/specialist. An eminent surgeon, judge or entrepreneur. Medical, financial or legal specialists. Someone who cares for the welfare of his employees and others. An extremely conscientious worker. Loans. Insurance, banking, investments. Building future assets. Taxes. Inheritance. Home improvements. A lucrative family enterprise. Domestic products, trade and personal services. Nurse. Hospitals and related services. Illness and recovery. Forced adjustments. Threatening financial situation. Serious health issues, health crisis, threat to life. Surgery. Family upheaval/crisis. Family or business power-plays. Family, trade or business severance. Travel. Treachery and betrayal.

Gifts: Ascension. Promotion.

69

Tarot Equivalent: The Ace of Pentacles

Opportunities: 9 intensifies 6. Born wealthy. Acquired or increased wealth. Enterprise. Global trade. Domestic enterprises with global marketing possibilities. Property. Real estate. Money-making capabilities. Leaving legacies to posterity. Gain/loss/regain of wealth. Sound, legal judgement. Love, romance and commitment. Home improvements, extensions. Changes within the domestic situation. Heated domestic scenes. Family dramatics. Care of a family member. Serious illness in the family. Domestic violence. Incest. Affairs. Dissolution of a family or business enterprise.

Gifts: Instinctive judgement regarding money-making possibilities. Ability to develop a global enterprise or do things on a large scale. Multi-tasking.

96

Tarot Equivalent: Substitute: King of Swords, The Devil and The Lovers

Opportunities: The masses. Global service industries. Domestic services. Nursing homes. Job networking. Make a million, lose a million. Idealism. Marriage. Possessiveness. Facing your fears. Freedom from restriction. Life altering experiences and decisions. Adjusting to altered circumstances, beliefs and goals. Compulsive obsessive tendencies. Vast responsibilities. Renewed hopes and dreams. Advisor, counselling roles. The wider community. Championing a cause. New beginnings from shattered beliefs and dreams. Loss of faith and hope. Shattered confidence in judicial system. Separations or severances in relationships. Family estate. Family grievances. Divorce. Love affairs. Alimony. Family legal disputes. Emotional outbursts. End of a line of work. Break away tendencies. "Putting in the knife".

Gifts: Release from the mundane. Devotion. Spiritual aspiration.

78

Tarot Equivalent: The Ten of Pentacles

Opportunities: Denotes wealth, success and a happy and contented conclusion to one's life. Marriage. Working towards a bright and happy future. Eventual success and security from very poor beginnings. Completion. End of a cycle or phase. Voluntary settling for less to achieve a desired outcome. Choosing fulfilment rather than the reward. Warns of redundancy and the possibility of taking some or all of the glitz away from a comfortable and happy retirement. Being forced to settle for less. Loss of work. Down on your luck. Sometimes death.

Gifts: Wisdom. Retirement.

Appendix 1

87

Tarot Equivalent: Substitute: King of Swords, The Devil and The Lovers

Opportunities: Mastery. Great achievement. Specialised areas of skills or business. Research. Investigation. Occult specialist. Metaphysics. Relocation. Home improvements. Travel to a new home. Passing on personal insights to others. Taking advantage of the good nature of others. Severe manner or treatment. Says it as it is. Honest opinions. Too blunt. Unaware of words hurting others. Treachery. Perversion. Theft, daylight robbery. Material loss. Loss of home or family disintegration. Loss of assets. Loss of power. Giving in to weakness. Embezzlement. Sedition and treason.

Gifts: Giving others the benefit of personal insights or gifts. Discrimination.

79

Tarot Equivalent: Substitute: 7 of Swords, The Tower and The Chariot

Opportunities: 9 fortifies 7. The people's or family's champion. Persistence, stamina, tenacity. Purposeful. Decisive. Unwavering. A never give in attitude. Sees things through to the end. Handles large undertakings. Scientific thinking. Researcher. Great thirst for knowledge. Inquisitive. An analytical mind. Reserved and/or gregarious. Financial planning and advice. Illusory beliefs. New romance. Sudden surprises. Bizarre occurrences. Insensitivity to others. Total selfishness. Ruthlessness. Anarchy. Love/hate relationships. Hot/cold relationships. Clandestine or illicit affairs (also 97). Sexual deviance.

Gifts: Completion of a great work. Metaphysics.

97

Tarot Equivalent: Substitute: 7 of Swords, The Tower and The Chariot

Opportunities: Someone or something that has universal appeal. Guru. Evangelistic tendencies. Preaching. Dissemination of specialist knowledge. Counselling abilities. Group counsellor or counselling. Empathy. Group leader. Charisma. Pursuit of a worthy cause. Diviner. Huge victory or coup. Surprising events. Great perseverance. Great insight. An intellectual. Self-imposed isolation. Holds own counsel or has a mind of their own. Sceptic. Eccentricity. Dual personality - likes to be needed or likes solitude; either loves you or cannot abide you; love/hate relationships. Gregarious and/or reclusive. Schizophrenic tendencies. Perverted mentality. Perverted perceptions. Despot. Sexually indiscriminate. Paedophilia. Lack of conscience. Ruthless.

Gifts: Inspiration. Genius. Awakening.

The Life Diamond

⟨89⟩ Tarot Equivalent: Substitute: 3 of Pentacles, The Star and Strength

Opportunities: 9 makes 8 stronger. Huge financial resources. Enjoying the fruits of labours. Securing of financial future. Receiving recognition for vast knowledge and talents. Stock market. Global or large financial institutions. Tying up legal affairs to do with real estate, loans or trade agreements. Costly lawsuit. Police and legal events. Agitator. Lobbyist.

Gifts: Immense talent in a given field. Fame and fortune.

⟨98⟩ Tarot Equivalent: Substitute: 3 of Pentacles, The Star and Strength

Opportunities: Public acclaim or disgrace. Public lawsuit. Global terrorism. Campaigner. Dissenter. Insurance claims. Lawsuits. Prosecution. Litigation. Contesting of a will.

Gifts: Mediator for peace. Environmental activist.

APPENDICES

APPENDIX 2:
0 - 78 NUMBERS APPENDED TO THEIR TAROT KEYS

THE MAJOR ARCANA

The first 22 Keys represent our latent, undeveloped and unexpressed spiritual potential - our endless possibilities. The word *arcanum* (plural *arcana*) means secret or hidden knowledge relating to Cosmic Laws. They depict different aspects of the esoteric counterpart hidden deeply within our nature that relates to our spiritual and psychological makeup - the intangible aspects of ourselves that need to be meditated upon, probed and acted out to be able to bring them into manifestation via daily expression. These Keys symbolise in pictorial form archetypal images of Higher Forces that ingeniously describe our spiritual journey. It is suggested that you consult Tarot resources that give a comprehensive description of these amazing keys, as to do this here, is beyond the scope of this book.

Esoteric titles follow each Key's number and name. These titles are those given in various esoteric texts. The ruling astrological correspondences of the Major Arcana Keys are then listed beside each followed by their Hebrew letter's name and what it represents. Note that *Aleph* is the first letter of the Hebrew alphabet naturally corresponding to number one although situated on "0" of The Fool". Hence, the actual number of each Hebrew letter is one ahead of each Tarot Key because the first letter is assigned to The Fool, at "0".

This added information for each Key often provides further insights when interpreting numbers for those who are seeking deeper esoteric insights.

0 The FOOL – "The Spirit of the Aether". URANUS. Hebrew letter: *Aleph* meaning *An Ox*. Relates to super-consciousness. An omnipresent pregnant state.

1 The MAGICIAN – "The Magus of Power". Relates to self-consciousness. MERCURY. Hebrew letter: *Beth* meaning *A House*. Creative endowment. Life vs. powerlessness, impotence, death; rational vs. irrational thought.

2 The HIGH PRIESTESS – "The Priestess of the Silver Star". Relates to subconsciousness. MOON. Hebrew letter: *Gimel* meaning *A Camel*. Peace vs. war or opposing forces.

3   The EMPRESS – "The Daughter of the Mighty Ones". VENUS. Hebrew letter: *Daleth* meaning *A Door*. Fertility vs. aridity; wisdom vs. folly; grace and sin.

4   The EMPEROR – "The Son of the Morning; the Chief of the Mighty". ARIES. Part of Body: Head. Hebrew letter: *Heh* meaning *A Window*. Sense: Sight. Logic, law and reason vs. lawlessness.

5   The HIEROPHANT – "The Magus of the Eternal Gods". TAURUS. Part of Body: Neck as link between head and body, throat, mouth, nose and ears. Hebrew letter: *Vau* meaning *A Nail or Hook*. Sense: Hearing. Virtuosity vs. sensuality.

6   The LOVERS – "The Children of the Voice Divine; the Oracles of the Mighty God". GEMINI. Parts of Body: Lungs, shoulders, arms and hands. Hebrew letter: *Zain* meaning *A Sword, Knife or Weapon*. Sense: Smell. Discrimination. Decision vs. procrastination.

7   The CHARIOT – "The Child of the Power of the Waters; the Lord of the Triumph of Light". CANCER. Parts of Body: Breasts, ribs and stomach. Hebrew letter: *Cheth* meaning *A Fence or an Enclosure*. Sense: Speech. Control vs. chaos Protection vs. exposure.

8   STRENGTH – "The Child of the Flaming Sword; the Leader of the Lion". LEO. Parts of Body: The heart, sides, back and spine. Hebrew letter: *Teth* meaning *A Snake*. Sense: Taste. Courage vs. cowardice; Offence vs. defence.

9   The HERMIT – "The Magus of the Voice of Light; the Prophet of the Gods". VIRGO. Parts of Body: The intestines where digestion is completed. Hebrew letter: *Yod* meaning *An Open Hand*. Sense: Touch. Wisdom vs. ignorance.

10 WHEEL of FORTUNE – "The Lord of the Forces of Life". JUPITER. Parts of Body: The thighs. Hebrew letter: *Kaph* meaning *A Fist; to grasp*. Cyclic changes. Wealth vs. poverty; gain vs. loss; progress vs. inertia.

11 JUSTICE – "The Daughter of the Lord of Truth; the Holder of the Balances". LIBRA. Parts of Body: Kidneys (elimination), the loins and lumbar region of the spine. Hebrew letter: *Lamed* meaning *An Ox-goad. Work. To prod*. Justice vs. disparity; work vs. indolence; education vs. ignorance.

12 The HANGED MAN – "The Spirit of the Mighty Waters". NEPTUNE. Parts of Body: The feet. Hebrew letter: *Mem* meaning *Water*. Reversed awareness from mundane to spiritual.

13 DEATH – "The Child of the Great Transformers; the Lord of the Gates of Death". SCORPIO. Parts of Body: Sex organs and reproduction. Hebrew letter: *Nun* meaning *Fish*. Sense: Movement. Transition, transformation, continuance.

14 TEMPERANCE – "The Daughter of the Reconcilers; the Bringer Forth of Life". SAGITTARIUS. Parts of Body: Thighs and hips that support the weight of the body when standing or sitting. Hebrew letter: *Samekh* meaning *Prop*. Sense: Anger. Synthesis of seemingly incompatibilities to create something new.

15 The DEVIL – "The Lord of the Gates of Matter; the Child of the Forces of Time". CAPRICORN. Parts of Body: The knees that we are brought to in prayer by our sense of bondage and personal insufficiency. Hebrew letter: *Ayin* meaning *An Eye*. Sense: Humour. Non-attachment vs. attachment; liberation vs. bondage.

16 The TOWER – "The Lord of the Hosts of the Mighty". MARS. Hebrew letter: *Peh* meaning *Mouth as organ of speech*. Arousal vs. apathy; awakening from stagnation; truth vs. illusion.

17 The STAR – "The Daughter of the Firmament; the Dweller Between the Waters". AQUARIUS. Parts of Body: The shins and ankles. Hebrew letter: *Tzaddi* meaning *A fish hook*. Sense: Imagination; meditation. Hope vs. despair.

18 The MOON – "The Ruler of Flux and Reflux; the Child of the Sons of the Mighty". PISCES. Parts of Body: The feet. Hebrew letter: *Qoph* meaning *The back of the head; an ear*. Sense: Sleep. Cyclic change vs. rigidity; reorganisation vs. maintaining the status quo.

19 The SUN – "The Lord of the Fire of the World". THE SUN. Part of Body: The face. Hebrew letter: *Resh* meaning *A head, face or countenance*. Fertility vs. sterility.

20 JUDGEMENT – "The Spirit of the Primal Fire". PLUTO. Part of Body: Sexual organs. Hebrew letter: *Shin* meaning *Tooth, digestion*. Spiritual rebirth. Realisation vs. ignorance.

21 The WORLD – "The Great One of the Night of Time". SATURN. Part of Body: The skeleton and teeth. Hebrew letter: *Tau or Tav* meaning *A cross, mark or signature*. Advancement vs. stagnation; administration vs. anarchy.

22 The FOOL – "The Spirit of the Aether". URANUS. Hebrew letter: *Aleph. An Ox* meaning *Cultivation*.

THE MINOR ARCANA

These Tarot Keys are more *specific* in nature, describing life's everyday activities in accordance with their element. They perfectly describe how various people participate in our lives, as well as the everyday events, situations and circumstances that we experience in our personal worlds. Therefore, they are best interpreted as representing opportunities and lessons according to what they denote in everyday life.

There are fourteen cards in each suit. The royal, or court cards, which begin each suit depict mastery over the qualities of the particular element and attributes that they belong to. They also indicate mixing in society and/or corporate affairs in general. When the King or the Queen are present in a person's numbers, expect that person to display certain of that King or Queen's qualities and attributes which gives them the latent ability to develop outstanding qualities and attributes and rise to the top of their chosen field.

The presence of a King or a Queen also characterises others who hold prominent positions in the life, such as a parent, partner or figureheads in society. Companies and organisations are also represented by each royal family. For example, the Cup royal family represent all aspects of the media industry. It would be advantageous to have either the King or the Queen if one is a writer, or the Knight if an illustrator or the Page if a reporter. As can be said for all cases, the royal family's highly developed characteristics can be positively or negatively expressed or balanced, e.g. one can be a compassionate and kind leader or a self-serving tyrant or one who mediates and is just and fair.

The Knights are as their name implies - crusaders and defenders of the qualities and principles that each suit portrays. They represent people and matters coming into and out of the life. The Pages personify young people or things in their early stages of development relative to a suit's particular representations. They tend to be daring, foolhardy and mischievous and lacking in maturity, yet spontaneous, ambitious and willing to do whatever it takes to succeed in their respective fields.

When the royal cards depict other people in the life, which they often do, they invariably describe those who have entered one's personal world, bringing with them their own specific lessons to pass on, whether directly or indirectly i.e., what it is that one needs to know or master as described by the Keys' qualities and element.

The powerful Aces follow the royal cards. Their power can be equated to that of a King (note the power suggested in their esoteric titles below). To aid in delineating the minor Keys, keep in mind that the smaller the numbers of each Key, often greater the difficulty is experienced in achieving what it depicts. This makes sense if you know that each of the four Aces are placed at the top of the "Tree of Life" in "KETHER, the CROWN", with the 2s and 3s being the next highest on the tree, and so on until the four 10s are found in the last sphere at the bottom of "The Tree" in "MALKUTH, the "KINGDOM (Earth)" which depicts the densest of the Tree's "Worlds". Simplistically, The Tree of Life is a symbol that represents our manifest universe. It is a diagram composed of ten spheres named *Sephiroth,* and twenty-two connecting lines called Paths. Together, they epitomise the *Thirty-two Paths of Wisdom.* (To elaborate on the "Tree of Life" further, is to go way beyond the scope of this book. However, The Tree is well worth your investigation – see *Recommended Reading* at the end of book.)

The esoteric title for each of the 78 Keys appears alongside their numbers. These titles have been taken from those made public knowledge by the members of the "Order of the Golden Dawn". Knowledge of this nature may further assist in their delineation by including this additional information.

The order of each suit follows the orthodox pattern, which begins with spirit and ideas (Wands), desires, emotions and feelings (Cups), intellect and thoughts (Swords) and results of the former (Fire, Water and Air) being manifested and expressed in material, everyday affairs (Pentacles or Coins - Earth).

THE SUIT OF WANDS

Wands relate to the element **Fire** - your spiritual attributes. They reveal how creative self-expression is demonstrated in enterprising ways stemming from intuition, inspired thoughts and creative ideas that have their source in superconscious realms - the Kingdom of Spirit. Basically, they govern the sphere of ideas, inspiration, imagination, idealism, energy, enthusiasm, virility, vitality and enterprise. They indicate when things are in their initial stages, showing much promise and potential for future development and extension. Wands also depict property, business and medical matters. Wands can be antagonistic and quarrelsome when negative.

23 = King of Wands - Air of Fire
24 = Queen of Wands - Water of Fire
25 = Knight of Wands - Fire of Fire
26 = Page of Wands - Earth of Fire
27 = Ace of Wands - The Root of the Powers of Fire
28 = Two of Wands - Dominion
29 = Three of Wands - Established Strength
30 = Four of Wands - Perfected Work
31 = Five of Wands - Strife
32 = Six of Wands - Victory
33 = Seven of Wands - Valour
34 = Eight of Wands - Swiftness
35 = Nine of Wands - Great Strength
36 = Ten of Wands - Oppression

TIP: With this suit, select cards that have a special affinity for you as reference points, such as major personal Keys, or commit the King, Queen, Knight and Page and Ace to

Appendix 2

memory as being ideal reference points. To place the 10 of Wands as this suits' final Key in your memory would give you a further anchor on which to draw. Whatever, it is best to find and employ your own methods that help to gain rapid access to these Tarot Keys. Memorise their pictorial details as well. Visual recollection of each Key and its symbology is an extremely helpful skill to develop to radically speed up delineative work. Committing a few keywords from each Key to memory is another essential skill to acquire in order to speed up interpretive capabilities.

THE SUIT OF CUPS

Cups relate to the element **Water** - the realm of the emotions, feelings and desires. Like water that has many states and moods, expect its qualities to be in a state of constant flux and change. The Cups very basically rule love, marriage, relationships, friendships and associates, and emotional security. They also rule the love of luxury, pleasant surroundings and company, comfort, entertainment, addictive behaviours and self-indulgence. Artistic talent and/or an appreciation of beauty in all forms are common traits because Cups rule the Creative World of forms. Cups can be quite nasty and perverse when extremely negative.

37 = King of Cups - Air of Water
38 = Queen of Cups - Water of Water
39 = Knight of Cups - Fire of Water
40 = Page of Cups - Earth of Water

(Cup court cards can signify self-delusional tendencies, a love of luxury, self-indulgence, day-dreaming and be addiction prone)

41 = Ace of Cups - The Root of the Powers of Water
42 = Two of Cups - Love
43 = Three of Cups - Abundance
44 = Four of Cups - Pleasure
45 = Five of Cups - Loss in Pleasure
46 = Six of Cups - Joy
47 = Seven of Cups - Illusory Success
48 = Eight of Cups - Abandoned Success
49 = Nine of Cups - Material Happiness
50 = Ten of Cups - Perfected Success

TIP: This is the easiest suit to commit to memory because many of its *unit* numbers correspond to its Tarot Key. For example, the "Ace of Cups" = 41, so the unit, **1**, relates to the **Ace**. Unit **2** in 42 = the "**2** of Cups". Unit **3** in 43 = the "**3** of Cups", and so on until you reach **49** which is the "**9** of Cups". The **0** in 50 equates to the **0** in the 10 of Cups. **50**

The Life Diamond

is an easy number to impress on your mind as being the *final* Key for its suit. Unit **1** in **51** begins the *next* suit - the suit of Swords. It immediately directs your attention to the *beginning* of this suit.

THE SUIT OF SWORDS

Swords relate to the element **Air** - the realm of the mind, discrimination, truth and justice. They can be quite severe and often forceful. Therefore, they relate to serious concerns, struggle, strife, setbacks, attacks, disappointments, depression, losses and separations. Swords often indicate illness, medical intervention and death. They also indicate the services of specialists, doctors, judges, solicitors, psychologists and police. Because the swords are double-edged, one must be on the lookout for contradictions, hypocrisy and double standards, such as; illness/recovery; restriction/movement; work/rest; truth/lies; hope/despair. Swords mainly describe situations that contain an element of force or severance - the thrust and parry of life. They bestow the ability to cut to the Truth and achieve planned accomplishments from the realms of ideas (Wands) and desire (Cups). They represent the "pain of adjustment" when negative.

51 = King of Swords - Air of Air
52 = Queen of Swords - Water of Air
53 = Knight of Swords - Fire of Air
54 = Page of Swords - Earth of Air

(People or situations indicated by Sword court cards, can be two-faced or double-dealing)

55 = Ace of Swords - The Root of the Powers of Air
56 = Two of Swords - Peace Restored
57 = Three of Swords - Sorrow
58 = Four of Swords - Rest from Strife
59 = Five of Swords - Defeat
60 = Six of Swords - Earned Success
61 = Seven of Swords - Unstable Effort
62 = Eight of Swords - Shortened Force
63 = Nine of Swords - Despair and Cruelty
64 = Ten of Swords - Ruin

TIP: This is another easy suit to commit to memory because its suit numbers have immediate correspondences to their Keys. For instance, from **55** the **Ace**, through to the **10 of Swords**, you can mentally use their *root digits* to link them directly to their Keys! Take particular note of each root digit of the following key numbers: 55 (**1**), 56 (**2**), 57 (**3**), 58 (**4**), 59 (**5**), 60 (**6**), 61(**7**), 62 (**8**), 63 (**9**) and 64 (**10**). They all help you to remember to locate each Sword's placement from the Ace through to the 10. <u>Interesting point</u>: **55** is the only master numbered Ace in the deck. This fact should help you to quickly store it in your memory.

THE SUIT OF PENTACLES or COINS

Pentacles relate to the element **Earth** - daily activity, work, finances and acquisitions. They provide the fertile ground upon which foundations can be laid for the creative manifestation of spiritual, emotional and intellectual ideas in daily life. Coins represent the end product of the initial undifferentiated idea (Wands) to its form (Cups) to its constitutional parts and mechanisms (Swords) and finally to its end product. They basically represent results in the form of business, industriousness, assets, material security, property, resources, values, priorities and measures of status and success. The Pentagram inscribed on the coins represents man's eventual control over all of the dominions in nature. (Refer to Chapters 2 and 3.)

65 = King of Pentacles - Air of Earth

66 = Queen of Pentacles - Water of Earth

67 = Knight of Pentacles - Fire of Earth

68 = Page of Pentacles - Earth of Earth

69 = Ace of Pentacles - The Root of the Powers of Earth

70 = Two of Pentacles - Harmonious Change

71 = Three of Pentacles - Material Works

72 = Four of Pentacles - Earthly Power

73 = Five of Pentacles - Material Trouble

74 = Six of Pentacles - Material Success

75 = Seven of Pentacles - Success Unfulfilled

76 = Eight of Pentacles - Prudence

77 = Nine of Pentacles - Material Gain

78 = Ten of Pentacles - Wealth

TIP: This suit does not lend itself to easy ways of committing it to memory unless you have major Keys holding certain positions within it. If this is not the case, then you can follow the tips given for the Wands suit by memorising the numbers and their Keys that hold the Royal, Ace and final positions. My way of quickly locating these Keys is to memorise **69** as the **Pentacle Ace**. Then, from the numbers 70 to 78, mentally *add 2 to each **unit** number*. For example, **70** (0+2) = the **2** of Pentacles, **71** (1+2) = the **3**, **72** (2+2) = the **4** and so on until you reach **78** (8+2) = the **10**. Use this ploy to add 1 to the units of

The Life Diamond

the Wands Keys to quickly place them in their suit. The easiest Keys to remember and place will always be the ones that equate to one of your major numbers. They provide excellent anchor points from which to begin memorising them. In keeping with true Pentacle nature - perseverance pays!

TABLE: EASY REFERRAL TO 78 TAROT KEYS NUMBERED IN SUITS

MAJOR ARCANA	WANDS	CUPS	SWORDS	PENTACLES
0 The Fool	23 King	37 King	51 King	65 King
1 Magician	24 Queen	38 = Queen	52 = Queen	66 = Queen
2 High Priestess	25 Knight	39 = Knight	53 = Knight	67 = Knight
3 Empress	26 Page	40 = Page	54 = Page	68 = Page
4 Emperor	27 Ace	41 = Ace	55 = Ace	69 = Ace
5 Hierophant	28 = 2	42 = 2	56 = 2	70 = 2
6 Lovers	29 = 3	43 = 3	57 = 3	71 = 3
7 Chariot	30 = 4	44 = 4	58 = 4	72 = 4
8 Strength	31 = 5	45 = 5	59 = 5	73 = 5
9 Hermit	32 = 6	46 = 6	60 = 6	74 = 6
10 Wheel of Fortune	33 = 7	47 = 7	61 = 7	75 = 7
11 Justice	34 = 8	48 = 8	62 = 8	76 = 8
12 Hanged Man	35 = 9	49 = 9	63 = 9	77 = 9
13 Death	36 = 10	50 = 10	64 = 10	78 = 10
14 Temperance				
15 The Devil	**TIPS:**	**TIPS:**	**TIPS:**	**TIPS:**
16 The Tower	1. Mentally **REDUCE**	1. Mentally **convert**	1. Mentally **ADD**	1. Mentally **ADD 2**
17 The Star	whole numbers	unit digit from	whole numbers	to *unit digit*
18 The Moon	from **ACE** ⇒ 36.	41 ⇒ 50 into **SAME**	from **55** ⇒ **64** then	from 70 ⇒ 78.
19 The Sun	Then +1 to root digits.	**DIGIT**. Eg 41 = 1;	**REDUCE:** Eg 55=10=1	Eg 70+2=**2**; 74=**6**;
20 Judgement	**Eg 33=6, 6+1= 7.**	44 = **4**; 50 = **10**	Eg 59=**5**; 64=**10**	77=**9** & 78=**10**
21 The World	2. Memorise ROYAL Keys and ACE	2. Memorise ROYAL Keys and ACE	2. Memorise ROYAL Keys and ACE	2. Memorise ROYAL Keys and ACE
22 The FOOL				

APPENDICES

APPENDIX 3
DELINEATIONS FOR THE 78 TAROT KEYS

NB: Appendix 3 is by no means exhaustive as whole books are written on this subject. It is made up of rudimentary interpretations to be used as a convenient starting-point. Therefore, it may be necessary to have Tarot reference books in your possession to access a variety of Tarot Key delineations.

The ORDER of TAROT KEYS from 0 to 78

0 - The FOOL: Feeling joyous, carefree and pure of heart and in touch with the essence of life. Living in the moment. Optimism and enthusiasm. Taking a quantum leap into the void and hoping for a safe landing/conclusion. Strong inner urge for change or to initiate something new. The beginning of a new cycle. Turning-point. Ready to move on regardless. Restlessness. Choices can be impulsive, reckless, daring or unplanned and not always based on full information or sound judgement - they may succeed or fail dismally. Foolishness. Wasted creativity, energy and resources. Many distractions. Scattering. Lack of focus. Poor choices. Misfit. Inertia. More desirable goals set aside due to other matters taking precedence. Presence of unforeseeable factors.

1 - The MAGICIAN: Enlightened self-direction. Mental efforts. Goodwill. Giftedness. Multi-talented. Developing skills, leadership, independence and self-awareness. Dominance issues. Ability to develop and capitalise on latent potential for good or evil. Ability to exploit leadership potential, ingenuity, creativity and learned skills for good or evil purposes. A willingness to take command of a needy cause or situation. A willingness to cooperate. To be versatile. Abuse of powers, talents, time and energy. Inhibited self-expression, speech impediment and/or learning disorders.

2 - The HIGH PRIESTESS: Mother figures. Innate wisdom. Wise or superficial. Heightened clairvoyance and intuition. Psychism. Mysterious forces. The paranormal. The unknown and the unforeseen. Secrets. Diplomatic. Can be overtly uncooperative or passively resistant. Avoidance behaviours. Travel. Commerce and trade.

Appendix 3

3 - The EMPRESS: Fertility, full and plenty, fruitfulness and exertion. Material gain. Happiness and fulfilment. Romance, marriage and pregnancy. Brings out talents and giftedness. Creative imagination. Tendency to overdo or over imbibe. Can be a 'Jack of all trades but a master of none'. Self-indulgence, impulse spending, weight gain, over-eating and drinking. Immorality and licentiousness. Infidelity. Untrustworthy. Lies. Sterility or infertility. Miscarriage or abortion. Signifies the head, the breast and the solar plexus.

4 - The EMPEROR: Father figures and mentors. Family mores, ties, conditioning and issues. Upbringing. Ambition. Authoritarian and confident. Executive ability. Stability of purpose. Building and consolidating security. Setting firm foundations and routines. Leadership. Executive and administrative abilities or authorities. Lessons in control over self and others. Strength or weakness. Tractability or intractability. Ability to be in command eroded by poor choices. Others' influence or outside influences. Autocratic. Wilful. Undisciplined. Disorder. Unjust, unreasonable. Short-sighted. Apathetic. Immature. Insecure. Inability to break from restricting, unhealthy or dysfunctional family ties.

5 - The HIEROPHANT: Depicts a person of great knowledge and wisdom who can be an inspirational or heinous leader. Desire to be seen as a pillar of virtue. Wise counsellor. Teaching by example. Help and support from another wiser or more knowledgeable than you. Those in religious or social welfare institutions. Bereft of outside advice forces falling on own resources to make the best of a situation. Those in authority get it wrong. Self-righteousness. Hypocrisy. Misrepresentation. Insincerity. Marriage or divorce.

6 - The LOVERS: The promise of purification through enlightenment and right living. Discrimination between virtues and vice. Faced with an imposing choice that once made has far reaching consequences. Forming bonds based on love, honour, commitment, trust or devotion. Soul unions. Lessons in versatility, resourcefulness and flexibility. Love, marriage and divorce. The voice. Solving life's riddles. Pro-active decision-making and consequential adjustments. Attraction of the sexes. Coercion, seduction and infatuation. Allurement of unworthy thoughts desires and deeds. Inner conflict. Illusion and self-delusion. Vacillation. The path of truth as opposed to the path of evil. Corruption. Basing decisions on erroneous information. Disaster.

7 - The CHARIOT: The ultimate triumph of spirit over matter. The victor or conqueror. Fame and reputation. Consciousness of purpose. Putting necessary knowledge, plans, discipline, structures, routines and actions in place to ensure success. Combines faith and intellect. Resolving difficulties and life's opposing forces. Restores balance and control. Staying on track or pitching pell-mell into chaos. Imbalance. Unrealistic beliefs or expectations of life and others bring failure. The power of speech and silence. Controversy. Defeat, destruction, ruin and downfall. Death.

8 - STRENGTH: Purity. Illumination. Holiness. Saint and sinner. Will and determination. Overcoming adversity, shortcomings and base instincts. Opposites in thoughts, emotions, speech, deeds and endeavours. Degrees of strength and weakness in health and sickness, wealth and poverty, courage and cowardice and power and subordination. Sophisticated or ignorant. Mastery and commonplace. Industry and indolence. Arrogant. Remorseless. Belligerent. Combative. Judgemental. Trials and triumphs. Attraction and repulsion. Bonding and separation. Promise and menace. Bullying. Terrorism. Weak will. Lack of self-discipline. Inertia. Degradation. Disgrace. Inheritance. Death and taxes. Medical practitioners. Medical intervention.

9 - The HERMIT: Governs the internal and the external senses which are memory, meditation, imagination, common sense, smell, sight, hearing, taste and touch. Enlightenment. Virtuous. Way-shower, mentor, teacher, counsellor, religious. Visionary. Wisdom. Humanitarian. Selflessness or selfishness. Experienced. Fruits of labour. Hermit-like tendencies. Happy in own company. Humility. Lowest expression can be iniquity, temptation, deception, hypocrisy, lying, charlatanism, malcontents, mischief-makers and drama queens. Sobriety or addictive behaviours. Extended family.

10 - The WHEEL of FORTUNE: Prophecy. Rise and fall. Gain and loss. Force of necessity, manifestation and power. Cycles of life. Opposites. Expansive and karmic rewards or retribution. Reaper of own good and bad deeds. Destiny at work. Good and/or bad fortune. Drastic change. Beginnings and/or endings. Ability to create your own Destiny. Increase, progress. Advancement and improvement. Atonement for one's actions. A time of reckoning. Justice. Karma. Refusal to go with change. Clinging to the status quo for fear of the unknown or the challenges that change brings. Rigidity. Atrophy. Death. Rebirth. Involution and evolution.

Appendix 3

11 - JUSTICE: Legal issues. Just or unjust outcomes. Innocence and guilt. Contracts and agreements as settled by the law, e.g. marriage, divorce, intestate, financial, alimony. Judges, lawyers, arbitrators and conciliators. Politicians. True understanding. Discrimination. Right use of reason. Elimination of useless, outworn ideas, beliefs, attitudes, habits, people and things. An inward urge or drive towards self-discovery, motivation and direction. Realisation that actions speak louder than words. Education, direct experience and attentiveness are the teachers. Teaching. Struggle to regain balance, harmony, equilibrium and right wrongs. Inequalities. Intolerance. Bias. Chaotic conditions.

12 - The HANGED MAN: Spiritualisation gained from labour, sacrifice and suffering. Sudden about-change. Reversals in life, love and relationships. A martyr's viewpoint. Life-altering experiences that can be in the form of a religious 'awakening' or an initiation. Intuition. Self-preoccupation with own affairs or beliefs. Asserting independent ideas or actions that run counter to others'. Delays. Taking time out to consider future action. Changing priorities or clinging to the outworn. Retiring from social activity in order to develop new goals, perspectives and life direction. Lack of faith. Victimisation. Ridicule or lack in esteem for being 'different'. Unworthiness. Persecution. Persecution complex. Feeling 'crucified'. Surrender.

13 - DEATH: Reminds us that nothing remains the same and that growth and progress inevitably issue from one door closing and another opening. The impermanence of life. Clearance of clutter. Sometimes extreme lifestyle changes or view of yourself, beliefs, attitudes and behaviours or perception of the world. Fear of change and inertia can trigger forceful elimination of someone or something that would have been best to let go of voluntarily. Total destruction necessary for transformation and reconstruction. Clearing clutter to allow new developments to take root. The bare bones of a situation. Surgery to remove a diseased body part. Loss of limb. Skeletal problems. Death. Liberation.

14 - TEMPERANCE: Focus. Synthesis. Multi-tasking under pressure. Coordination, combination and cooperation. Moderation. Innovation due to changed or forced circumstances. Ability to juggle several important issues at a time or during a crisis. Vacillation between extremes, whether emotional, behavioural or circumstantial. Confusion. Scattering of time, energies, resources and talents. Ignorance and forgetfulness. Discord. Sexuality. Self-focus needed to solve problems. Ordeal, hardship and dangers from natural forces.

15 - The DEVIL: An effort to overcome base desires such as being a slave to self-delusion, temptation, greed, ignorance and material pursuits, to those that are virtuous and spiritual. Someone or something you have tied yourself to that inhibits well-being and growth. Making a commitment to someone or something that may be detrimental. The lessons are learning to know what is. Prioritising. Taking things at face value. Non-attachment to materialism. A process of personal re-evaluation. Checking imbalances. Breaking bonds that tie. Blind to own faults. Self-sabotage. Overindulgence. Addictive behaviours. Weakness. Submission to corruption and depravity. Sexual obsession. Rape. Paedophilia. Death.

16 - The TOWER: Spiritual awakening. Enlightenment. Transformation. Changes for the better. Sudden release from inhibiting conditions. Unexpected surprises and outcomes. Sudden change and disruption. Complete disintegration of an existing way of life. Seeing where your life is built on false premises. Reversals. Opposites. Adversity. Operations, accidents and catastrophes. Destruction. Shame, defeat and danger. Weakness and subversion. Being stuck in a rut until things change or *you* change. False speech. Fall from Grace. Imprisonment or threat of. Death.

17 - The STAR: Spiritual unfoldment. Germination of ideas. Concentration. Meditation. Dedication. Hopes and wishes fulfilled or dashed. Unusual creative expression. Development and recognition of a specific skill. Recognition, honours. Fame, being in the limelight, becoming a 'star'. Entertainer. Attracting attention to oneself. Clairvoyance or psychic attributes. Occult discoveries and research. Metaphysical interests. Healing. Rewards for effort. Defeatist attitudes. Defamation, vilification and libel. Self-doubt and lack of faith, trust and confidence in others. Problems with sexuality, sexual identity or sexual expression. Sex related crimes. Death.

18 - The MOON: Visualisation. Unfoldment of latent powers. Adaptation. Temporary states of being. Esoteric psychology and Sciences. Subliminal forces. Intuitive insights. Psychic sensitivity and phenomenon. Spiritual healing. Intuitive healer. Limbic massage. Occult teaching. Dreams. Being forced to accept the status quo. Self-deception. Disillusionment. Harsh realities. Bad judgement and associations. Treachery and deception. Emotional displays. Being stuck in the past. Lack of direction and will. Escapism. Avoidance behaviours. Self-delusion. Refusing to change. Depression. Childishness. Tormented love. Psychiatrists, psychologists, welfare workers, psychological counselling.

19 - The SUN: Spiritual rebirth. Enlightened self-direction. Attainment. Leadership. Esteem. Honour. Celebrations. Recognition of creative, academic or scientific works. Inventiveness. Dreams of success. Religious leanings. Children. Parenting issues. Children's issues. Children's success, awards, notoriety. A child's learning difficulties or behavioural problems. Good or bad health. Failure. Vanity. Disrespect. Self-initiated conflict. Unhappy relationships. Broken unions. Separations. Cancellations. Poor health. Low vitality. Oasis or desert. Death.

20 - JUDGEMENT: A wake-up call! Revelations. Renewal of the spirit. Completion. Being forced to address important matters and decisions that need to be made otherwise greater problems ensue. Severe conditions. Tests, trials and triumphs. Commendation. Great achievements and success despite difficulties. Overcoming obstacles despite many setbacks and obstructions. Coping with delays to plans due to others. The unknown and unforeseen. Serious health disorders. Censure. Condemnation. Disapproval. Finding fault. Rejection. Termination. News of death. Inheritance. Wills.

21 - The WORLD: Advancement. Moving forward and up, i.e. spiralling growth - evolution. Progressing to the next stage. Change in status. Promotion. Success. Wealth and prosperity resulting from personal sacrifices and arduous labour. Joy in achievement. Tying up loose ends. Closure. Developing new perceptions, approach and outlook. Forward planning. Dealing with pressing matters. Resolutions. Periodic endings and beginnings. Travel. New directions. Possible change of place. Stagnation. Incompletion. Failure. Death.

22 - The FOOL: The Fool in this position marks the ending of a phase and the beginning of another. Revolutionary. Inspirational. Intuitive. Psychic. Mediumistic. Healer. Mystical experiences. Occult practices. Loves a good joke. Fearless. Rash. Audacious. Courageous. Mistake-prone. Foolish. Misunderstood. Misfit.

The Life Diamond

23 - The KING of WANDS: Spiritual. Visionary. Idealistic. A gentleman. Chivalrous. Adviser. Successful. Irritated by trifles - interested in the essence not the details. Conscientious, enterprising, inspirational leader or corporate head. Warm, witty, full of charm and generosity. A loving family man. A born salesperson. Detached and aloof. Obstinate. Autocratic and ruthless. Spineless and fatuous.

24 - The QUEEN of WANDS: Administrative abilities. Business-like. Enterprising, hard-working, ambitious, energetic. Loves the countryside and travel. Loves the thrill of attainment. Motherly, warm-hearted, loyal, fierce protector of children. Domineering. Controlling. Insensitive. Temperamental. Runs others' lives often in the guise of helping. Egotistical. Seeks the limelight. Can be nit-picking, whingeing, critical, spiteful and cruel. Also unfaithful, elusive, secretive, withholding, back-stabbing and vengeful. Signifies rural life, farmers, keen gardeners and florists. Loves pets, especially cats or is allergic to them.

25 - The KNIGHT of WANDS: Inspired leadership. Focused intent. Great potential and enthusiasm. Nobleness and refinement. Passionate. Chivalrous. A mighty crusader for a cause. May lack follow through. Can be distracted by something more interesting or fun. Can be selfishly driven and self-serving when true intentions are exposed. Motivated by 'what's in it for me'. Gains strength and confidence from experience and successful handling of adversity. A keen observer. Prone to cause and effect. Has wit, energy and fortitude. Great courage and daring. Heroic. A dashing individual. Chivalrous. Travel. Selfish pursuits, intentions, ideas. Anarchy. Forced to act, change direction or mind.

26 - The PAGE of WANDS: Bursting with news. Making an announcement. Opinionated, excitable and talkative. Developing qualities of intuition, eagerness, devotion, piety, loyalty and optimism. New ideas in their formative stages of development. Things getting off to a quick, enthusiastic beginning. Inspirational entrepreneur. Can symbolise disaster and ruin from unwise speculation. Amenability to scams and get rich quick schemes. Unlucky to form bad partnerships motivated by greed. "A fool and his money are easily parted". Struggle. Disappointing, upsetting, surprising news. Sudden changes of direction or mind. An agitator. A braggart. Quarrelsomeness. Domestic animals.

Appendix 3

27 - The ACE of WANDS: Spiritual strength. Inspired. Original ideas. Creative. Talented. Fruits of an inventive mind. Creator of beneficial works. Global aspirations. Energy, verve and dynamism applied to appealing interests and enterprises. Natural forces and flow. Aborted ideas, schemes and plans. Blocked energy. Lethargy. Unproductiveness. Easily disillusioned. Corruption. Spiritual lack. Death.

28 - The 2 of WANDS: Successful undertakings. Luck. Profitable enterprise. Perfection of an idea. Authority figures. Executives. Merchants. Investors. Eye for a bargain. Delayed progress. Broken contracts. Unrealised dreams, potential. Poor profits, loss or break-even point. Inflexibility impedes progress. Struggling against the clock. Injuries at work. Dodgy contracts. Fear of the unknown.

29 - The 3 of WANDS: Concretisation of ideas. Fruitful endeavours. Proud of accomplishments and efforts. Celebrating good news, results and returns. Capitalising on opportunities that have promise. Deception and fraud. Failed enterprises. Workplace disagreements.

30 - The 4 of WANDS: A period of quiescence, consolidation and contemplation. Family working in peace and harmony to achieve goals. Family projects or arrangements prove profitable and amenable to all. Joint solving of family problems. Sibling rivalry. A broken home. Successful completion of a project. Prosperity. Time for celebration, relaxation and enjoyment of fruits of labours. Creative arts, dance, entertainment, writing. Publishing. Problems caused by inaction, too much pressure or over anxiety. Working on false hopes or information. Building upon poor foundations.

The Life Diamond

31 - The 5 of WANDS: Harmony via conflict. Struggle and strife. Competition and opposition. Struggle with the self, with life in general, duties, health and relationships. Struggle to overcome inhibiting forces. Struggle to develop own powers. Desire to succeed despite indomitable odds. Wrestling with the inner/outer self. Wanting the impossible. Temporary state of limbo. Feeling overwhelmed by opposing forces or the insurmountable. Getting bogged down in petty squabbles. Superficiality. Litigation.

32 - The 6 of WANDS: Professional success. Public acclaim. Charismatic leader. Riding high. Satisfaction. Receiving adulations for work well done. Promotion to a leadership position. Pride or ego sabotage success or block progress. Falling from your perch.

33 - The 7 of WANDS: Self-empowerment. Valour. Overcoming personal difficulties. Remaining steadfast and vigilant. Holding your ground against others. Conquering overwhelming difficulties. Standing up for yourself. Protecting your reputation. Maintaining your principles and purpose. Courage in the face of adversity. Strength and determination ward off adversaries. Vulnerability. Feeling outnumbered and hemmed in by competition. Others block progress. Teaching, lecturing and writing skills.

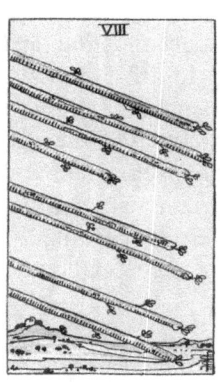

34 - The 8 of WANDS: Sudden endings or reaching sudden conclusions. Success on the horizon. The situation requires swift action. Taking swift action frees up restricting conditions. Initiating communications to gain necessary information. Manifestation of ideas. Applied force in productive ways. A wonderful opportunity to deal with several outstanding matters. Outdoor activities. Active pursuits. Travel or sudden cancellations. Delayed action results in lost opportunities or loss. Overdoing things. Rash behaviour. Unforeseen changes to plans. Embezzlement or theft. Impatient, impetuous and forceful. Self-undoing.

Appendix 3

35 - The 9 of WANDS: Defiance. A 'never give in' attitude. Victory due to courage and dogged assiduity. Ready to face opposition come what may. Thinking of the best action to take. Waiting for ideas or things to unravel. Taking the time to assess a situation. Many things pressing on the mind. Anxiety. Improved health. Excessive worry or health concerns temporarily hinder progress. Possible surgery. Doubting your abilities. Fear of failure. Faking. Being something you're not, like outer courage with inner fear, outer success with inner doubts. Many accomplishments yet one more hurdle to cross.

36 - The 10 of WANDS: Hard-won acclaim, success and wealth. Hardship. Great responsibilities. Ability to withstand and endure huge pressures and demands. Compulsive/obsessive tendencies. Back-breaking work. Carrying the world's problems on one's shoulders. Rounded shoulder; dowager's hump. Biting off more than one can chew. Great expenditure of resources and effort produce meagre results due to others' interference, deception or carelessness. Meddling in others' affairs. A busy-body. Failure due to tardiness.

37 - The KING of CUPS: Spiritually inclined. Psychic sensitivity. A man of authority, in his prime or at the top of his career. Doing things in style. Lavish accruement. Indulgence. Enjoys the best that life has to offer. Loves the arts and sciences. Passionate about work or interests. Combines work with pleasure. A pillar of strength and virtue. Ambitious. Benefactor. Sympathy and empathy. Power for good or evil. Easily loses interest in those, or that, which does not excite him. Extremely perverse when negative. Can be secretive and manipulative.

38 - The QUEEN of CUPS: Spiritual. Mystical and prophetic. Psychic. Gifted. Highly artistic and creative. Very loving, kind, compassionate and affectionate. Super-sensitive. Good listener. Generous to own detriment. Lover of beauty in all forms. Loves and surrounds the self with beautiful people, home and things. Spendthrift tendencies. Happiest when able to help and support others. Lives in a world of fantasy and imagination. Highly in tune with others as well as environmental conditions. Immoral. Double standards.

39 - The KNIGHT of CUPS: Spiritual aspirations. Psychic abilities. Seeker of perfection. Chivalrous. Virtuous. Refined. Loves the arts, entertainment, parties and music. Charismatic. Romantic. Sex appeal. Sensual. Marriage proposal or a rival in love. Teacher. Pride in appearance. Vain. Dandy. Dreamer. Self-delusional. Creating excuses for lack of will, direction, motivation or apathy. Bone-lazy. Self-indulgence. Self-pampering. Weak willed. Addictive behaviours. Sexual deviant. Pornography. Living in the past. Does the barest minimum. Holidays. Spending sprees. Scattered goals. Easily distracted from true path.

40 - The PAGE of CUPS: Intuitive messages, guidance, flashes. Intuitive grasp of a situation in its early stages of development. Creative, imaginative, sensitive, kind and psychic. Reflective. Changes to plans stem from new ideas, feelings and attitudes. Self interests govern motivation. Announcing an engagement, marriage or birth, celebration, special outing or holiday. Birth of an enterprise. Tendency to get lost in own dream world. Circumstances may be such that own needs must come first. Indication of fragile new beginnings in order to regain trust, confidence or self-esteem after experiencing bitter disappointments, woundedness, maltreatment or betrayals.

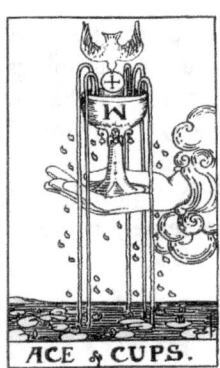

41 - The ACE of CUPS: An Ace of sharp contrasts. Joy and sorrow. Full and plenty. Fertility and barrenness. Emotional stability or instability. Love and hate. New relationships and friendships or erosion of same. Fidelity and infidelity. Peace and war. Wealth and poverty. Birth and death. Aesthetic tastes. Creative inspiration and drive. Feeling blocked or abandoned. New creative pursuits. Disappointment in results or profits from efforts.

42 - The 2 of CUPS: Marriage or union. Seeking the perfect union or soulmate. Mutual respect and friendly cooperation. Pleasant company, outings, entertainment, reciprocal visits/presents. Bickering, misunderstandings, breakdown in relationships. Separations and divorce. Broken contracts or partnerships. Emotionally charged meetings. Conflict of interests.

Appendix 3

43 - The 3 of CUPS: Celebrating festivities, anniversaries, happy occasions and achievements. Friendship and sharing of mutual interests. Enjoying the company of those with like minds and tastes. Reciprocal visits and present giving. Surprise visits. Delight over successful conclusions. Healing of rifts. Celebrating improved health. Negative effects from over-spending, over-indulgence, neglect of health routines, proper rest or indiscriminate sexual activity. Infidelity. Disloyalty. Rifts or separations caused by a meddling third party.

44 - The 4 of CUPS: Seeking help from within. An unexpected surprise. A gift that may be ignored or not appreciated or fully developed. Opportunity knocks but a divine discontent prevails which puts up a 'blind'. Extremely hard work or circumstances. A period of quiescence, consolidation and contemplation. Boredom and disgruntled feelings and attitudes inhibit fulfilment of potential. Sitting on one's talents instead of capitalising on them. Inability to move on from a setback. Dissatisfaction. Lost opportunity, failure or forced to let something of promise go. Need to develop more positive attitudes and set future goals in place. Time to get off the proverbial backside and get moving!

45 - The 5 of CUPS: Deep sadness. Grief. Nostalgia. Depression. Depressing conditions. Life seems to take a turn for the worse. Daunted by the uncertainties of life. With deep remorse and regret one grudgingly succumbs to rejection, defeat, misfortune and loss without acknowledging that all is not lost. "Throwing the baby out with the bath water". Focus on self-pity loses friendships and bright prospects. Always wishing or hoping for more due to an element of greed. Strength and hope return. Redemption.

46 - The 6 of CUPS: New developments. Revisiting old familiar places. Nostalgic memories. Return of old friends or people from the past. Rekindling an old love acquaintance. Past efforts reap future rewards. Success depends upon breaking entrenched family codes, beliefs, thoughts, attitudes and habits that inhibit self-development. Childish behaviour. A time to dispel bad memories from the past. Get rid of clutter. Ongoing health issues, tests. Warns of family problems and disruptions. The need to break with negative family ties that bind you to the past. Desire for new start in life. Do not dwell on past upbringing or mistakes - forgive, heal and move on. Death.

The Life Diamond

47 - The 7 of CUPS: Abundance of creative talent and energy. Discrimination. Remaining focused and in touch, regardless of being faced with multiple choices, avenues or opportunities. Need for application of self-discipline. Making the best choice from several options. Only right choice or direction reaps success. Attending to necessities. Beware of what you wish for, you just might get it! Reaping what has been sown. Self-delusion. Seduced by glamour and illusion. Inability to see the forest for the trees.

48 - The 8 of CUPS: Answering to a Higher Call or inner yearning. Spiralling growth. Searching for the meaning of life. Turning toward something more promising. Travel. Unforeseen circumstances that may necessitate leaving all that is known and familiar behind to begin a new life despite fears, uncertainties and emotional pulls. Topsy-turvy or life-altering events. Reversals. Life-changing decisions. Endings and beginnings. Abandoning a relationship, way of life or project that fails to fulfil. Being abandoned.

49 - The 9 of CUPS: Fulfilment. Contentment. Satisfaction. Well-being. Enjoyment of rewards for efforts. Known as the "wish card". Wastefulness. Prodigality. Conceit. Self-indulgence. Greed. Abstinence. Complacency. Self-defeating behaviours bring about loss, disparagement, criticism, lowering of self-esteem and failure. Costly mistakes. Financial duress or plenty. Money-making schemes.

50 - The 10 of CUPS: Abundance. Wealth. Happiness and joy. Family celebration. Family holidays or visits. Things going the way you want them to. Happy endings. Emotional poverty. Loneliness. Anger. Guilt. Sudden disturbance to happy, stable family life due to children, the elderly or unforeseen circumstances. Family turmoil. The proverbial "house of cards".

Appendix 3

51 - The KING of SWORDS: Imposing, formidable, self-assured, wise. Has stolid love of truth and justice backed by firm moral convictions that are unswerving but often without compassion. Though harsh and severe, disburses fair judgements. Commands high respect. Doing what needs to be done regardless of personal cost. Pulling on inner strength. Can be sceptical, suspicious and cautious. Asserts authority, knowledge or power or being at the mercy of another's. Extremely loyal in commitment to friends and equally as committed to hatred of enemies. Extremist tendencies. A hypocrite. A tyrant. Police involvement.

52 - The QUEEN of SWORDS: A woman who subtly yet amiably puts forward her opinions with the hidden expectation that they will be accepted or followed without question. These queens possess great courage, fortitude, will and determination. They are trenchant and forces to be reckoned with. They either say it as it is, or are devious in their expression and demeanour. Represents a woman who has experienced much sorrow. A widow or a divorcee. A woman on her own. A person who counsels from life experiences. Intimate knowledge of pain and suffering is used to comfort and support others in need. Ability to bear what life dishes out. Vicious tongue. Ulterior motives.

53 - The KNIGHT of SWORDS: Purposeful, incisive, focused, impetuous, leadership. Brings things to a swift conclusion. Bestowed with a brilliant mind and sound judgement but often lacks sensitivity and empathy concerning others, racing rough-shod over them in his flurry. Mind on overload with thoughts racing in and out. Cutting through the dross to reach the heart of the matter. Often selfish and ruthless in pursuit of personal goals or the mission which he deems to be its saviour. May lack the patience to see things through to fruition. Self-undoing through impetuousness. Jumping to the wrong conclusions. Going on a wild goose chase. Creates unrest due to boredom. Formidable. Sexual indiscretion. Pillager.

54 - The PAGE of SWORDS: An idea or a plan that contains great promise. Bright, clever but generally aloof. Insensitivity and insincerity. Only in touch with own emotions. Into blame and shame. Libellous speech and actions. Defamatory comments. Gossip-mongering. "Foot-in-mouth" disease. Court action due to fraud or libel. Secret plots and schemes. Sent to Coventry. Uncertainty. Temper tantrums. Regretful actions. Self-defence. Withholding vital information. Lying by omission. Announcing need for rest and recuperation, a holiday, time-out or medical tests or hospitalisation. Fatigue. Illness. Possible news of separation, divorce or death.

55 - The ACE of SWORDS: New beginnings. Great power. Triumph. Strength in adversity. A force for good or evil. A complete change of attitude, methodology or environment. A crisis. A life-changing event. Complete reversal of a way of being. Self-destructive behaviours. Fighting against negativity. Willing yourself to be positive and constructive when old negative patterns resurface. Forced to cope with undesirable change.

56 - The 2 of SWORDS: Communing with higher self or realms. Ability to reach higher spheres of consciousness. Soul searching. Taking time-out for contemplation and consideration of pressing issues. Trying to reach just and fair conclusions to help settle differences. Quarrels and conflict. Fear of direct confrontation. Fear of change. Avoidance behaviour. Reaching a temporary stalemate or impasse. Suspension of activities. Intractable behaviours. Being diverted, delayed and obstructed from achieving desired goals. Being taken advantage of. Weakness.

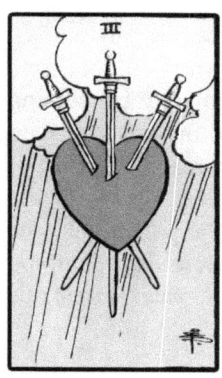

57 - The 3 of SWORDS: Facing problems squarely and honestly puts them in perspective. Finding creative solutions to problems. Heartache and/or heartbreak. Bitter disappointment. Betrayals. Sorrow. Separation, rejection, loss, grief and death. Distressing issues surrounding a loved one. Vexing worries and anxieties. Fearing the worst. Suffering threats and/or physical abuse. Alienation. Much pleasure in stirring, retaliation and venting of wrath (often only thought about - not always acted upon). Disappointed in choices made.

58 - The 4 of SWORDS: A period of quiescence, consolidation and contemplation. A time for relaxation, rest, retreat, going within, pondering the future, meditation, relaxation, convalescence and recuperation. A form of forced or self-initiated confinement. Hospitalisation. Imprisonment.

Appendix 3

59 - The 5 of SWORDS: The victor and the vanquished. A 'might is right' attitude. Annihilator. Aggressor. A well-armed aggressor. Tyrannical behaviour. Jumping to the wrong conclusions. Bully. Ability to see and take advantage of the chinks in the enemy's armour. Being able to disarm another/others. Taking unfair advantage of a person or situation. Dishonour, degradation and humiliation in defeat. Knowing when to give up the fight. Abject surrender.

60 - The 6 of SWORDS: Travel. Leaving unpleasant situations behind. Certain amount of detachment or distancing required to resolve family issues. Putting a space between yourself and your problems. Persistent stress instils need to get away from it all. Need to take a different tack. Search for health treatment. Seeking ways to relieve financial strain, stress, pain and emotional or physical restraints. Feeling beset by trouble and strife. Unresolved tension.

61 - The 7 of SWORDS: A tactician. Being in a situation that requires stealth and cunning. Being satisfied with partial success. Lowering of standards. Compromise. Need for wise counsel before action taken. Irrational behaviour. Shrewd. Astute. Knows when to retreat with the goods! Can lie, cheat and steal. Plots and schemes. Need to analyse options and take appropriate action. Running from a dishonourable act. Terrorist activity.

62 - The 8 of SWORDS: Temporary impasse. Facing opposition, legal wrangles, struggle, conflict and angst. Being stuck in a distressing situation that appears blocked. Careful consideration of your problem brings a solution - you are not paralysed - there is a way forward. See your situation realistically as fears and indecisiveness may be the ties that bind causing constraints and feeling imprisoned or tied down. Enabling others or situations to interfere with your mind/plans. Feeling powerless. Self-paralysis. Self-pity. Psychosomatic illness. Using illness as a crutch. Lacking motivation. Failing to take action. Making excuses for indolence. Paranoia. Mental conflict, turmoil or confusion. Escapism. Ignoring or avoiding responsibilities. Grief.

63 - The 9 of SWORDS: Fear of failure. Obstacles and problems. Imprisonment. Fear. Guilt. Shame. Disturbed sleep patterns. Recurring nightmares. Constant worry and anxiety. Bothered by bad memories. Frightening flashbacks. Depression. Thoughts of suicide. Many problems preying on the mind. Melodramatics.

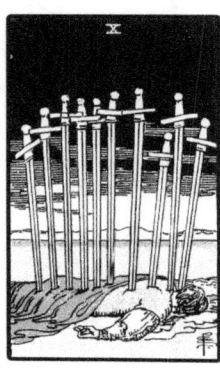

64 - The 10 of SWORDS: Betrayals. Back-stabbing. Ruin. Sudden upsets with dire consequences. Pain and suffering. Sunshine after a storm. Light at the end of the tunnel. Debilitating health problems. Spinal complaints. Collapse. Medical intervention. Life-threatening experience. Struggle for survival. 'Dark night of the soul experience'. Blocked chakras. Death.

65 - The KING of PENTACLES: A corporate leader. Astute businessman. Success oriented. Focused on achievement of financial and material goals. Seeks prosperity and riches. Reliable. Self-indulgence. Avaricious. Self-sufficiency. Resourcefulness. Attention to detail. Power hungry. A brute. Stunted progress.

66 - The QUEEN of PENTACLES: Practical and down to earth women. This queen is shrewd and has an eye for a bargain. Loves the thrill of haggling. Keeps cool under duress. Happiest when serving others. Unorthodox practitioner/ medicines. Naturopath. Healer. Psychic abilities. Ability to cultivate dreams. Works hard to achieve future security then spends her life enjoying the fruits of her labours. Can achieve riches. Health issues. Disavows responsibility. Use and abuse of power or friendship. Out for own gain. Self-serving interests. Calculating. Can be crafty or naive in business.

Appendix 3

67 - The KNIGHT of PENTACLES: A kind, patient, conscientious, staunch, faithful individual but can be slow to act and seem boring. A time to take stock of the situation to achieve clarity before moving on. Slow, laborious progress. Patient and persevering qualities. Never losing sight of the goal and a never give up attitude. Setting achievable objectives. Loves children. Careful execution of duties. Protector. Lover of nature. Things grinding to a halt. Reality and practicality of a situation requires cancellation of intentions or plans. Plodding. Boring. Jealous and envious of others' good fortune.

68 - The PAGE of PENTACLES: News and views pertaining to the following aspects of this Key. Future plans in the making. Goal-oriented. Beginning of a new business enterprise. Money-making opportunities seized upon. Finances required for travel and study purposes. Diligent. Sombre, serious approach to work and attainment of goals. Sensual. Materialistic. Pragmatic. Down-to-earth.

69 - The ACE of PENTACLES: Beginning of a financial enterprise or a financial proposition. Rewards commensurate with labours. Status and achievement, security and wealth. Successful business dealings. Sound business sense and practices. Financial settlements. Investments. Real estate. Material gain, wealth and prosperity. Inheritances. Loss of wealth and status.

70 - The 2 of PENTACLES: Going with the flow. Multi-tasking. Skilful manipulation of duties and obligations. Mastering difficulties. Dealing with financial fluctuations. Dealing with constant flux and change. The juggler. Many things on the go at one time. Perfected skills. Procrastination. Confusion. Walking on egg-shells.

The Life Diamond

71 - The 3 of PENTACLES: Craftsmanship. Apprenticeship. Industriousness. Architecture. Home improvements. Accolades from peers or superiors. Support from colleagues or superiors. Scholarship. Faithful adherence to plans that achieve self-improvement through studies, application of skills or financial success. Doing whatever is necessary to overcome obstacles and difficulties. Abandoned success. Indolence.

72 - The 4 of PENTACLES: A period of quiescence, consolidation and contemplation. Material gain confused with identity and status. Emotional security tied to financial status. Taking stock of your financial situation. Evaluating your life. A collector of memorabilia. Stalemate. Afraid to move out of comfort zone and take risks. Staying in uncomfortable situations much longer than necessary. Rigidity. Persisting in a course of action even though it is wrong or inappropriate. Financial ruin. Failed projects. Need for financial advice.

73 - The 5 of PENTACLES: "Impoverished" due to loss of inner light. Lack of emotional and physical support in needy times by relatives, friends, banks, church or welfare institutions. Broken rules and trust by loved ones, church and welfare employees. Dealing with hypocrites or broken promises of assistance. Loss of trust, hope and/or faith. Emotional or financial hardship. Struggle. Harsh times and/or illness elicit resourcefulness and independence and accountability for choices and actions. Redoing others work. Unemployment. Bitterness. States of feeling impoverished. Feeling "crippled" by harsh circumstances. Ruin. Isolation due to partner's travel, work or different interests. Feeling deprived or abandoned. A loner by choice.

74 - The 6 of PENTACLES: Benefactor. Generosity. Sharing good fortune. Assisting those less fortunate. Selfless service. 'Good Samaritan'. Philanthropist. Giving or receiving financial or material aid. A productive period. Recognition for your achievements. Sale of goods. Balancing finances. Reaping just deserts. Victim/saviour tendencies.

Appendix 3

75 - The 7 of PENTACLES: Cultivating particular talents, skills for material gain. A time for assessment and re-evaluation of achievements. Pride in one's work. Charitable work for little material reward. Work for the love of it. Seasonable labour. Bent on seeing results from labour. Unexpected surprises that may be extremely beneficial or disappointing. Disappointing results commensurate with effort. Rewards belie invested time, money and effort.

76 - The 8 of PENTACLES: Great skill. Acumen. Industry, enterprise and perseverance. Dedication. Conscientiousness. Enthusiastic devotion to work or cause. Skills that can be turned into moneymaking concerns. Securing one's future through diligent labour. Envious of others' skills and good fortune. Abuse of skills. Unanimated. Lack of ambition. Purposeless.

77 - The 9 of PENTACLES: Wealth. A person who has everything. Great accomplishment. Contentment from efforts. A successful single woman. The widow. Gross displays. Meanness. Lording it over others. Lack of faith. Spiritual wealth or poverty.

78 - The 10 of PENTACLES: Wealth. Fulfilment. Retirement. End of a phase. "Protector" element either due to a silent benefactor or wise mentor or one who makes their "guardianship or generosity" public knowledge. Security. Death and taxes. Inheritance. Defamation. Besmirching the family name. Loss of work. Financial ruin.

RECOMMENDED RESOURCE LIST

The Tarot - Paul Foster Case, B.O.T.A. Publications revised addition, 1990

Numerology and the Divine Triangle - Faith Javane and Dusty Bunker, Para Research, 1985

Tarot Prediction, *An Advanced Handbook of Images for Tomorrow* - Emily Peach, The Aquarian Press, 1988

The Numerology Workbook, *Understanding and Using the Power of Numbers* – Julia Line, The Aquarian Press, 1985

Numerology, *The Romance in Your Name* - Juno Jordan, De Vorss and Company, 1989

Easy Tarot Guide - Marcia Marcino, ACS Publications, 1990

Seventy-Eight Degrees of Wisdom, *A Book of Tarot. Parts 1 and 2* - Rachel Pollack, The Aquarian Press, 1983

The Pictorial Key to the Tarot - Arthur Edward Waite, Samuel Weiser, 1984

The Mystical Qabalah – Dion Fortune, Samuel Weiser, 1984

FORTHCOMING TITLES

THE YEARLY DIAMOND – *YOUR DESTINY IN ACTION*

Yearly Diamonds are Life Diamonds' companions. Their comprehensive, yearly forecasts are derived from the same integrated, esoteric system used to decode the Life Diamond. Yearly Diamonds are quickly and easily calculated from the *current age* and *Life Path Number*. They produce profound, yearly forecasts with unprecedented depth, detail and accuracy from their 4-month cycles, constellations and magickal facets. Nothing in this sacred science exists that can provide at a single glance, such a personalised representation of precious soul-based directions, new and exciting possibilities and warnings for each Personal Year as Yearly Diamonds.

As well as Yearly Diamonds, **Monthly** and **Daily Diamonds**, **Decade Cycles** and **Decade Diamonds** and **Yearly, Monthly** and **Daily Tarot** *spreads* are introduced. They, plus **Personal Year, Month and Day** *Number Families*, reveal an even finer definition of life's smaller steps within larger time-frames. The ultimate aim of utilising these predictive divisions of numerology is to uncover their spiritual and everyday secrets so that personal objectives can be updated, refined and modified, if applicable, and then acted upon to achieve present and future possibilities as and when they arise.

Many case studies and diagrams accompanied by a variety of in-depth interpretations and helpful tips highlight ways to search out personal insights and directions from each revelatory, numerological configuration being presented for exploration. Do not be surprised if these configurations grow to become your favourite divinatory tools; your personal Wayshowers for all time. The only thing that restricts their prognostic applications is the knowledge and skill of the interpreter.

MORE MAGICKAL DIAMONDS

This book applies the same integrated, esoteric system which merges numerology with the Tarot, mystical symbology and psychology to uncover soul-based directions from a selection of old and new areas of numerology. The technique of constructing numerological diamonds is applied to each area to open them up as never before. They uncover greater, personal insights as a means of heightening self-awareness. These insights uncover personal aptitudes, vocational leanings and strengths and weaknesses as well as an understanding of what you are attracting into this life and why certain things happen. Accompanying diagrams, interpretation guidelines and helpful tips are major features throughout each chapter.

Diamonds are applied to the **Achievement Number** (old), the **Shadow Achievement Number** (new), the **Life Experience Number** (new) and the **Destiny Number** (old). In particular, the **Higher Purpose Diamond** (new) is exceptional. It reveals your chosen quest and/or vocation by highlighting specific paths that lead to fulfilling your mundane and/or spiritual Destiny. **Personality Diamonds** (new) uncover esoteric insights from names that give a comprehensive, perceptive analysis of a person's personality traits. A new, fast, esoteric way of "reading" names is also introduced. It graphically exposes the "gifts" and potential hidden in all names.

Perhaps this book's most significant contribution to numerology is in its chapters that explore families, groups, and relationships. **Relationship Diamonds** reveal a relationship's compatibility status as well as its strengths, weaknesses and directions. The introduction of an unparalleled technique that *progresses* **Relationship Diamonds** enables forecasts to be made for all types of relationships which uncover unfolding yearly trends – something to really get excited about.

Another exciting feature is the Appendix which contains new esoteric/exoteric interpretations for the 26 letters.

www.ingramcontent.com/pod-product-compliance
Lightning Source LLC
Chambersburg PA
CBHW081805300426
44116CB00014B/2241